Linda Neil is a musician, writer and radio producer. Her documentaries have won awards at the New York Radio Festival and have been short-listed for the United Nations Media Peace Prize. She has a PhD in creative writing and a degree in music from the University of Queensland, where she has taught creative and professional writing and media and cultural studies. She is currently working on *My Year of Singing Love Songs,* a music documentary for ABC Radio National. *Learning How to Breathe* is her first book.

LEARNING HOW TO BREATHE

Linda Neil

UQP

First published 2009 by University of Queensland Press
PO Box 6042, St Lucia, Queensland 4067 Australia

www.uqp.com.au

Text design and typeset in 11.75/15.25pt Adobe Jenson Pro by Post Pre-press Group, Brisbane
Printed in Australia by McPherson's Printing Group
Author photograph by Amelia Schmidt

This project has been assisted by the Commonwealth Government through the Australia Council, its arts funding and advisory body.

Sponsored by the Queensland Office of Arts and Cultural Development

Cataloguing-in-Publication Data
National Library of Australia

Neil, Linda
Learning how to breathe

ISBN 9780702237348 (pbk)

Neil, Linda. Neil, Joan. Mothers and daughters – Biography. Caregivers – Biography. Parkinson's disease – Patients – Biography. Musicians – Biography.

362.0425

As this is a work of memory and not of journalism, all care has been taken to protect the privacy of those involved. Except for family names, all names, including those of institutions, have been changed. Some dates, timelines and physical descriptions have also been altered for reasons of privacy. As well, some characters appear as amalgams of several people.

to joan ben chris
cat stets pa
paul kym finn kel
hannah lily and rose

CONTENTS

Two things happen today. My mother falls and I foresee my own death. These two things may or may not be connected. My mother's falling precipitates a moment of clarity in which I know that through her falling I will be changed forever. I know as I watch her fall that, contrary to the habit of a lifetime, I will not walk away. I will not disengage myself from her falling and by engaging in her fall I will fall myself.

I watch her fall from where I am standing at the kitchen sink. She falls at the clothes line and as she stumbles she grabs hold of one of her favourite old tea towels, one she'd had when Dad was still alive, and slowly rips it in two as she tries to steady herself.

It's a strange thing to watch your mother fall. The only way I can describe it is by saying that, as I watch her temporarily frail body hit the ground and hear the oddly resigned whoosh of air escape her as bone scraped against the concrete path – the one that Dad put in for her so that her bare feet wouldn't feel the prickles as she walked from the laundry to the line – I can feel my heart break a little. This breaking is also a falling, a shedding and perhaps a death.

Book One

THE POLITICS OF SADNESS

RETURN

My mother sometimes told her singing students that they must make singing look easy. They should stand before their audience with a calm relaxed posture, and a serene face and manner, and sing with clear natural diction to enable the audience to feel they could do the same with a couple of lessons. Introducing the song was also an important part of the performance, she stressed. It is best never to mumble or feel embarrassed in any way. Being in control, or appearing to be, was one of the tools of a competent singer. 'Maintain the appearance of serenity, even if you are dying inside,' she wrote in an article for the Music Teachers' Association of Queensland. 'A performer should never worry an audience; they should give the impression they are doing something completely natural. Mechanical matters such as resonance, articulation, breathing, and all the difficulties which we know are part of the process must disappear from our minds – and theirs – as we begin to sing.'

'But is it really possible to make it look that easy?' she concluded. 'And, if so, does this bear out the old adage: Art begins where effort ends?'

Mum used to refer to the years after my father died as 'my time'. The time before what she referred to as 'my time' was, I imagine, the time to care for my invalid father, and, after he died, the time to grieve. Then, one year after my eighty-year-old father was buried in a cemetery in Brisbane after a church service at their local parish of St Lucia, my mother, seventeen years his junior, celebrated the season of 'her time' by embarking on her first overseas adventure, a trip through Europe with her friend Miriam, followed by a visit to her two sons, Paul and Stephen, living in London at that time. The following years, she told me later, were rich with such travels and adventures. Released from a life of duty and work during which she had seen all her children travel the world while she stayed at home in the house her mother had once owned, she enjoyed the surprising and fruitful freedom of these years. 'Her time' stretched from the year 1993 until 1998, the year she returned from a trip overseas – the last she would ever make – with my sister Cathie, who accompanied her on this last grand adventure through Canada and America where they attended singing and choral workshops and music and theatre festivals, including the Shaw Festival at Niagara Falls.

Two months after her return, for no apparent reason Mum began to feel sad. This sadness came upon her incrementally; she interpreted it at first as exhaustion and did what she had always done to combat exhaustion or weakness of any kind: she kept on working. A few days after landing back in Australia she flew north to Gladstone to adjudicate in the Central Queensland Eisteddfod. There she noticed a pain in her right hand and arm as she wrote her comments for the dozens of vocalists who sang for her over the three-day competition. These initial niggling irritations then developed into a sudden lack of mobility in her right shoulder and the habit of waking up in the morning crying. Crying is not something my mother did. Later I will joke with her that crying was something I did brilliantly; I'd been crying, in fact, for years. It was my area of endeavour and accomplishment. Hers, on the other hand, was singing and the teaching of music. The art of the voice and the breath. Of channelling feeling into song. The art of not crying.

Her tears led to uncharacteristic phone calls to my brother Paul, her eldest son, whose wife Kym was expecting their first child. He suggested she go to a doctor to get something to help her. But exactly what sort of help she needed and exactly what was wrong with her was unclear. A visit to her GP of over thirty years resulted in a prescription for antidepressants. These helped neither her insomnia nor her sadness.

My mother used to tell me that there was no perfect time to start anything. There would be no ideal moment when everything would be aligned and balanced in support of any new venture. No matter how much you believed in the stars, or the gods, or the fickle hand of fate, if you waited too long for the perfect moment you might well die before ever starting anything. I doubt whether my parents or my grandmother thought much about the significance of dates, or names, or numbers for that matter. They were too practical for such esoteric interests and would have told me never to rely on anything so intangible and unscientific to decide the course of my life. They would have told me to get down off my high horse, give up all that airy fairy stuff, and just get real. Sometimes you have to pluck up your courage, dive into the chaos, and be prepared to get your hands dirty. So I will begin this story not at the very beginning or at the end, but at some time after and also some time before what might be the perfect place to start. I'll dive right into the mud of Bellingen in northern New South Wales, where I am wandering around ankle deep in slush at the Global Music Festival of Harmony in October 1998, embracing the chaos of a hippie festival that has brought me halfway to the border of Queensland, the Sunshine State.

The first music festival I ever played at was a youth orchestra festival in Aberdeen, Scotland, where orchestras of mostly teenage musicians from all over the world gathered to play symphonies and concertos, overtures and suites. It was my first overseas trip – I remember we played Shostakovich, Sibelius and Holst – and my parents had sacrificed a lot to put the money aside for me to make the journey. I doubt they would have been thrilled to know that, after all their trouble, I would one day be tramping around in the mud at a music festival for peace-loving hippies rather than lovers of classical music.

Bellingen is also a long way from the Queen Elizabeth Hall in London where I once played in a performance of *Peter and the Wolf*. Or the Roman Forum where I played Wagner and Mendelssohn. But Bellingen is where I have come to play with a band called *the new music collective*, a raggedy group of inner city musicians who play original songs with a fusion ensemble of instruments that include tabla, bass, bazouki, djembe, with me on fiddle. Original music – playing it, writing it, listening to it – has been my passion during most of the nineties in which my violin and I traversed a world a long way from the safe and secure musical life my parents would have wished for me. It wasn't just new music that interested me though. It was the new life that went with it. During my time in the musical wilderness I played all over Sydney – on streets and footpaths, in tunnels and arcades, in malls and public squares – with many different types of musicians for as many different types of people, before hooking up to amplifiers and sound systems on stages of pubs, clubs and medium-sized arenas, in recording studios and sometimes even in television studios, improvising and composing what my grandmother might once have called 'the devil's music'.

A freak storm interrupted the festival opening the night before. Some people credited the unseasonal rain to the Indigenous elder who had welcomed us, or to the didgeridoo player beside him who made our bones rumble – and perhaps the clouds too – with his pulsing rhythms. But none of us was prepared for the deluge when it came, not even my partner Raphael, who once spent two years living without electricity in a hut on the hills behind Byron Bay. After sharing with him our own little hut by the sea for most of the previous two years, I know he is usually prepared for most natural things – disasters or otherwise – and thanks to him we spent the night undercover, huddled in the tent he managed to hastily fashion out of an old tarpaulin from the back of our station wagon, with my violin tucked away beside us in a canvas bag that Raphael had stitched together especially to protect it from the elements.

I am not good in natural emergencies, only, perhaps, musical ones. The day after the storm I am tired and grumpy as I wander around in the mud looking for the main stage where I'm supposed to play a gig that night. Raphael is away checking out organic garden stalls and catching up with other old hippies from the Northern Rivers. He always seems at home at events like these, but for me so far Bellingen has been a nightmare. A violinist especially dreads changeable weather because of how sudden climatic changes affect the tension of the instrument's strings and the clarity of its tone. I am supposed to be singing at tonight's gig and damp affects the voice too, along with the clouds of smoke I'm sick of walking through – tobacco, dope, and whatever other herbal concoctions the festival tribes are smoking this year. The chai tent seems like a safe haven to avoid the stoned line at the samosa van, but my head is already starting to spin from the thick smells of tea, patchouli and sandalwood as I stand in line. My phone rings. It is my brother Paul. He isn't ringing about the imminent birth of his first child, though. He's ringing to tell me there's something wrong with Mum.

He isn't any more specific, except to say, in his casual way, that she might need some help. This sounds all wrong: not just Mum needing help, but my family ringing to tell me about it. It has been a long time since I have done anything a good daughter or a good sister might do. Paul seems surprised when I say I'll drive up to Brisbane to stay with Mum for a few days. My family are not really the kind of people who ask for help. Or – perhaps – not from me. They are the kind of people who get on with things as best they can. Paul saying that Mum might need some help, even casually, suddenly seems to be a significant thing.

I bump up against another sweaty punter who, in return, spills a scalding mug of herbal tea all over me. Maybe Mum needs a break just like I do, I think. A break from my gypsy life feels like a good idea, along with a break from the rain, the mud, from camping, from Raphael, and even, for a while perhaps, from playing music.

Mum had a dream of music too. I watched it flicker into life when I was a little girl crawling around her feet while she played the piano. I listened, trembling, as she sang dramatic Italian arias and cried out for love's ruin while she cooked mince and potatoes in the kitchen of our suburban home. I had witnessed how it slowly flowered in our lounge room and in the lounge rooms and suburban music halls of Brisbane, where Mum worked, studied and taught singing and piano. I knew how hard she had struggled to attain her teaching diplomas, degrees and fellowships, and followed, albeit from a distance, how she built up her teaching practice so others could sing and flower too.

The gig tonight is huge. We play to hundreds of beautiful boys and girls blissed out on love and life and what the emcee announces is 'that shiva shakti energy'. For a moment I really feel I am shakti on the stage with my shiva in the crowd smiling up at me while I stand under a single spotlight and sing a song I've just written called 'Solitude'. I think for only a moment how strange it is to be playing a song called 'Solitude' in front of such a large crowd because it is so special to hear some of the audience singing the chorus with me, while outside the performance tent a full moon glows bright orange in the black sky. Even while I sing, I still hear another voice whisper, as I have for so much of my life. The divine whisper, Raphael calls it in his cosmic way, the one I hear when I play music. Tonight I might even say that the whisper is calling me home – if I had ever really believed in such a place.

Next day, I refuse Raphael's offer to drive north with me to Brisbane to see Mum. He jokingly enfolds me in his muscled arms etched with tattoos, pretending not to let me go.

You are coming back, aren't you? he whispers close to my ear.

Don't be silly, I say, turning to him to return his embrace, but really only because I know it is what he needs to hear. Raphael is a sensitive man, though, and knows I have already left him, especially since my temporary move back to Sydney from Byron Bay – for supposed musical reasons – a few months before.

I notice a woman look at him admiringly as she passes. I feel an ache and hate myself for being possessive.

I've kept as far away from her as I could, I suddenly tell him. *The last thing in the world I ever wanted to do is go home to my mother.*

Maybe that's why you can't settle, he says, not without sympathy.

I'm afraid, I tell him, as honest as I've ever been with him. *Being round my family always makes me feel like a freak. I mean, I know they're good people. That's why I feel so guilty around them.*

I know you're afraid. But always remember fear is only something that's in your mind, he tells me.

When I hear him say things like this to me, I understand why I wanted to be with him. He is a balm for my mind.

And you're brave, you know, he presses deep against me. *Braver than you realise.*

I breathe him in. *I wish I was a better girlfriend,* I say, snuggling back into him.

You're not such a bad girlfriend, he teases me. *It's just that I can never really pin you down.*

He pretends to capture me; I try to wriggle free.

What exactly are you afraid of? he asks, letting me go.

I sigh deeply. My answer could take days, I think. A lifetime.

That one day I'll be so afraid I'll stop breathing altogether.

We all will eventually, he says, before laughing. At me, with me. At himself. Raphael always spreads his laughter around.

I know. But you always said, didn't you, that we should face the things we're most afraid of?

Ha, he says, ruefully. *I never knew you took that much notice of what I say.* He uncoils himself from me then, a tall bear of a man letting me go. *Drop me a line sometime,* he smiles.

I'll only be a few days, I tell him casually.

Yes, of course, he echoes, *a few days.*

Just for a final laugh, he holds out his hand for me to shake, a formal goodbye between the friends we are becoming, rather than the lovers we have been. But I have already begun to rev the engine of my station wagon to set off for the trip north. I don't really know whether I am lying or not. Whether I will only be a few days or whether the divine whisper might be heading north as well.

It takes me a whole day of driving, with stops at Byron Bay and the Gold Coast, as well as a sushi bar in Toowong, to finally make it to St Lucia by dusk. So it is early evening by the time I pull up outside the family home in Warren Street. The street has changed a lot since I last visited. More and more of the old wooden family homes which lined the footpath when I was a girl have been knocked down in favour of the townhouses and home units that accommodate the large numbers of international students who attend the University of Queensland two streets away.

We used to call Warren Street the rabbit warren for no particular reason, though later, when we got to know some of the stories about large Catholic families, we made the connection in our own minds between our street and the fact that people of our particular religion were supposed to breed like rabbits. We did not have a particularly large family, not by local standards anyway – three girls and two boys: three with saints' names, Cathie, Paul and Stephen, and two without. I was named after a movie star called Linda Darnell and my sister was named Janice because Mum liked the sound of it. Five was a modest number of children compared to other families we knew of, like the O'Hares, who had ten, the Kellys, who had eleven, and the O'Gradys from Durham Street, who had twelve. Even the humbly named Meekmans from Indooroopilly had seven kids and an even smaller house than ours.

Though there was not enough room in our small old wooden worker's cottage with the besser bricks at the front and fruit trees at the back for everyone to have their own bedroom, it was at least in the realm of possibility that we might one day. And so we did: with judicious building underneath the upper storey of our house and some sacrifices – which included the banana, mango and lemon trees that were cut down in an effort to create more space – we all eventually had our own rooms.

The best feature of our house, though, with its haphazard extensions and tiny rooms, was the long veranda that ran right along the back. Winter Sundays were often spent in the sunlight that flooded the corner of the veranda and on summer nights a cool breeze always seemed to find its way across the gully at the back. This gully ran through a piece of land that was always unoccupied – 'Thank God,' Mum used to sigh – due to an obscure council regulation, and so from all angles and in all seasons the University of Queensland was clearly visible from the rear of our home.

The university had always loomed large, literally and metaphorically, in my vision from the time I was a little girl. When he was alive, Dad would mow a path through the long grass at the back of our house, even though it did not belong to us any more than it did to the snakes and creepy crawly things which inhabited its undergrowth. 'I'm mowing the path to your future,' he would call back to us as he bent over his Victa motor mower and pulled the zip starter, his slim but broad back curving over, his favourite floppy gardener's hat pulled right down over his forehead like Gilligan from *Gilligan's Island*. Dad had been involved in education since he was given a scholarship to study with the Christian Brothers and had been a teacher for all of his adult life. The university was a metaphor for everything he believed in and loved: learning, reading, contemplating, imagining, examining things, being examined, bettering yourself, and sometimes being bettered. It was his goal for all of us that we would ascend from our desks to these towers of education, whose turrets and flags were symbols throughout our childhood of where we were headed.

I walk up the front stairs and knock loudly on the security screen door but there's no sign of Mum. I rattle the handle of the screen door and find it is locked, so I call out through the thick mesh. Inside, the house is in darkness. The television is on with the volume turned down very low, as I remember it always was, tuned to the ABC seven o'clock news.

Mum appears at the end of the hallway. I can hardly make her out in the shadows.

Mum, I call out. *It's me.*

She seems uncertain. I adjust my eyes to the gloom and press my face against the dusty screen so that I can see her more clearly. I try the door handle a few times. Mum was always too devoted to her teaching and singing to ever be an avid housecleaner. But though her home was always regularly maintained, now even the door itself, with its grime, seems exhausted.

I can't get in, Mum, I call to the darkness inside. *Can you unlock the door, please?*

Oh, it's you, Linda. She comes forward, a tiny figure in a white nightie and printed dressing gown. *The bulb's gone in the light.*

Then I've come just in time, I joke feebly as she fumbles with the lock on the other side of the reinforced screen that was installed, along with one at the back, soon after my father died.

It's the wrong key, I think, she says, walking back into the darkened room before returning with the right key.

You look well, she greets me finally, holding up her cheek for me to kiss. When we hug she feels smaller, more fragile than I remember. *Put the kettle on will you, Linda. I need to lie down.*

I make us some tea then get my violin out of the car. I know that perhaps she'd prefer to hear me play than talk. We've never really discussed anything personal. Maybe it is my own self-consciousness that makes this difficult, but Mum rarely asks 'How are you?' She prefers to begin our conversations with 'What have you been doing?' rather than 'How are you feeling?' I don't think any of us really minds. In fact, often it feels good to have a mother who is interested in our professional or creative activities, rather than probing us about our personal lives.

Mum seems distracted as she drinks her tea and does not look directly at me. Though she is thinner, her face is round and rosy and her skin, genetically blessed like her mother's, remains unlined and smooth.

I still don't dare ask how she is as she hovers uncertainly near me, restlessly rearranging her body in and out of the lounge chairs. Her blue eyes seem unusually large and her white floral nightie and flimsy dressing gown keep falling from her narrow shoulders. I suddenly want to hold her, to envelop her in my flesh, just to stop her restlessness.

But I don't hug her. Instead, I do what I normally do these days in times of crisis or uncertainty. I take my violin out and play; this time, I play an old French tune my grandmother loved, called 'Meditation', from an opera by the French composer Massenet.

Mum closes her eyes and listens. A smile breaks lightly across her pale face as I begin to play and I remember again how she is – how all our family is – transported and energised by music.

It always seemed as if it was Grandma Chris who was most delighted by music, but perhaps this was because for her it was only ever a dream. It wasn't hard work and practice like it was for Mum, or, later, for us. It wasn't listening to words and poetry, as it seemed to be for Dad. Gran had been too poor and perhaps too practical to ever have had a chance at seriously pursuing music. But she was the first one who shared its secrets with me, who told me breathless stories about violinists like Yehudi Menuhin and Jascha Heifetz the way other matriarchs might have whispered about movie stars or ballad singers. It was Gran who played me old records of gypsy music when I was young. According to family folklore it was Grandma who first suggested to Mum that I learn the violin, who first put the instrument into my hands. The truth might be more prosaic. Mum just might have wanted all her daughters to learn music – though, curiously, the boys were never given lessons – because that is what girls did while their brothers played sport. The main thing was to keep us occupied with something, because, as Gran used to say, 'Idle hands – and minds – do the devil's work.' But learning music may also have been one way for Mum's daughters to – literally – play with her. And for her to play with us.

When I finish playing, Mum says: *It always brings tears to my eyes. And you play like an angel,* she continues. *Your father and your grandmother would be so proud that you've kept it up.*

I thought they were horrified about what I've done with my music. This role of the prodigal daughter is an old refrain. Even as I say the words I wish I would just shut up and listen. *I thought they thought I'd gone off the rails.*

She looks directly at me as she says: *You've always expected the worst from us, Linda. Perhaps we understood more than you realised.*

I know she's right, but I am surprised to hear her say it. After the circuitous route I have travelled to arrive back here in my mother's lounge room, I am not prepared to delve more deeply into such misconceptions, mine or hers, so soon after coming back home. I change the subject.

Sitting down on the arm of her chair, I ask: *So what do you think is up with you, Mum?*

She looks at me for a moment, as if I am an old, strange woman returned from a long long journey.

Remember when you were a little girl? she asks me. *You told the McDonalds down the road that you wanted to be the best violinist in the whole wide world.*

It is one of those things parents remember more than children. I don't remember it, but Mum does. It still has meaning for her now.

She settles back into her chair and looks away again. *I remember you were wearing those ridiculous red shoes of your grandmother's. The ones with the wedge heels.*

She smiles as she remembers this childish image of me, a little girl in shoes that are too big for her.

You liked how they made you taller, she continues. *You were in their garden playing the violin for them in those silly red platform shoes.*

I nod my head, even though I have no recollection of the McDonalds or the red shoes.

And Flo McDonald asked you what you wanted to be when you grew up . . . She trails off, her head leaning to one side in an expression of reverie.

I try to jog Mum's memory gently. *And I said . . . ?* I ask her.

You told them that . . . She cannot finish her sentence.

I wanted to be the best violinist . . . I prompt her.

Yes . . . in the whole wide world, she finishes.

I hop off her chair and sit on the floor at her feet.

Well, you know, Mum. Kids say things. Anyway, I was never good enough to make it in the classical music world.

Too impatient, she scolds me. *Remember? Little steps add up to a big journey.*

Maybe I just needed to go out and do my own thing, I tell her.

But perhaps it's come true, she smiles at me. *Perhaps you are a great violinist.*

Now I know something is definitely wrong with you, I giggle, avoiding her compliment. I was ok on the violin; I wasn't a virtuoso but I felt natural making up music on the instrument. I'd played on quite a few albums while I was in Sydney with musicians who were well known in the business and people seemed to like it. But it wasn't music that people knew, music that I'd grown up with. It was new music, spontaneous music. Improvised music. Sometimes wild, unpredictable music.

She straightens herself up a little. *I'm not saying you're perfect, Linda. God knows, nobody is. All I'm saying is that you do let the music sing.*

Mum trained me not to 'have tickets' on myself and I still can't accept compliments graciously.

Oh, come on. Mum. It's me, Linda.

She looks directly at me. *Yes, I know who it is.*

I think about the business of dreaming, the dreams I had as a child. Here I am, returned from the dreaming of these dreams, to the place where they began.

She leans towards me. *I haven't been able to sleep,* she tells me tentatively.

Pianist's hands, I think as I reach over and touch her knuckles. You can always tell a pianist's hands by their suppleness and flexible fingers. I'd never thought much about

Mum being a musician, not the way you start to think around musicians when you've been out on the streets listening to people playing music in order not just to survive, but to stay alive, mentally, emotionally, as well as physically. But here she is, my mother, with her pianist's hands.

You must be so tired, I sympathise, holding her hands lightly in mine. Up close her eyes are bloodshot and weary.

I haven't slept a wink in nearly a month, she tells me.

You don't doze off in front of the TV? I smile as I remember her habit – and Dad's as well – of nodding off in front of the television in the evenings. *Like you used to with Dad?*

Oh, she sighs, *if only things were that simple now.*

She sighs again. Our conversation falters. I make her another cup of tea and go back out to the car to get my guitar from the heap of clothes and instruments which are piled in the back of my station wagon. It suddenly feels unseemly to be here with my dusty car full of junk outside the lawns of my parents' house, which, like the rest of the lawns in the street, are neatly mowed and maintained.

Even the idea of casually getting out my guitar to sing in Mum's lounge room feels inappropriate. The suburbs seem no place for a minstrel used to playing and singing out on the road and I cringe with embarrassment, as I sometimes still do, that I have travelled such a long way from the place where I first heard my mother singing. People sing scales in this house, they practise vocal exercises and learn 'proper music'; they study for exams, compete in eisteddfods, and perform in recitals. I was familiar with all those music rituals as a violinist and was, for a while, a 'professional'. But even Sister

Mary Immaculate Conception, my first violin teacher, once said to Mum: 'I don't think the violin will ever be enough for her.' Perhaps she was right. The violin became a tool for other kinds of discoveries, not just musical ones. I travelled with it like a friend, an explorer, sometimes, when things got tough, like a soldier. There was something deliberate and symbolic, though, in how I had put my violin bow back in its case and started to strum the guitar or the violin to accompany myself as I sang my songs. Musically speaking, it made me naked. It gave me nowhere to hide. Abandoning the violin, and what the violin brought me in terms of work, had sometimes seemed like a kind of madness. But I knew I had to find the song inside me, the song I hadn't heard yet, even though my voice was weak and untrained. I was ok with my choices and used to people asking me to stop singing and play the violin instead. But I still feel nervous playing and singing in front of people who knew me before, as if they all might secretly think as they listen: 'Oh my God! What the hell happened to her? She had such a bright future ahead of her.'

I take a deep breath to calm my nerves and carry my guitar back up the stairs so Mum can hear my song. I say nothing as I begin to strum and watch as her eyes close and her breath starts to ease.

In my solitude / I know you'd be here if you could

I sing the song I performed last night in Bellingen.

In my solitude / Oh please don't think me rude

I understand about the solitude, Mum says after I finish. *So soothing.*

Are you lonely, Mum? I suddenly ask, wondering if this is what she really means.

Lonely? Good god no. I like to be on my own. She says it as if she means it. *After your father died I got used to the quiet. I looked forward to it. Lying on the couch at night watching the television. Not thinking about anything. Not having to do anything for anybody.*

She starts to cry then, not quietly or discreetly, but loudly and abruptly. Her tears are both a shock and not entirely unexpected; when I hear them they are at once alien and as familiar as the lounge room of my old home, which has hardly changed at all since I was a little girl – the dull plush carpet, the old scratched furniture, the heavy linen curtains hanging in front of dusty alcoves, the cheap, laminate entertainment unit that holds French, Italian and German books and old videos. In among the mismatched utilitarian furnishings, though, there are two beautiful things: a silky oak china cabinet that Mum bought before she was married, filled with old china cups, saucers and plates, all purchased before she became a wife and mother and then hidden away behind locked doors as soon as her first baby was born. And in the corner the one thing in the room that really gleams: Mum's mahogany baby grand piano.

Oh, Linda. She holds out her hand to me; I take it in return. *You are going to stay for a while, aren't you?*

Of course, Mum, I say, hugging her.

I don't know why I say 'of course' the way I do, as if this request and my casual answer are the two most natural things in the world. For the first time in years she seems lost for words. Or else she has just temporarily misplaced her voice. She says nothing as she leans close into my shoulder, so close that only the sound of our breathing is the music between us.

Three weeks after I arrive back in Brisbane, Mum's first grandchild is born at Westminster Hospital in Toowong. The days between my arrival and this birth are filled with meetings and gatherings, with excursions to shopping centres I have not visited since I was a teenager, and sudden, unexpected encounters with old neighbours in the streets where I grew up. Mum's friends drop by to visit and exclaim their surprise at seeing me again. They are warm, welcoming, connected to me because they are connected to my mother. I answer their questions cheerily enough, but my ease is artificial. I feel abstracted, hardly tangible in this world of once familiar things. Mum is proud to have me back, though, and often refers to me as *my daughter, Linda.*

Her daughter, Linda.

I study myself in mirrors and discover a woman who doesn't appear to fit the place where she is. Even my long red curly hair feels too spontaneous among the short cuts and perms of my mother and her friends. I don't do anything as drastic as cutting it all off, but I mousse it for the first time in my life and twist it into the same kind of ringlets Grandma used to fashion from my hair when I was a child. The resulting curls give me such an old-world look that I feel as I did when I was first sent to violin lessons with Sister Mary Immaculate Conception, who taught in an old room of the oldest building in my mother's old school – a young girl with an old-fashioned hairdo, playing old music on an old woman's old violin.

During the days that lead up to the birth I couldn't ignore Mum's growing unresponsiveness to what was going on around her. Because she was reticent about using the phone, I took over the task of making daily phone calls to my sister-in-law, monitoring the pregnancy's progress. When the due date passed, Mum commented that it must be a boy as boys are always late.

And why is that, Mum? I asked, laughing, trying to draw her back from the absent space into which she now seemed to regularly disappear.

Because they find it harder to leave the womb than girls, she replied. *Except for you. We all thought you would be a boy because you took ages to come out.*

Maybe I was scared to leave the womb, I laughed, aware of how my symbolic interpretation of things often used to make her eyes roll.

Not like your sisters, she told me. *They couldn't wait to get out. They were just raring to go.* She trailed off as she often does these days, withdrawing into her own thoughts. I am left to fill in the gaps she leaves by her silence, imagining words, inventing fragments that hang in the air between us.

THE LONELIEST GOATHERD

My nephew, Finn Neil, is born on 14 November, my father's birthday. When Paul rings to announce his son's arrival, I have never heard him so happy.

He looks just like a Neil, Paul tells us on the phone from the hospital.

What the hell does that mean? I ask, receiving his joy and giving it back to him. *What does a Neil look like?*

I know his answer will be different to mine. To some, the Neil side of the family is a handsome lot: classically proportioned, refined, with large, well-shaped foreheads – to 'contain all the brains', as my grandmother used to put it. I always thought Dad's relatives were a broody bunch; their overhanging lids and downward curving eyes seemed to indicate deep thinking, worry, and secrets held inside. According to some sources, Neil means 'a king from Scotland'. Others say the name means 'Irish chieftain' or 'champion'. In the Gaelic tradition it means 'of dark complexion';

in a Cornish context it means 'power'. In another – my favourite – it signifies 'a cloud'.

Just like Dad did, Paul replies with unrestrained delight in his voice. *But then again a friend reckons all babies look like their fathers so that the fathers will fall in love with their own image and not leave.*

But you don't look like a Neil – small, dark and handsome, I tease him. *You're fair and cute like Mum's side of the family.*

The Cottrells, my mother's side of the family, were humbler, more practical, less snobbish than the Neils. The Neils were dark-haired and brown-eyed, the Cottrells fair and blue-eyed. The name 'Cottrell' means 'cottage' or 'cottager': he or she who owns a cottage. My grandmother, Christina Augusta Cottrell, perfectly embodied this name – acquired through her marriage to my grandfather Albert – by originally owning the two cottages that our family lived in. The cottage at St Lucia was enlarged eventually into something big enough to be called a house; the fibro shack at the Gold Coast – where Grandma originally lived before selling it to Dad for us to use as a holiday house – was hardly roomy enough to qualify even as a cottage. If names signify something more than the letters that form them or a legal necessity, the type of union suggested by the names Neil – dark-complexioned champion king – and Cottrell – he or she who owns a cottage – was embodied by the marriage of my mother and father. When Dad, dark haired, olive skinned, newly departed from a position as head of the Strathfield seminary – a fallen king – co-joined with my practical, industrious, cottage-dwelling blonde-haired mother, it was more than a union of the dark and the light, it was a merging of a kingly man without a cottage with a humble young woman whose mother owned two.

My brother shares the Cottrells' practical streak. Now, to top it all off, he has been practical enough to beget a child to carry on the name of those Celtic champions. We rejoice in some more trivial banter, this bubbling celebration of new life.

I can hear gurgling sounds in the background as I continue. *And his eyes? What colour are his eyes?*

Well, they're blue at the moment, Paul tells me, *but that'll change in the next few days.*

I give the phone to Mum. She is reluctant to speak even though this is a milestone for her – her first grandchild, from the son most likely to produce one for her, the only one of Mum's five children who is married and who, he tells me later, she feels is happy with his life. I know Mum sometimes fretted about her unmarried daughters, but she never pushed the idea of marriage onto us. If she ever brought up the subject she might have understood perfectly well if I had told her that while many girls were dreaming of weddings and gold rings, I was dreaming of being a female explorer, a research scientist, a discoverer of new things. *Perhaps we made you too independent,* she later wondered about me and my sisters. *You're all just too used to doing your own thing.*

Mum loved her sons. Her 'boys'.

Joan: Boys need to let off steam much more than girls. I used to dread the days it rained because the boys couldn't go outside then. They'd be inside all day throwing their cricket balls

> against the walls. I put my good china away just before my first child was born and never took it out again. Your father knew it was best to get the boys to run around as much as possible, to wear them out so they'd just come home when they were tired or hungry and not be so loud around the house. He was good like that. He thought sports would be better for the boys than music.

According to Mum, Paul, the eldest of her two boys, was one of those lucky people who expected to be loved from the moment he was born. He has always been a man who seemed at ease with himself, who liked to get on with people, who liked being married. We all thought he would be a wonderful father. When I became interested in names and their meanings I thought that it might have had something to do with his name, which means 'humble'. Perhaps a humble man is considered a good man, a man worthy of love. My other brother, Stephen, a name that means 'crown', which seems to perfectly suit his intellectual and refined demeanour, was also well loved, but more discreetly, I suspect. My two sisters also have names that would seem to bode well for the flowering of their finer natures: Cathie means 'pure' and Janice means 'gracious'.

I wave the phone in front of Mum, encouraging her to speak to this humble man whose good fortune it is to be so blessed with this expectation of always being loved. But she is distracted and worried about her state of mind and unsure if she can feel properly joyful at this milestone.

* * *

On the way to Westminster Hospital we stop at the Taringa Five Ways to buy fruit and flowers. Unable to even offer a smile, Mum waits in the car. It is a glorious November day in Brisbane. An unseasonable cool breeze is blowing while I pick out the most luscious bunch of flowers, but Mum is neither calmed nor cooled. She seems dislocated and anxious as we drive along the Brisbane River towards the hospital. Her face is tense and held in; I detect a clenching of the jaw and notice how distractedly she grips the armrest with her hand. I chat casually, encouraging her to breathe her way through her discomfort, trying to lighten the guilt she might feel about her lack of enthusiasm for this visit, marvelling too at the way fate works: that after years away from family duties I have returned for this day, while my mother, who has always ably fulfilled all her responsibilities, seems hardly able to enjoy it at all.

She leans on my arm as we walk up to the maternity ward from the hospital car park.

I'm so tired, she says wearily. *How did I get this tired? I don't know what I should do. Tell me what I should say. I should be happy, shouldn't I? I should feel happy. I know I should.*

I put my arm around her shoulders and propel her gently up the driveway. *I can't tell you what to say, Mum. Just say what you feel.*

She begins to cry again. *I don't know what I feel. I just feel tired.*

To distract her, I take her for coffee and cake before we head up to the maternity ward. The hospital's little café is staffed by volunteers; one is an old acquaintance of Mum's.

As I order tea and lamingtons, I notice how Mum shies away from contact, how she can hardly breathe from the fear she now feels at being out in public.

When I first see Finn, he is wrapped in a white flannelette sheet lying under a halo of light on a baby table in the middle of a small hospital room. Close up, Finn looks like a tiny version of a fully grown man. I love him deeply straight away. It enters me unexpectedly, this genetic bond, this wanting to linger near his breath, to smell his fresh skin, to be close to his murmurs and cries. I have to stop myself from becoming animal, from taking him to a corner of the airless private ward and holding him close to my heart, oblivious of any other claims on his little body, to hold his tiny face up to the light and offer him to the perfect blue November sky as a sign of new life and renewed possibilities.

Instead, Paul and I joke briefly about the coincidence of his birth falling on the same day as Dad's birthday.

Perhaps he's a reincarnated spirit, I tease him. *Perhaps he's Dad come back to watch over us.*

We all laugh, drawn closer by our shared love for the new child. I feel the biological pull as a kind of birth of something inside me too, a sense of something that wasn't there before, reflected in the tiny body, the little crushed face, the sleepy eyes and curled fingers, and matted black hair brushed forward like an old man's. *Dad,* I whisper out of earshot of the others who might take offence at my presumption. *Finn,* I sigh, nestling my cheek on his. *Dad. Finn.* For the first few hours, in the dislocated ecstasy of sudden love, the two names seem interchangeable.

Mum seems a little confused by the occasion as she hangs back from the cluster of love in the centre of the room. Finn is placed into her arms by his mother, a girl from the country just like Mum, who also believes in the value of these simple family rituals.

Joan, look what Paul and I have done. Kym smiles, exhausted yet radiant. *I remember what you told me about how you forget the pain it took to get them here the minute you hold them and now I understand.*

It is easy to see the sudden arousal of love between Kym and Paul, who seems giddy with happiness. Their bubble of emotion is so private and palpable that I back away and pull up seats for Mum and me near the window. From here Mum can look at the newly flowered poinsettia trees outside if she needs a distraction from the emotional business of this birth.

I'm sorry, Paul, she finally says. *I hardly sleep anymore.*

Paul has always been a generous man and is so happy now that he is not offended by Mum's state of mind. *That's ok, Mum,* he tells her, beaming. *We're just glad you're here,* he reassures her.

I know Mum is overjoyed at seeing her first grandchild but as I witness her behaviour in the maternity ward I understand that there could be something quite serious happening to her. It is unsettling for all of us to see. If our family had sometimes seemed like a whirlwind of music, sport and rowdy activity, Mum had always been the strong centre of the storm. She herself sometimes compared mothering five children to being a general in charge of a small army. But I hadn't always been such a good soldier and in the family I was sometimes known by the term my Uncle Charlie first coined for me: 'the little rebel'.

When I was eight one of my first acts of rebellion had to do with the song 'The Lonely Goatherd' from *The Sound of Music,* which my mother had volunteered all three of her daughters to perform wearing bibbed skirts and babushkas and holding puppets dressed in lederhosen and alpine hats. Along with four other boys and girls, the three of us were supposed to represent the von Trapp family in a draughty room in one of the back streets of inner city Brisbane, the premises of Russell's Music and Dance Academy.

Unaccredited by any official organisation, these Academies of Song and Dance, these Schools of Voice, Strings, and Keyboard, were a kind of underground network of music teaching in Brisbane run by men and women like Russell, who may once have done a stint in the chorus of a show in Sydney or Melbourne before heading north to set up shop in Brisbane. They operated in a secret, lowbrow world, never directly referring to the Conservatorium of Music, which in those days and right up until the new millennium did not regard any academies that taught American show tunes, music hall medleys and tap dancing as either legitimate or musical.

My mother worked at one of these academies playing the piano for Russell's singing and dancing students. Russell was a short, boisterous man who fulfilled Mum's dreams of being a professional musician by paying her a few dollars an hour for weeks of evening rehearsals for his regular *Gala Night at the Academy* shows. 'The Lonely Goatherd' was Russell's idea, and it seemed logical that the three extra girls needed to complete the faux von Trapp ensemble would be provided by his eager-to-please accompanist.

Despite how hard she worked and how little she was paid, I know Mum loved the thrill of being involved with these shows and thought her daughters should be equally as thrilled. It was also a feat of organisation for her to have all our meals cooked and frozen in separate containers – individually marked with our names according to our particular culinary tastes – so that each night of the week she was away at rehearsals we would have a different meal – with dessert accompanying each of them. But I had already begun to wage battles with Mum over the matter of violin practice and I was in no mood to cooperate over a goatherd, no matter how lonely he was. My refusal to wear the coordinated floral outfits made from the curtains in Russell's mum's lounge room, or to participate in Russell's choreography, which involved making our puppets dance and do somersaults during the instrumental interlude, or, in the end, to perform at all, would become another step in my campaign of musical independence.

It wouldn't be the last piece of music I sat out, but it was the first major strategic withdrawal I made from the sound of my mother's voice. In the end, looking bored and refusing to open my mouth did the trick. I was quickly sent off-stage by an exasperated Russell, in cohoots with my mortified mother. My protest was nonviolent and only partly successful; even though I was no longer expected to sing, dance or wear the pink floral babushkas and pinafores, I still had to accompany my mother and sisters to all their rehearsals, where I would sit slumped and sulking while Russell commanded his troops and my mother, his second-in-command, thumped away on the piano. I was also obliged to be in the audience for what turned out to be a charming and very melodious ensemble piece which the audience greeted with stamps and howls that Cathie and Janice absorbed with wide, exuberant grins lighting up their pretty faces.

I was envious of their success, but not of the tortuous negotiations which rehearsals turned out to be, with Russell alternately barking and cajoling his inexperienced singers into performing professionally. Mum never said 'I told you so' about this triumph. Not directly. And neither of my sisters tried to rub salt into my wounded and stubborn pride. They didn't have to. When they were asked to give a reprise performance at a bigger hall for an even larger and more boisterous crowd, I was – not unexpectedly – left out; as I was the next year when Russell decided to dress up his singing troupe as a group of Asian children to sing 'I Whistle a Happy Tune' from *The King and I*. But despite realising, even then, that my stubbornness could isolate and marginalise me, as well as exasperate my mother, there was no way, I whispered to myself when, as well as being left out of the concert I was left at home through all the rehearsals – the loneliest goatherd of all – that I could whistle anything, let alone a happy tune, with the extravagant Russell in charge of both my mother and the music.

I still can't whistle at all. Both my brothers are virtuosos. Paul – who uses a unique technique that involves throwing his head back and clenching his teeth in a half-smile – is a brilliant whistler. He could certainly have whistled that happy tune – if he'd been asked. I imagine he made Kym swoon and giggle with his perfect whistling of Cole Porter's 'Night and Day' during their courting days, and he could make us all laugh with his whistled interpretations of any number of songs by Frank Sinatra or Fred Astaire. He was a wonderful, natural singer too, favouring supporting roles in amateur theatre productions of such musicals as *South Pacific* and *Guys and Dolls* in which he once sang the part of Nicely-Nicely Johnson for the Ignations Musical Society at Toowong. I went along, probably grumbling, to one of his performances with Mum, who attended every production in which her kids appeared or played in.

I was surprised, even shocked that evening as I had no idea that my sports-mad, musically untrained brother could sing as beautifully as he did. I recall Paul's buoyancy on stage, his ready grin, his slightly kooky charm, the obvious pleasure he took in wearing the nifty suit and rakish hat that was part of his costume. Most of all, though, I remember him hitting some high notes at the end of a song in such a pure falsetto voice that I felt I was being lifted up out of my seat. I turned to Mum in astonishment to see if she was as surprised as I was, but she was too busy beaming to return my look, perhaps overcome herself at how unexpected and joyful those fleeting sounds were.

At the hospital now Paul isn't singing though, he's whistling a quite comical kind of lullaby to Finn, with sound formed through his trademark gritted teeth, as I steer Mum out of the room in search of tea and sandwiches.

Perhaps a change of scenery will help calm her emotions, which at the moment seem to ebb and flow depending on her surroundings. We walk arm-in-arm to the cafeteria singing a little as we go and Mum is almost jovial by the time we run into Jonus Nicholson, a prominent doctor at the hospital and also one of Mum's most dedicated singing students. Jonus is a vigorous, palpably confident man, who is also noticeably deferential to Mum.

So do we call you Grannie now, Joan? he asks.

She gives Jonus a comical withering look. *Believe me, Jonus, no one is going to call me Grannie.*

I can see that only politeness stops Jonus from clapping Mum on the back as he would any other colleague.

That's the spirit, he says instead, bowing slightly. *You'll always be young at heart, Joan. We all know that.*

He prepares to move on – an important man in an important hospital has little time for chitchat. As his singing mentor, though, Mum has claims on his time. She calls him back with a theatrical whisper and asks to speak to him privately for a few moments.

He offers her a seat near the nurses' desk.

Sure thing, Joan. What exactly is the problem?

She sits down heavily, as her eyes well with tears. *I haven't slept for nearly two months and I just can't take it anymore.*

Jonus seems mortified as she begins to sob quietly. *Oh, come on now,* he blusters. *Where's our strong dependable Joan? This isn't like you at all.*

That's all very well for you to say, Jonus, she whimpers, visibly embarrassed by his manner. *But I just can't go on like this. I need to rest. Even for one night. I just don't feel like myself at all.*

Sensing that something serious is happening, both to my mother and to their relationship, Jonus immediately takes charge, as I suspect a man of his energy might. His friendly tone changes slightly as he straightens up beside Mum's crumpled body.

First thing tomorrow, I'll book you in for some sleep therapy, he announces. *It looks to me like a long rest will do you the world of good. Get your body back into its old routine. Believe me, I'd go in there myself if I had half the chance.*

You have a special ward for sleep therapy? I ask, marvelling that such a place might exist in a traditional hospital.

Ward 6B, he replies briskly.

Ward 6B, I echo.

Ward 6B, he snaps back, with a comedian's timing. *Joan, you can stay there for a few days, a week if you want to, and get back on your feet. You'll be as good as gold in no time,* he promises, and, unable to restrain himself a moment longer, he taps Mum lightly on the back. *We can't have you getting sick and stressed on us,* he continues. *We all need you too much.*

He springs to his feet as he prepares to move on. *I'll get cracking on getting you a bed,* he promises. *So you can get better and get cracking on the music for our Anzac Day concert. Is it a deal?*

He holds out his hand for a shake. Mum takes it limply, exhausted, I imagine, at the thought of doing anything at all, let alone organising a concert for this energetic, overwhelming man.

He drops Mum's hand quickly and takes mine instead before leading me a little way up the corridor. *Your mother's not herself,* he tells me, hanging an arm around my shoulder and steering me away from Mum. *What's been the problem?*

I don't really know, I answer honestly. *I know she hasn't really slept at all for weeks.*

Letting go of my shoulder, he signals confidently back to Mum. *Well,* he says, turning abruptly back to me, *we can fix that problem for a start and then see what happens. Ring Ward 6B tomorrow and check that your mother's bed has been organised and then bring her in as soon as possible.*

As he begins to move on, he calls back to Mum who is slouched over on the seat, dabbing at her eyes with a handkerchief. *Righteo, Joan,* he assures her. *We'll get you back on your feet before you know it. And then we'll all be singing again. Remember the vowels . . . A-E-I-O-UUUU . . .*

He sings an arpeggio for each vowel sound as he backs away from us down the corridor, deftly swerving around nurses as he goes, as if, along with his many other skills, he also has eyes in the back of his head. Then he is gone, a whirlwind of activity and advice. I sit beside Mum and smile reassuringly.

Sleep therapy sounds good, do you think? I ask, teetering between optimism and anxiety.

Anything sounds good, she answers.

On the way out we call in to see the baby again, but Mum is restless to leave. Driving home, we discuss the possibilities of sleep therapy. I imagine soft music wafting through corridors, meditation tapes lulling the sleep-deprived into slumber, soft curtains blowing in the spring breezes. I once spent a summer playing meditation music in the hills behind Byron Bay. I saw ex-junkies, incest victims, the bored, the depressed and the broken-hearted soothed by the vibrations of peaceful music. I always hoped that these things would one day slowly creep into the mainstream and even believe for a moment that they may already have arrived at hospitals for the wealthy and the well-insured.

It turns out Ward 6B is the hospital's psychiatric ward, something I discover when I ring the hospital the next day to confirm Mum's bed.

Is there anywhere else she can go? I ask the nurse in charge of admissions. *I mean, she's not mentally ill. She's just tired.*

Oh, don't worry about it. She sounds eager to get off the phone. *Lots of women come in here to regulate their sleep patterns. You'd be surprised by how many patients we see with similar problems to your mother's.*

But there will be some kind of therapy, won't there? My unease is immediate, as is my sense that things are moving forward too quickly.

The nurse, though, presses on. *Absolutely,* she insists. *The doctor will see her and decide what course of action to take.*

Will they talk with Mum about ways of dealing with stress? I ask anxiously. *Relaxation? Meditation?*

You'll have to talk to the doctor about all these things, she says, obviously not wanting to waste any more of her time on the phone. *All I can do for the moment is tell you that your mother's bed is ready and she can come in anytime.*

I don't feel comfortable about taking Mum to the hospital and try to dissuade her from this first step into institutional care. But I have been away too long to establish trust between us so quickly. In her eyes I am still the rebel daughter, used to opposing everything she says, just for the sake of it. So I buy her some new undies, help her pack, even joke with her that we should just look at the whole thing as an adventure and that things will settle down and get back to normal in no time.

During the drive to the hospital, the weather seems too perfect for such an occasion. The jacaranda trees, so recently hung in hazes of purple, are lush and benign even though their time of full flowering is over. We're in Mum's car for this trip: a blue Hyundai Excel, the first of its kind in Australia, which she and Dad bought with his superannuation back in the late eighties. It runs more smoothly than my old car and after regular cleaning and servicing it smells as if it's still new. Mum is not entirely comfortable with me at the wheel; she still associates me with many wayward things, including driving recklessly. I can't really blame her for this; my lifestyle has hardly given her reason to think I am one hundred percent reliable about practical things. But she is insecure about driving herself now, so has conceded the keys to me for the first of many drives I will make with her in the passenger seat.

The psych ward is in one of the oldest sections of the hospital. I imagine I can smell sweet antiseptic and Dencorub long before we arrive there. Mum is suddenly uncertain, just like I am, when we arrive at the hospital doors. I feel her resistance beneath my arm as I guide her through the main entrance, past the chapel, the reception desk, the newsagent, gift shop, café and chemist. We walk carefully, arm in arm, looking around us like children from a fairytale about to enter a dark and forbidding place.

The head nurse meets us at the psych ward's reception desk. Gloria is large and soft, a physical combination that seems to perfectly reflect her matronly demeanour. She is maternal and efficient with round, wet eyes. She begins her introductions in a breathy voice that gets breathier as she goes on. *The new ward we're building for our patients will be bright and sunny,* she says when she sees me look anxiously at the gloomy rooms. *I swear the rooms are like hotel suites.*

There are no private rooms available at such short notice, so Mum is allocated a bed in a large room at the end of the furthest corridor already occupied by two heavily made-up elderly women and a girl who introduces herself as 'Betty with bipolar'. While Mum's admission papers are sorted out, I stay close to her, sitting beside her in the plastic chairs which smell of Spray 'n' Wipe and lavender. I am still beside her when a nurse with a tray stops in front of us and hands Mum a pill at the same time that Betty strokes Mum's cheek and says 'hello' again. Betty wouldn't be more than fifteen, but she already smells stale and old. Her teeth are yellow under swollen red gums and her greying hair is a further shock in someone so young. She seems neglected, unnaturally puffy and hungry for attention. I look at Betty and then at Mum, and for a moment I can't bear to see the thread that holds them together, to see Betty's vulnerability reflected in my mother's tired blue eyes, in her slim body defeated by its fatigue, unable to remove herself, through either her will or her energy, from this irrevocable step.

Gloria gives Mum a glass of water to wash down the pill. I stand up and hover uneasily.

If you don't mind me asking, what's the pill for? I enquire. I try my softest, least threatening voice. *I'm Joan's daughter,* I whisper, stricken suddenly by some subterranean urge to apologise to this harried woman for being here. *I'm looking after her.*

There. I've said it. What I never thought I would say: I am looking after my mother.

Gloria smiles at Mum. *It's just to help you calm down, Joan,* she says. *That's what you came in for.*

Placing my hand on Mum's arm, I say in my most easygoing voice: *I thought she was coming in for some sleep therapy.*

Yes. Gloria places her hand on Mum's other shoulder. *We'll take care of that a little later. We've just got to settle her in now.*

Mum seems oblivious to the subtleties of what is taking place above her: her daughter and her nurse, like two sentries standing guard over her. Gloria's in charge, though, as she helps Mum up, encourages her to swallow the pill quickly and move away from me.

All the information's been sent down, she tells me. *You should go and have a rest yourself while we take care of Mum.*

She calls my mother 'Mum'. Generically, I suppose. How many mothers who come into the psych ward for a rest does she call Mum? Perhaps it's too hard to remember so many names. Perhaps she calls everybody Mum, even women who haven't given birth. I've always believed that we are capable of mothering and fathering each other, so it's nice if she calls everyone Mum. Does she also call the male patients 'Dad'? My mind races around these ridiculous thoughts as I watch Mum being led down the corridor towards her room. They're trained in this sort of thing, I think more rationally now, trained to deal with families that don't want to let their loved ones go, that don't trust complete strangers to understand what is at stake when their mother or father walks through the hospital door and away from the familiarity of their care.

Four days after admitting Mum, Gloria pulls me aside on my way to visit Mum. She wheezes slightly when she breathes and I notice an asthma inhaler sticking out of her front pocket.

Have you noticed a lot of changes in your mother since she's been here? she asks, obviously concerned. *We've been having trouble getting the dosage right. The average patient we get in here has a far greater tolerance for these sorts of medications than your mother seems to.*

Gloria is solicitous and courteous, but her gaze is constantly distracted, like a sentry, I think, still alert after a long watch.

The problem is that your mother's never taken sleeping pills or tranquillisers of any sort before, has she?

I know Gloria wants a shorthand answer, something she can fit on the black dotted line on the hospital form, not an in-depth analysis. So I ask, in as friendly a voice as possible: *Is this a problem?*

Most women over the age of fifty, she tells me, *are taking something to help them sleep or settle their mood. And most women who come in here have already developed a certain tolerance for medication, so we prescribe accordingly. Your mum, however, is different.*

I don't know how to address Gloria's assumptions about what 'most women' do, but I can hear Mum's voice somewhere in my head telling me not to ask so many questions, telling me to just go along with things. I am in her world now, the world she trusts. I owe her, at least, my effort to be polite, to try to support what she would do in regards to her own body.

I keep my voice even as I finally speak: *As far as I know Mum never took anything to help her sleep.*

My answer appears to satisfy Gloria who seems prepared to end our conversation. I'm not satisfied, though.

We actually thought there was some sort of sleep therapy program in here, I query.

Most of our patients want the sleeping pills, she asserts gently.

I understand. But I'm sure Mum doesn't want to become dependent on sleeping pills, I reply, already feeling like a troublemaker. I've got to 'pull my head in', I remind myself, doing a passable imitation of Mum admonishing me. She'd be right too. Using the word 'dependent' is too pre-emptive. But after years in the music scene I'm paranoid about drugs of any kind.

It's not a question of becoming dependent, Gloria continues evenly. *Your mother hasn't slept properly for weeks. Months perhaps. And her body needs a chance to catch up. We're just trying to facilitate that process.*

Facilitate the process. I feel uneasy, as if I am hearing a foreign language. *How long will this process take?* I ask. *What I mean is, how long will she be in here . . . on the medication?*

She glances over my shoulder.

Well, that's not for me to say, she answers briskly. *You need to talk to your mother's doctor. Do you have authority to do that?*

She seems keen to end our conversation. I feel guilty, demanding.

What authority do I need? I ask without guile. *I'm just staying with Mum for a while.*

There is a commotion in a nearby room. Gloria has a quick gasp on her inhaler as she walks away without answering my question. It sounds like Betty, who, in the short time I've been visiting the hospital, has revealed a compulsive habit of hopping into bed with the other women patients. From the outside, it looks more logical than mad, this lonely sick girl wanting to cuddle these maternal older women, whom even Gloria calls Mum. But in here it is crazy. Or it is driving everyone else crazy.

My throat feels as dry as Betty's sounds. I listen intently as her screams are muffled. I still feel uneasy, but I remind myself to take a deep breath and then a few more. Inhaling and exhaling lightens my mood and calms me down. I tell myself as I breathe that I can come and go as I please. Hospitals such as this one are a part of my mother's world to which I am making a brief visit. I only intend to stay a little while with Mum, until she's better, then move back to my own life.

I walk on past the open door of a small single room in which I can see Betty being comforted by two nurses. I keep walking. Years of travel have taught me how to keep moving, how not to get involved. There are some basic conventions of the stranger passing through: you keep your eyes and ears open and you say as little as possible. So I smile sweetly and make a promise to myself as I head down to Mum's room that, like a traveller in need of rest, I will only stay a little while longer in Brisbane – at least until Mum is weaned off the pills which are being prescribed for her and which she is now taking every night to help her sleep.

ONE FINE DAY

When I was a teenager, after I'd forgotten my dream of being the best violinist in the whole world, I dreamed of being a forensic scientist. Another dream was to be a private detective, to uncover the secrets lying beneath the surface all around me. Later, these occupations never presented themselves to me as real possibilities, but during the time I am in Brisbane with Mum I begin to tape many conversations and interviews with family members and with friends. I don't do this secretly, as a real private detective might; there are no hidden microphones or clandestine operations involved.

Later, I will translate these recorded voices, conversations and dialogues with family members and friends into words, stories, and sometimes into songs. These testimonies also contain stories about my father and my grandmother, who I will subsequently come to know much better long after their deaths. Many of the recordings I make, though, are with my mother. I do this as a kind of research, to have a record of our relationship and the experience of coming home. They are also a record of Mum's voice, the only thing about her I had ever really known. But other things emerge as I go through this process of recording, transcribing and reading Mum's words – a sense of exploration and discovery, the things I had longed for as a child. This adventure does not unfold in faraway exotic countries, though, but in the house where I grew up. This is the greatest discovery, perhaps, of this homecoming. Through this process, I will also have a chance to finally get to know my mother and learn to hear her voice as the instrument through which her own divine whisper speaks.

I can't really say I ever knew my mother. I knew who she was; I knew her name and what she did. I can describe her activities (and in her many letters over the years she presented herself as a sum of her and her family's activities) and perhaps the timetable into which she fitted her – and our – life. I can say she was a singer, a teacher, a student, as well as a mother and a wife. I would never think to say she was 'just a housewife', even though she was a wife who also did most of her studying, teaching and singing in the house. But the divisions between her home life and her work life were hardly distinct. She did like her restful moments, though, and was a great fan of the afternoon soaps on television. She liked to plop down on the couch in the lounge room to watch them in the interlude between her afternoon and evening activities. These included teaching, writing articles on singing and teaching for newsletters, as well as talking to parents about their children's music practice and exams and – when her kids were still at home – preparing afternoon tea and evening meals for the family.

But I can't say I knew her. Not on the inside. Not the way that later I knew others. Or came to know myself. I only ever sensed her through the soundtrack she provided for my life, from the past to the present, from the songs she sang around me when I was a child to the songs I wrote myself and sang to her when I returned to care for her and the disease which eventually will claim her voice, the only thing about my mother I ever really knew.

As a child, in the absence of this knowing, I became connected to other things. I became a blind person in a world of sound and vibration. I crept into the furthest corners of our chaotic house, lay under pillows, behind dusty curtains, my feet wedged into the star-shaped holes of the besser brick that covered the front wall of our house, and tried to imagine what it would be like to be dead. I listened for ghosts and ghostly sounds. Sometimes, when the house was suddenly quiet, when even the constant music had stopped, I thought I could conjure up the sound of the past, both recent and distant, and train my ears to discern the intricate melodies within these invisible things.

Many of the details of my childhood are about listening: to songs, to melodies, to words, to radios and record players, to birds and cars and children and cricket and football and conversation, to stories, both real and imagined. But we were bodies as well as voices, which, according to my mother, are one and the same thing, so there are some indisputable things that can be listed. Details about the relationship between Mum and me include the fact that she rarely discussed hair, makeup or wardrobe issues with me during my childhood or adolescence, except for the times I was performing music, when the matter of clothes seemed to become important. When I was first learning the violin, she had also painstakingly and painfully played note after note on the piano in order to 'drum the pitch' into my ears. She wanted me to be practical like my grandmother, who had once earned money by 'taking in sewing'. I never quite understood what it meant to 'take in sewing', even after I was, literally, taken to sewing lessons in an old building in town after I had twice failed sewing in Grade Four, when Sister Mary Serenity had written on my report card that the stitches on my sampler reminded her of 'dog's teeth'.

We never had much money and apart from our school shoes we often only had one extra pair of shoes for the whole year. But I remember that Mum once bought me a pair of brown vinyl Mary Jane shoes with a gauze bow after she found me crying on my pillow one night because I was so sad at having such 'ugly old things' to wear to school birthday parties. She also let my grandmother curl my hair around old rags at night, turning them into ringlets when I went to my local primary school during Grades One and Two. I loved my neat, perfectly curled, hopelessly old-fashioned hair and was devastated when for 'practical reasons' Mum cut it all off after I was sent to the big St Hildegard's School in town to begin Grade Three. A couple of years later when I learned some more Biblical stories I compared the loss of my ringlets to the shearing of the sleeping Samson by his cunning Delilah. I felt small, ugly and powerless with my formerly luxuriant mane now cropped close to my head in a hairdo that an older cousin once compared to a curly swimming cap.

It was the sort of hairdo old ladies wore after their hair turned blue or purple, the sort of hairdo that, I was told, I would grow into. Gazing up at all the short permed hairdos that women seemed to wear after a certain age when, as far as I could see, aesthetics no longer had any bearing on their choices of clothes, shoes, handbags or hairdos, I was horrified by the thought that it would probably be forty or fifty years before I would 'grow into' the hairdo my mother had chosen for me and that all I had ahead of me was a lifetime of looking hideous and old before my time.

Mum remains in hospital for two weeks and returns home like a newborn herself, and I cancel music jobs in Sydney and the New South Wales north coast in order to spend Christmas with Mum for the first time in years. The sleeping pills she began to take while staying in Ward 6B give her the sleep she craves, but their side-effects make her body feel increasingly disorientated and exhausted. Other problems develop as well: she stops driving her car, becomes more reluctant to speak to people on the phone, and seems less and less capable of taking care of her own needs. I become the designated driver, her secretary, her personal assistant. Over a period of weeks, then, and with little conscious choice, I become her carer.

It will only be for a couple of months, I tell Raphael, who is becoming increasingly wistful as I regularly forget to ring him back when he leaves messages asking how I am and for me to call him. *A couple of months till she is back on her feet,* I now say enigmatically whenever a friend from Sydney or Byron Bay asks when they might expect to see me again. The truth is not so simple, nor as vague as I make out to them.

I like being home. This comes as a surprise to me. I like being with Mum. A couple of months turns into three, then four, then more, until, at the end of March 1999, I arrange for my things to be sent up from down south, set up house in the flat at the back of my mother's home, and, on the advice of Mum's doctor, apply for a full-time carer's allowance. Later, I will see this step as a milestone of sorts. The day I sign on for this allowance marks a demarcation point that officially brings me home again to my mother's house in a full circle. I am no longer living an artist's life out in the world, no longer playing and recording music, or exploring love. The art I am developing now is altogether different.

WE'LL MEET AGAIN

Dad was always considered the literary one of the family. But later, when I go through Mum's things, I discover piles of old newsletters issued by the Music Teachers' Association of Queensland, to which she regularly contributed notes about singing. I discover passages that illuminate more than just the simple mechanics of the voice: they reveal my mother's devotion to her craft and the sharpness of her mind.

Mum was never fascinated with the voice itself as a musical instrument. She felt that singers should mould their voices into flowing, correctly shaped and meaningful words. 'We should work for beauty and resonance,' she wrote in July 1990. 'Big is not necessarily beautiful. It is better to be light and right than strong and wrong. Singing is a flowing living language that can speak of joy and sadness in ways that words cannot.'

Mum wrote a lot about being nervous. How not to be nervous. She studied many books about how to calm the nerves, as well as the reasons why they were there in the first place. Finding a way to rise over the chaos of emotions and feel peaceful and balanced was a kind of personal quest for her that wasn't only to do with performing music. She tells me that as a young woman she struggled with feelings of timidity and that she had to work hard to develop a strong mental approach, not just to singing, but to every situation in life.

She knew how loud the destructive dialogue could be inside your head and encouraged all her students to identify and discard the negativities that tightened up the throat and made a full clear tone difficult to produce. She knew how many of her pupils had been told when they were children that they could not sing to save their lives, that singing was something other people did, that singing should remain in the bedroom or the bathroom. She also understood how easily a singer's terror could transmit itself to an audience and she worked hard to build confidence in all her students.

As for me, Mum pushed me year after year to perform, in exams, in competitions, for eisteddfods and auditions. Without her, I would perhaps have just stayed in my room reading books and dreaming of other lives I might have led. Without her encouragement, I would never have attended my first audition for the local youth orchestra and found myself ushered straight into the First Orchestra rather than having to do my time, as so many others had to, in the minor orchestras as a prelude to 'making it' to the big one.

Despite all her encouragement, though, I never stopped being terrified when I had to perform classical music. My fingernails were bitten down to the flesh and my knees used to quiver uncontrollably whenever I had to play in public. So it could have been me she was addressing when, in 1988, she wrote: 'Try to perform with ease, assurance and artistry. This gives the listener a feeling of pleasure and relaxation. Nervousness is catching, but so is assurance.'

On 25 April 1999, Mum's birthday, the traditional Anzac Day Benefit Concert at the Westminster Hospital takes place for the first time without Mum accompanying her singing students, who have always been – and will be this year for the last time – an integral part of the occasion. After a depressing birthday lunch at a Chinese café – neither of us feels like eating – we drive to the hospital where Jonus Nicholson is hosting the concert. The program promises us a patriotic show consisting of old war tunes and slides celebrating 'the glory and sorrow of war'.

First up is Hilary, a young secretary from Wynnum. For the past five years she has travelled to St Lucia every week to learn singing from Mum. Hilary loves musical comedy and before the concert she tells me she would one day like to teach singing in a room underneath the house where she lives with her young family, just like Mum did. In the concert, Hilary sings 'We'll Meet Again' with such emotional precision that by the end of the song many in the audience are crying. Their tears might also have something to do with the slides that are shown on a screen behind her while she sings – of diggers and soldiers, young men and old men, leaving for and returning from wars. But I sense also that there is something inside

Hilary's body as she sings, some feeling she is trying to access and translate into vocal timbre and resonance. Beside me, Mum is feeling those things too, willing them from her body into Hilary's body, as if she is singing along, a strange duet of teacher and student, bound together through resonance.

The concert is long and Mum is fatigued by half-time, but stands bravely beside me among the crowd sipping champagne and nibbling on small cakes and pies. Occasionally, we are discovered by one of Mum's old colleagues, or by the families of Mum's students who are starring in the concert.

Jonus finds us after we have both sat down exhausted behind some potted palms. He is jubilant. So far the concert has been a great success. But he is still anxious for Mum's approval.

Well, Joan, he says. *How do you think I sound?*

It's a question that needs a tactful answer. Despite his other career achievements, Jonus is especially proud of his singing ability, even though during the first half of the concert he had bellowed off-key British war tunes with the sort of confidence and poise that suggested he may have been tone deaf.

Well, Jonus, Mum offers weakly, *it's certainly getting better. Just keep listening to your tapes like I told you to. And it will keep on improving. Just remember the first rule of performing – don't let your nerves get the better of you.*

A lot of the performers at the Anzac Day concert are nervous, but most manage to hide it. Their training has made it possible to overcome what normally constricts the ability of the diaphragm to expand and suck in air. Though none of

Mum's students will ever be well known, they have achieved enough of their potential to have their own moment of glory on Anzac Day.

One of them is Geoff from Morningside, a beefy truck driver whom Mum took on as a student after he'd been rejected by both the university and the Conservatorium of Music. Before he begins to sing, Mum whispers to me that Geoff is a rare find: a bass baritone with real charisma. Though he's only in his early twenties, Geoff sings with a resonance you might expect from a mature man. His voice is rich and vibrates with warmth and power and his diction is clear and flawless. *Both the conservatorium and university rejected him because he wasn't educated and spoke so roughly,* she tells me, quickly growing weary from the effort of speaking. *They couldn't look beyond the surface and see and listen to what was underneath. So they sent him to me.*

After the concert, Geoff comes up and gives Mum a kiss on the cheek. She beams at him maternally, yet I can see she is distracted and confused by the attention from so many students and friends who have not seen her for months and who crowd around her when the concert is over.

Whaddya reckon, Mrs Neil? Geoff asks in a broad ocker voice. He towers over her: a giant man and a little woman. But his demeanour is respectful and it's obvious her words carry weight for him.

Wonderful, Geoff. Now you really ought to go and audition for the opera company next. If opera companies have one thing in common it's that there are never enough bass baritones, she flatters him.

Geoff shakes my hand effusively before leaving us. Relieved, Mum takes my arm and leads me towards the door for some fresh air. Suddenly she is sanguine: *One of the proudest moments of my life was when he won the Grand Prize for Opera from Margaretta Eldridge at the National Eisteddfod in Sydney,* she tells me. *She wrote a glowing review of his singing. That showed them – all the knockers – that you should always try to give everyone a chance, no matter where they come from.*

On the evening of Mum's birthday, inspired by what I have heard and seen at the Anzac Day concert, I record the first of many interviews with Mum about her work as a singing teacher.

Linda: Do you remember how you always seemed to take on pupils who everyone else had rejected?

Joan: I prided myself on getting ordinary people with ordinary abilities and teaching them, first of all to do the most basic things like sing in tune, the rudiments of good diction, then teaching them that a song was a story told in music and that they had to mean every word for the song to get across to the listener.

Linda: I remember sometimes we'd hear your students from upstairs. Some of them were so awful.

Joan: I don't like words like 'awful'. Who decides what's awful? I didn't think that people should be denied the opportunity to do what they loved to do just because they may not have any natural ability. And how do you know, if you rejected people out of hand, that you might be letting go of

> something precious and meaningful, not just in their own lives but for us, the audience as well? People can be taught a lot of things: how to have good diction, how to produce resonance, how to understand the mechanics of singing. But what they can't be taught is what's already inside them: their spirit and their soul. Singing really opens everything up. It opens up the singer and the one who is sung to as well. It was always a joy to me when students of mine with little or no ability got up to sing at a recital for the first time. The sense of accomplishment they had. The joy and happiness in their faces.

By the end of 1999 both Mum and I have lived through many new beginnings as well as endings. I join a gym and begin exercising regularly for the first time. I start yoga, meditation and chanting. Despite all these healthy efforts, though, I don't always handle my new life well. Sometimes I am ashamed to be back in Brisbane and go out of my way to avoid old acquaintances who see me across streets or in crowded shopping centres. Many nights I sob deeply into my pillow, missing my old life, missing Raphael and the friends I have left behind, as if somehow I have failed by coming home to my ailing mother, as if this was not some kind of life too, this return.

Not long after the Anzac Day concert in 1999, Mum teaches her last singing lesson. Her decision to stop teaching doesn't come to her in a sudden flash of clarity; rather, she just loses the will and the energy to do it. *It's something I used to live for,* she tells me. *Now the thought of it makes me want to cry.*

She continues taking the medication prescribed for her in hospital. As well as taking antidepressants and occasional sleeping tablets, she also begins to see a psychiatrist every now and then, not because she wants or needs to talk, but because these are the doctors who are involved in the treatment of the kind of vague malaise from which Mum now seems to be suffering. I am not comfortable about this. I sometimes wonder if Mum's medication might be creating more rather than fewer problems for her. But I have nothing to base my discomfort on. I only notice that she is turning inwards, growing increasingly unsure of herself and is tired a lot of the time.

She also abandons her morning walks, as well as get-togethers with friends. Long phone conversations are also things of the past. To fill the sudden gaps in her days and weeks, she finds new routines and interests. It is even fun for a while exploring the possibilities that change brings us. An adventurer at heart, I have always liked new things, but Mum is more a woman of routine and familiar things, and needs coaxing to take up new activities to replace those she has lost.

Other changes are valuable recompense for things I have lost. I get to know relatives again with whom I've been out of touch. Mum's brother Neville was once the captain of the Wallabies back when Rugby was neither professional nor lucrative. He and his wife, my Aunty Margo, are regular visitors to Mum's home. They also host her for frequent visits to their home at Mogill and during the drive to this outlying western suburb, Mum and I share stories from her past, she from her girlhood as the sister of a future Rugby Union star and me from my – often sanitised – life on what I laughingly called 'the road'.

Her new fragility makes her more tolerant of the kind of life that I have lived. Mum and I have dissimilar views about a lot of things: religion, politics, sex, race relations. Our differences once seemed crucial and fundamental, but now I barely notice them as we chat and laugh while driving along once familiar roads and highways.

Neville and Margo are kind and genuinely welcoming to Mum and to me. Margo especially sparkles when we visit and both she and Neville are concerned by Mum's problems, even though they are still unnamed, which are now making more changes necessary.

These changes incorporate Mum's belief, like her mother's, that an enquiring mind is a healthy mind. We look through the pamphlets for the University of the Third Age, which offers a variety of classes from which Mum chooses French, philosophy, and religion and spirituality. She enrols in each course, but attends class only once. I know she loves French, as Dad did, and once studied it at the University of Queensland. She also sang songs by Debussy and Ravel in their original texts, and enjoyed the occasional Charles Aznavour ballad, but now she says she cannot concentrate on anything so finely nuanced as the French language. Her supposed enrolment in secular philosophy is, she tells me, a clerical error, while the religion and spirituality class involves discussion about the philosophies of world religions, which leads Mum to decide that the matter of faith needed no deconstruction. *I know what I believe and that's enough for me,* she explains to me when I meet up with her after her first and only class at the Shingle Inn in Edward Street for tea and strawberry lamingtons, one of the simple pleasures that she is still able to enjoy. Later, when she joins the yoga and meditation classes for the over 55s at the City Hall, she often returns home in tears, unable to cope with the fear that now grips her when walking through city streets she has walked for most of her adult life.

She describes her mental state as somewhere between a buzz and a flame. Her eyes grow glassy from her medication and her coordination deteriorates to the point where she bumps into walls and doorways and begins to fall regularly around the house. She falls near the kitchen sink, on the cement driveway; she falls on the concrete path near the clothes line and tears the skin on both knees. Her thighs seem to be permanently bruised. Her skin grows thin, fragile, and is alabaster white; her scalp flakes constantly. For a woman who had been vital and working throughout her sixties, her sudden deterioration near the end of that decade is a shock. *I'm getting old,* she comments sadly. *And I don't know what is happening to my mind.*

THE RUSTLE OF SPRING

As a vocal teacher Mum's emphasis was always on the words and good diction. She thought subtlety was impossible without knowing the limits of your strength and power. 'Don't let the voice die away when singing softly,' she wrote in September 1988. 'Keep people on the edge of their seats with the intensity of your articulation. Keep the propulsion going. Work even harder with your waist muscles for soft singing.' She understood how important it was to recognise that each element contained its opposite element: softness needed strength, subtlety needed definition, force needed delicacy, and power, a light touch.

She concluded her article, as she often did, with a quotation from one of the dozens of resource books she consulted at our old dining room table as she wrote her commentaries for the singing teachers scattered all across the state. The one she chose in 1988 is particularly poignant in light of the coming years: 'This is the luxury of music. It touches every key of memory. It stirs all the hidden springs of sorrow and of joy. I love it for what it makes me forget and for what it makes me remember.'

Mum's mother, my grandmother Christina Augusta Cottrell, was left a widow at the age of fifty-two. After marrying relatively late to my grandfather Albert Cottrell, who was twenty years her senior, and having kids in her thirties, widowhood seemed to have energised rather than depressed her, though. After moving with her two children into the small house she bought near the university at St Lucia when the area was full of 'nothing but swamp, cows and professors', she cooked, cleaned, sewed and took in boarders to support her family. It wasn't easy for anyone in those days, especially for a woman who had left school when she was twelve. Mum was luckier though. She got to stay on at school till she was fifteen, when she had to turn down the senior school scholarship that a few lucky, bright girls were offered at the end of their junior year, a class Mum actually topped. Mum never resented this lost opportunity; in those days you did things that were 'good for the family' rather than 'good for yourself'. It wasn't in her nature to look back with regrets. She was like her mother and just 'got on with things'. She also never had a bad word to say about her father, whose deteriorating health had meant she had to start working as a stenographer to contribute to the family finances soon after leaving school. The bustle and activity of working life suited her. By the time she was fatherless three years later she was the head of the typing pool at Queensland Railways and a beautiful, blonde and budding part-time singer.

In the fifties and sixties, young women in Brisbane with singing in their blood had few opportunities to develop their potential. But Mum found teachers with names like Dulcie, Elsie and Ethel who taught singing in musty rented rooms high up in buildings in Queen, Edward and Wickham streets. Mum never called them by their first names and neither did we when we referred to them later. They were always Miss Dulcie Bolland and Miss Ethel Martin, L.Mus.A., A.Mus.A., as if their unmarried state was a matter for both public and private declaration, a badge of honour as important to them as the letters after their last names. It never occurred to me that Miss Martin may have been lonely or unfulfilled in her life. In photographs she looked beautiful. Mum spoke about her with love, respect and warmth, and when Miss Martin retired, Mum helped organise a special citation for her in honour of her teaching legacy.

Even we kids loved Miss Martin and never thought of using her first name. I used to think her title 'Miss' was honorary, like being called duchess or queen. I used to imagine that Miss Martin – and other women like her – were gatekeepers of a musical kingdom of order, tradition and theory that blossomed with flowers of song and melody. They looked like favourite aunts, but they were really mavericks and outsiders and subsequently were never part of that other kingdom – or queendom – of women who gave up their ambitions to sing after they married and who may have either pitied or envied the accomplishments of these pioneering women. Like the other religious women who had earlier schooled my mother, these nuns of music were also symbols of the few alternatives to marriage that were available to women of my mother's generation who had intelligence, talent, courage and a yearning for independence. And who, of course, could sing.

By January 2000, Mum is physically and mentally declining at an alarming rate. I sometimes wonder whether I am too complacent about what is happening to her, too lulled by my sense of 'coming home' to question Mum's doctors about the medication which seems to be making her increasingly vague. Perhaps I like how soothing this vagueness sometimes feels, even though I know it is out of character for Mum. Her doctors are still unable to specifically name her problem, but she now begins to refer to her 'mild nervous breakdown'.

The doctor says I may have had a breakdown, she whispers to me, not so much ashamed as relieved that there might be a logical explanation for her problems. A breakdown also implies the possibility of a recovery, if enough time and care are taken to repair her broken nerves. So we live in hope that such healing is possible – I still preface sentences with the phrase 'when you're better' – and that, like her mother and my father, she will continue to live a long and active life.

There are compensations for her problems, though, that neither of us could have foreseen. Because she isn't well enough to continue her old routines, Mum now has time for conversations and shared activities for which I have always been too absent: simple things like walking with me arm-in-arm around the streets of St Lucia, noticing the sounds and colours of the miner birds perched in their dozens along the telephone wires, the lorikeets that suck the juice out of the honey blossom trees, the sooty crows that wake us both every morning. We do things together that were unimaginable before. We observe changes in cloud formations, and the progress of the moon from evening to evening. We drive together to the University Lake and speak intently about the ducks that make their homes there. When our talking and observing is done, I bring out the songs I have written in my little flat at the rear of the house and perform them for the first time on the back veranda while Mum sips her evening tea. *Oh, that's a nice one,* she might say. Or: *I can't quite make out the words of that one.* Or: *Play that one again, will you? I love those high notes.*

I begin to write songs for her. With her. I collaborate with the energy of her sudden sadness, gratefully accepting her advice about enunciation and resonance. I gravitate towards minor keys. I experiment with the lower vocal registers. I practise the singing exercises I used to reject because they came from my mother. I begin to play the piano, her piano, her fruity, mahogany brown baby grand that is getting dusty because of my inadequate housecleaning. I tend to it now in another way, coaxing from its smooth white and black keys rhythms and melodies I had only ever played on a guitar or a violin.

I never expected to be writing songs in Mum's lounge room. It seems as if full circles really do exist. Instead of playing my songs to ferals, punks, artists and ordinary punters, I am now playing them to my mother.

Apart from singing, Mum could also make 'spring rustle' on the piano. 'The Rustle of Spring' was one of the piano pieces she practised over and over for her L.Mus.A., a diploma in piano from the Trinity College of Music in London. The sheet music for 'The Rustle of Spring' looked like something really was rustling across the page, which was covered in thick black arpeggios that expanded and contracted like accordion soundwaves turned into print. Apart from its musical manifestation, though, I don't know if Mum felt a special affinity with nature – after all, it was always Grandma who watered the garden at home – although I know she loved 'Winter' and 'Autumn' from Vivaldi's *Four Seasons*. Mum always preferred the cooler seasons; her fair hair and pale skin made the extremes of Queensland's summer months hard to bear. But I doubt she ever thought of moving, unlike her children, who all travelled as soon as they had the opportunity, scattering themselves across countries and time zones in search of adventure and experience, bringing back stories, photographs, music and songs so that she was able to vicariously enjoy years' worth of world travel without ever having to leave the comfort and safety of her own home.

I was the first to travel, courtesy of a youth orchestra that took me to different parts of the country and the world even before I left school. A few years later Cathie, who was teaching up in North Queensland when I returned home, travelled overseas and from exotic locales sent back photographs of herself smiling gloriously in a way I had never seen before, as if travelling had set her free. Janice, who moved to London in 1999, is also a traveller. Mum and Dad were thrilled for her when she became a professional singer and followed her radiant musical journeys through the programs and reviews she sent back from all her successes. Later I took off for India on my own and ended up working in Mother Theresa's hospital in Calcutta, work that had less to do with any charitable impulses to help the poor and hungry than with my own hunger for understanding what was going on in the world. Later, I travelled the country from north to south and back again in third-class carriages, lugging a backpack, a bumbag and a case full of notebooks in which I inscribed my travel diaries to go along with the copious letters I wrote back to Mum, Dad and Grandma so they could follow my travels too.

My brothers both moved to England at various times. Paul worked as a teacher in the East End of London, as well as, for a brief period, a photographer. He sent audiotapes back from his journeys through Africa and India for my parents' amusement. Stephen, who now lives and works in Melbourne, also mailed home hilarious accounts of his squatter's life in London.

Mum enjoyed our confidence and freedom in being able to satisfy our curiosity about the world. And no matter where we were, how we were living, or what calamity or wonder had fallen upon us, she wrote regularly to all of us, sometimes once a week if she sensed something amiss, but always at least once a month and often more. The arrival of her letters was as predictable as the weather she liked to remark upon; she sent snippets of news from home, comments on the changing seasons, stories about her students' achievements, as well as anecdotes about the minutiae of her daily life. Dad would add a few lines at the end of Mum's letters or write letters of his own in spare, elegant handwriting.

While we saw the world, Mum stayed home with Dad, studied, taught, played the piano and sang. As her teaching practice grew, perhaps she felt that the world was passing through her door, a population of would-be singers and pianists from multiple landscapes and territories, who shared the same simple dream that would connect them during all the travels they undertook, with Mum at their side, through the various geographies of music.

The buzzing in her head that Mum begins to describe during the first year of my return could be that musical soundtrack imploding in her brain. I listen and listen in the silence that grows around her, but all I can hear are her sighs, the soundtrack, now, of her loss.

THE POLITICS OF SADNESS

Cathie: I remember vividly getting a call from Mum in my office at school in early 2000. I only found out later that she was in the psychiatric ward. Mum was hysterical and was weeping down the phone for me to come and save her and take her home. I had never heard my mother like this before – ever – and did not know what to do. This was the beginning of the sensation of total helplessness that I felt and I am sure we all felt to varying degrees at various times.

At this time, no one knew what was wrong with Mum. She had never been a woman who let depression get to her. She has always had her walking and her music to get her through the low times. So this state of mind was foreign to us, as was the ease with which the medical profession seemed to prescribe drugs for women who said they felt sad.

It seems the only available places for people to go while doctors sort out their antidepressant medication are the psychiatric wards of mainstream hospitals or private hospitals for the mentally ill. Stepping through the doorways of these institutions often feels like crossing portals into other worlds. We go first as travellers, hoping to just pass through on our way back home, but find ourselves staying longer than we first expect.

During the next few years, I spend a lot of time in these places with Mum, who is still confident that her problems can be solved with the right treatment and medication, and by following what I humorously refer to as 'doctor's orders'. Though Mum's insurance ensures she stays in well-equipped wards with state-of-the-art facilities, our sojourns in the psych wards are not always what I would call comfortable. It isn't easy to watch women being wheeled down corridors for electroconvulsive treatment. Or to argue with doctors who advise Mum to undergo the treatment herself. I find myself once again in the position of Mum's advocate – even, sometimes, with her. I shudder at the violence of the treatment as well as, often, at how bloody-minded I am accused of being. Family and friends tell me stories of relatives and acquaintances, of ailing aunts and depressed uncles, grief-stricken grandparents, as well as, I suspect, recalcitrant teenagers, who all benefited from shock therapy. I'm surprised by how many people feel undisturbed by this approach to emotional problems, one that destroys short-term memories while, I suppose, making longer-term memories bearable. I plead with Mum to stand her ground. Memories tell the story of life, I argue. I am greedy too: I want to hear her memories, to know what her life has been. In the end, Mum probably refuses the treatment just to please me. Or perhaps just to shut me up.

Mum is first admitted to Woodlands private psychiatric facility when her doctor advises another hospital stay. Apparently, Mum's antidepressant medication, which doesn't always appear to be working, needs be monitored more closely and the best place to do this is in hospital. There are no beds available in the Westminster psychiatric ward so Mum is assigned a bed at Woodlands, a private hospital in a neighbouring suburb. I still marvel at the ease with which Mum is now considered a psychiatric patient, even though she has, to my mind anyway, only ever exhibited normal emotional responses – that is, worry and sadness – to the changing state of her health as well as the incremental losses in her life.

Still, we heed the doctor's suggestions, often because there seems to be no choice. I have also been warned that it isn't fair of me to present alternatives to Mum. *It only confuses her more*, I am told, *if you question the efficacy of her treatment*. She needs to feel confident in her doctors and the medication plan they have prescribed. I don't understand how having access to as much information as possible can be harmful, especially as no one really seems to know what is happening to Mum. But often now she is too overwhelmed herself to consider other options.

While Mum is still strong she greets me during my daily visits to Woodlands like the queen of a new kingdom, introducing me graciously to her fellow residents, the majority of whom are women. Some I meet just seem tired; some of them are scattered and anxious. Others have entered these institutions unwillingly, at the urging of family and friends. Others rage against the authority and use their voices to resist the easy labelling of themselves and their fellow patients as 'mad'.

One of Mum's new friends is called Grace. Her name seems appropriate; she is overweight – from too much lithium, she tells me conspiratorially – but she moves with the finesse of the ballet dancer she once was. Grace describes her encounters with her doctor, who regularly recommends her for ECT treatment, in absurdist terms, detailing the side-effects of her medication with off-hand humour. *I told my doctor he was driving me bonkers,* she says over morning tea. *He stared straight at me and said, 'I wouldn't worry about that, love. You already are bonkers.'*

Grace's stories confront the voice of authority that prevails in hospitals. Her humour is both contagious and unsettling: *I looked at my CD player for an hour the other day, and for the life of me I couldn't figure out what it was,* she tells us, gleefully gobbling up home-made scones. *Last time I went home I tried to insert a CD into my toaster. My daughter was more worried than I was. I said to her: 'You know what they say, love, the less you remember the less there is to forget.' And who wouldn't want to start forgetting with some of the things you see inside here?*

I discover that Grace had never 'presented' any symptoms of the dementia she is now being treated for until after her first stay in hospital.

During Mum's intermittent stays at Woodlands as well as Ward 6B at Westminster, she and women like Grace become good friends. I admire Mum's gift for these brief yet supportive friendships that seem to flower between women in places like psych wards and mental hospitals. I imagine new mothers share a similar bond: a recognition that another rite of a woman's passage is upon them, through which they will discover their strength, alone and with each other, to handle the changes in their bodies and minds brought about through biology, chemistry or medical technology. Mum will rarely keep in touch after she and her temporary friends leave hospital – to go home or pass on to new facilities – but she is easy in the company of others like her, sent to these places to 'rest and recuperate', or to be observed while their medication regime is 'finetuned' only to find themselves categorised as 'unstable', or 'subject to mood swings'. Or worse.

One of the consequences of her being admitted to psych wards or psychiatric hospitals, even though we are regularly told it is 'just to work out the medication', is that Mum now thinks she might be going crazy. Or, perhaps worse, that other people might think she is. These doubts about the state of her mental health begin to worry her as much as her as-yet unnamed illness. After the first few days of her stay at Woodlands, Mum begins to question her own sanity.

Do you think I'm going mad? she asks me one day in the middle of one of our walks around the hospital corridors. It is shocking to think that she could feel so upended when, barely a year before, she had been adjudicating eisteddfods and travelling the world. I wonder at the circumstance that puts a tired woman into a mental hospital where she begins to doubt the stability of her own mind.

If it's the word itself you're afraid of, I say gently, feeling her uncertainty, *we could always pick another one.*

To amuse her, I bring Dad's old thesaurus with me next time I visit. *We'll find you an alternative word for mad,* I announce that day as we munch on vanilla slices in the visitors' room.

I suggest 'unsound' might be a better choice, although when I investigate further I decide that for my musical mother a word that suggests the negation or absence of sound might not be appropriate. Nor would its other meanings: 'unhealthy, diseased, or suffering from wounds or injuries'. I try 'senseless', but we both feel that a word which implies a state of unconsciousness or of being destitute, deprived of sensation, or physically insentient is also best avoided.

She admits to often feeling a little foolish, as I do too, but decide against 'foolish' as a substitute for the word 'mad'. 'Rabid' is another word which we reject. *I am not a mad dog yet,* she observes wryly. Nor is she, outwardly anyway, 'furious, raging, or violent in behaviour'.

You are prone to infatuation though, I scold her playfully as I wipe off some leftover crumbs of vanilla slice from around her mouth, *especially with the good-looking doctors who flirt with you when they want you to take your antidepressant medication.*

I didn't know infatuated meant mad, she whispers, disappointed that what she had always considered a harmless and fleeting pleasure could be taken as a sign of mental imbalance.

There it is, in Roget's Thesaurus, I show her, *in plain print.*

Then who isn't, or hasn't been mad at sometime or other, she says, *and if so, shouldn't everyone be thrown into the madhouse?*

Sensing her melancholy, I move on quickly to the next word.

How about wild then? Do you think perhaps it is better to be known as a wild woman than a madwoman? I ask her.

Linda, I'm tired, she whimpers as her shoulders slump, a sign of a sudden mood change.

Come on, Mum, I say, trying to rouse her out of what I sense is an oncoming depression. *Just a couple more.*

Ok. A couple. Not more. She sighs again. It reminds me of her sighs when I was a child. I always wanted to go that extra little bit further while she would have preferred to stop. I understand now that the effort she makes to rouse herself is for my sake, not hers.

Now, where are we up to again? Do you think perhaps it is better to be known as a wild woman than a madwoman? I repeat meekly.

Not where I come from, she answers solemnly. She puts on her glasses and takes the book and reads aloud the words beneath my fingers. *'Animal-like; living in a state of nature; not tame, undomesticated; uncultivated or uninhabited, desolate.' No, definitely not wild. Absolutely not.*

What about 'alternative', Mum? I ask, surprised to find this word as a substitute for mad. *Would you rather be known as alternative or mad?*

She looks exasperated as she peers up at me. She sees I am on a roll.

I don't quite understand what that word has to do with mad, although I know that you have often preferred alternative music to the music of your own mother, she says. *Do you think I could go back to my room now?*

What about 'divine madness', I ask her as I link my arm through hers and steer her back in the direction of her room. Her new room-mate, Flo, short for Flower, is walking towards us from the other end of the corridor, accompanied by a nurse. Flo has just had electric shock treatment. I keep talking in the hope that Mum will be distracted from noticing Flo's blank face and slow shuffle.

'Divine madness'. As in 'fervent with poetic or divine inspiration'? Or would you prefer to be 'stupefied with astonishment, fear or suffering' rather than mad?

I walk slower so that Flo can get settled into her bed before Mum reaches her room. Last time Flo got the treatment she didn't remember Mum for days. *Or perhaps you could just be carried away by or filled with enthusiasm or desire, or just wildly excited?*

When Mum doesn't reply, I laugh, trying to distract her. *I know. How about 'discombobulated'? It was one of Dad's favourite words. Remember?*

Discom – what? Mum whispers as she suddenly notices Flo's progress down the corridor. She stops, hanging back on my arm until the procession takes a left-hand turn into Flo's room. Up close I can see that I have only imagined the changes in Flo. What I thought was her blank stare is her usual expression and because of longstanding arthritis she always walks slowly. There are only subtle signs that there is anything different, but incrementally after each treatment we have noticed Flo becoming more of a stranger in this strange place. As has, by association, my mother.

Discombobulated. I remember the word. I remember how it made me laugh when I first heard Dad use it, how it had sounded like a word that wore striped socks and funny shoes. Maybe Dad would have chosen this word for us now. For Mum. He always knew exactly the right word to use. The appropriate word that might lift us out of pessimism and gloom. *Meaning 'confused or disconcerted',* I tell Mum.

Mum stares silently down the now empty corridor and then back at me.

Discombobulated it is then, she tells me, uncertain whether I am joking or not. *You can tell that to the doctor next time he asks. You can tell him I am not mad, but that I am, quite definitely, discombobulated.*

DIVINE DISCOMBOBULATION

According to Dad, there were a lot of discombobulated people in the soap operas Mum liked to watch in the afternoon. *Not just discombobulated,* he would whisper to me in a theatrical aside, *downright mad.* He could do a pretty passable imitation of Victor, the aging hero of *The Bold and the Beautiful,* who went through the gamut of every dramatic emotion just by moving his right eyebrow, as well as the long-suffering Marlena from *Days of Our Lives,* who mysteriously looked younger as she got older, as if, Dad whispered to me, she had been given an elixir of youth by the gods. Dad never differentiated much between popular or highbrow entertainment. Despite his religious and scholarly past he always seemed, where culture was concerned, to be an egalitarian man who saw just as much soap opera and discombobulation in Shakespeare as he did in Mum's afternoon serials.

I never really understood why Dad used to call me 'ding-dong' when I was a little girl. I don't know whether he meant to insult me or liberate me. Or whether he thought I was slightly discombobulated. I was always laughing then and perhaps I made him laugh too. He had funny nicknames for his other kids as well – Pill, Stets, Cat and Pa – so I like to think now that he was encouraging me with my particularly embarrassing pet name to freely traverse those areas that were normally demarcated – by snobbery or genuine preference – and to enjoy Mum's soap operas the same way he might have liked me to appreciate a Shakespearean comedy or a Greek tragedy. Unlike the rest of the world, which seemed to easily divide things up between highbrow and lowbrow, our family, apparently, had no brows at all.

Around the time I first began to learn the violin, Dad gave me a book called *The Myths of Greece and Rome* in which I read about Madness, Furies, Herculean tasks, Retribution, Patience, and the fickle nature of Gods and Goddesses. I read about a daughter cracking open her father's forehead – and giving him a terrible headache – in order to be born, a man rolling giant stones up a hill, and a cripple working in the bowels of the earth who was loved and healed by a beautiful woman. I read about a muscular, rapacious god overwhelming a young woman before carrying her off into the underworld, and how this girl's mother weeps and harries the earth until the ground opens back up to offer her a deal with the Lord of Darkness so her daughter could be returned – albeit only periodically – to spend the flowering days of spring above ground.

I became obsessed with these myths in my little room, which was always the messiest in the house. But even though the chaos of my room was a long way away from these other messier, more cataclysmic struggles between human beings and their darker natures, the stories still nourished me. I gobbled them up as hungrily as I ate the toast with honey and drank the tea that Dad made for me every day after coming home famished from school. Consuming words and fables of mythological history was sometimes more pleasurable than the physical act of eating itself, even though once, as a joke at the expense of my self-professed starvation at the end of a long day at school, Dad stacked onto my plate at least fifteen pieces of toast and honey and challenged me to eat them all up. I gave up after the tenth piece, proving Dad's point that my eyes – and words – were indeed bigger than my stomach and that the word 'starvation' did not – and could not – apply to me when there were children all over the world with nothing to eat at all. Slumped over on the table, bloated with toast and honey, I thus learned from my father the crucial lesson that I should use my words more carefully and meaningfully or one day I might really get myself into trouble. He may have been creating our own mythologies right there in our kitchen but at the time I couldn't see it. I only knew that reading connected me to worlds, times and spaces other than those immediately apparent in my bedroom with its walls so thin I could easily hear the television which Mum watched every afternoon in the next room.

Our preferred forms of entertainment were not that different. In both, there were life, death, love, calamity, retribution, trials, fury, and madness of varying kinds.

Mum knew the stories of Marlena from *Days of Our Lives* and Victor and his women from *The Bold and the Beautiful*, she knew about the trials of Susan and David from *Days of Our Lives*, and the fury of Stacy and Roman in *The Young and the Restless*. But I don't think she had any idea about the story of Persephone and Demeter. She lived through it with me, though, every time I fell in love and, like Persephone, descended into a sometimes calamitous underworld while she, stable, home-bound, eternal like the earth – and just as immoveable – remained above ground and waited for my return. I never sensed, however, that she searched or grieved for me, like Demeter, every time I disappeared. I am glad now that she didn't. She had too many other children to worry about. Or perhaps she was just too busy singing to notice. It was not in her nature to voluntarily make the descent, not like her second daughter who descended into the underworld – hopefully yet hopelessly – every time she fell in love.

Mum was engaged three times before she married Dad. Three broken engagements were unusual in Mum's time, but she was a beautiful young woman with a talent for singing, so she waited, worked, studied and sang, displaying the diligence and persistence that stayed with her all her life. The first two engagements, in her early twenties, seemed to have been explained away by the admission that she was 'young and didn't know any better' and was just marking time until she met the boy I always suspected figured in her dreams as the 'lost love of her life' – a country boy called Damien. With his lean, lanky, movie star looks, Damien was the perfect physical match for Mum's ingénue beauty. They went dancing together and held hands on moonlit walks. In photos from around that time she looks like a teenager, as virginal as she was in reality and still with stars in her eyes.

There was, though, a major problem with Damien: his possessive mother, who threatened to withdraw his inheritance if he married 'that showgirl harlot'. The first time I heard that phrase in relation to Mum, I laughed out loud. Mum looked the very opposite of a harlot with her cherubic face and pink lips. I even searched for evidence of ill-repute in Mum's old photos, but all I found was the glow of energy and life in her eyes and her wide open face as she threw her head back and sang.

Grandma's steady wisdom eventually prevailed. On an extended rail trip she and Mum took together down south, Mum's ardour cooled. Returning to Brisbane, she ran into my newly secular father at a concert in the Brisbane City Hall. Dad was handsome, older, educated, stable, and that most desirable catch for a good Catholic woman: a 'retired' religious man who had been trained from an early age to be obedient and self-sacrificing. Best of all, he was not a drinker and therefore perfect husband material. Neither Mum nor Grandma looked much further than these obvious virtues when Mum arrived home with him that night. A handsome, God-fearing man who loved Mum was the answer to their prayers.

My father wooed my mother with poetry and books, and she thrilled him with her songs and her loveliness. And while he was older in years than Mum, in experience with love he was far less schooled than she was. In photos they are a radiant, handsome couple: he, dark and wavy, she, fair and curly; he with the inward-looking curves and lines of a contemplator, she with the round, shining face of a performer. This image of the dark and light is deeply imprinted in my memory and my psyche; born from their duality, my life has sometimes been a search for the balance between these two polarities.

They were married at St Thomas Aquinas church in St Lucia just a short walk up from Grandma's house in Warren Street. Dad's mother did not attend the wedding; she was too old and ill to travel up from Sydney, but Mum's mother, who later recalled that the groom was 'so happy he was literally shaking', wept tears of joy, relief and gratitude, while Mum sang, especially for her new husband, one of his favourite songs: 'One Day When We Were Young'.

I never sang a song for my husband. I have not yet married. But I did sing one for Michael Franklin.

Michael Franklin. I can whisper his name now and I can still hear a song. My grandmother took one look at Michael Franklin and knew he would carry me down into an underworld from where I could only return with a broken heart. As a good Catholic she knew about the red burn of hell. But though I knew, thanks to my father's notes on Milton's *Paradise Lost,* that I might be 'overwhelmed/with Floods and whirlwinds of tempestuous fire', I didn't care. Not at all.

Michael was not the safe, nice boy Gran might have hoped for me, but he was other things that she understood through music: a barefoot angel who could make his violin sing. We first met as teenagers in a Youth Orchestra where we sat next to each other in the second violins. He was considered wild but so talented that he moved quickly up into the first violins and would eventually lead the orchestra while I was still scraping away in the second violins or at the back of the first violins. He was both fascinating and troubling to the status quo of the classical music scene and seemingly destined for a future overseas.

I resisted my attraction to Michael until I was, in my grandmother's words, old enough to know better. Nothing I did made any chronological sense anyway. Despite my inward rebellion I spent my teenage years being a serious, brainy girl and only in my early twenties did I go mad for love the way adolescents are supposed to – like Juliet for her Romeo or Cathy for her Heathcliff.

Before Michael Franklin, there were other boys who would never turn my world upside down the way Michael eventually would: a gentle cellist, a sensitive painter – all 'nice, intelligent young men' according to Mum. But I came from a house where love and music were inextricably connected: where each night as he washed the dishes after dinner Dad might have been contemplating whether music was indeed the food of love while Mum swept the kitchen floor and put away the plates as she sang another one of her favourite Rodgers and Hammerstein tunes.

Even then I was more interested in words and music I hadn't heard yet than those my parents sang but I still tried to be brave and follow my star. And I clung very close to my destiny when I thought it had arrived in the wiry, kinetic form of Michael Franklin and his red and golden violin. Although I was upended by passion, we both gave up things to be together: he abandoned his classical music future and while I did not have the brilliant future he did, I abandoned mine too. He began to compose and perform original music and I began to write my own words and songs. We played and moved around the country together, south and then north again; we even formed a band together. We survived a few mad chaotic years during which I used to dream I could hear my grandmother's voice calling down to me from the safe, serene, unchanging world above: *Mark my words, my dear girl, it will all end in tears.* Which it did.

I haven't cried over Michael Franklin for a long time, but I'm still shaken when I encounter him one morning on the footpath in West End outside a pub where we used to play in a band. I'm in West End to track down a treadmill for Mum from the *Trading Post*. Because she can't walk easily now she's had to give up her morning walk and really misses her daily exercise. The treadmill is to help her keep fit and this excursion in search of second-hand bargains is not my first on her behalf.

I haven't visited the area since Michael and I parted. I left town to start all over in Sydney while he ended up back in West End, married with a child. West End suits Michael. It used to be a working class area, where artists and druggies and other desperados hung out. But during the last decade, West End has developed like a lot of suburbs close to the heart of the city. Now the old pub where we once played, which used to smell of piss and vomit, is a bistro with an 'entertainment area', a menu artfully drawn in coloured chalk on a decorated blackboard, and outdoor seating under tasteful awnings.

Michael is staring straight ahead as he walks towards me, so I can easily veer off without him noticing me and avoid this encounter completely. In the past perhaps this is what I would have done. But this time I stop softly in front of him and say: *Hi, Michael.*

Mike looks as if he has changed too. He has always been tanned, but now his face is red, almost orange, and his hair is prematurely grey. He looks odd and distinguished. Even in his grungy barefoot days he always struck me as being the most graceful creature I had ever seen. Now he reminds me of an elegant, short-sighted, red and grey bird with his thin, lanky body, hooked nose, and glasses through which he looks down on me looking up at him. The patterned shirt and black jeans he's wearing make him appear individual, stylish and, at the same time, as if he doesn't care at all. Here he is, I suddenly think, after all these years, still a strangely compelling force of breezy lightness and angular movement.

He seems surprised and uncomfortable, and I wonder whether that is his natural state these days or whether I have made him feel like this.

Um . . . good to see you, he offers after a few seconds of mumbling hellos.

You look well, I say, peering closely at his face which, despite its deep red colour, is unlined and free of wrinkles.

You do too.

I wonder whether I do. I am fatter than when I knew him, but with the extra fat have come glowing skin and a plump face. I am also suddenly aware that I am wearing a low-cut baby doll dress with a push-up bra that gives me the kind of cleavage I never had when I knew Michael Franklin.

Um . . . what are you up to? Michael asks after a few more uncomfortable moments.

I wonder whether he really wants to know, or if he is just being polite.

I'm um . . . buying something for my mother, I manage to stammer.

He seems bored and looks away. Discombobulated, I think. That word again. The whole world has gone discombobulated. Including me. So there will probably be no long conversation forthcoming that might fill in the years I have lived since I parted company with Michael. No chance for a wise summation of the understanding I have gained since our break-up. Now there is nothing but this awkward man trying to get away from me outside a pub where we once played music.

Michael and I have barely spoken for nearly ten years since we parted. I was distressed when he married and had a child, but heartbroken when he did not reply to the letters I wrote him. I don't really know what I hoped to achieve by reaching out to him. Forgiveness. Understanding. Acknowledgement. I never wondered, as I do now, if perhaps he needed those things from me too. I didn't think he would reach back. He had moved on and he was not a man who could be reached, I eventually realised. At least, not by me.

Michael refuses my offer to take him for coffee. I am uncomfortable too, aware that, unlike him, I am childless and living with my sick mother. I feel pathetic, overeager. He seems anxious to go. We part casually, me pretending not to mind, he probably not minding at all. After saying goodbye outside the Boundary Street Hotel, I run into him again down the road towards Melbourne Street. He seems uneasy, sheepish that I have turned up in his path again.

After me blabbing for a few minutes, he starts moving away.

Got to go, he growls abruptly.

I feel hopeless, as if I am covered in wounds.

Sorry, he calls back as I move my hand towards him, offering a tiny gesture of farewell. *Got an appointment.*

I can't help myself. I am small, but I am compelled to make myself smaller. To beg, as I always have, for some thread of connection with this man.

Um . . . I've got some songs I've been writing, I call out. *I want to record them soon and I need a guitarist. A good guitarist.* Like you, I could have added. It is horrible to use music for such a purpose. I am ashamed, even as I say it, and try to back off. To find some dignity from this encounter.

He shrugs as he backs away. *Sure yeah . . . give me a call.*

Um . . . I don't know your number? I yell back, but he is quickly out of earshot.

I watch him sprint towards the traffic lights on Melbourne Street and then cross the street and head up towards the West End Market.

I feel pathetic, powerless at still not being able to say the words I want to say to Michael. To say to this person who moved on years ago: 'I want to know what I was to you. I want to own the part of my history that is also your history.' But I realise that I will never be known by him again. That I will never be able to speak. So while I stand there in Michael's smoky residue, I try not to think of the open-hearted girl I was when I first knew him, or the breakages that were to come.

I feel dizzy. My bones ache. I can hardly breathe. Suddenly I am glad I am on my way back home, back to Mum's house. I could never relate to her at all when I was with Michael. I resented her then, living my passionate, unruly life, blaming her for things I knew later I was entirely responsible for. But I have something to share with her today. We have something in common.

A singer is chanting on the car radio. I can't really understand the words he is singing, so I make up some of my own. *In all kinds of weather/ Forever and ever . . .*

I sing along, forgetting for the moment my own songs, or my old songs, feeling grateful that I am older and wise enough not to be too brave, too strong, but to feel my aching breath.

We're all in this together, I whisper into the rear view mirror. *Together.*

Forever . . .

I am halfway home before I realise I haven't gone down that cross street I was looking for. As in the past Michael Franklin has stopped me in my tracks and made me forsake my immediate plans. But I don't turn back. Mum can start to walk on her treadmill another day. As I can. I keep driving for home, where I will unpack my guitar, gather up all my spilled words, and strum a new love song for my mother as she lies exhausted and stiff in her bed.

IN A MOONLIGHT GARDEN

Mum's recently appointed physician, Dr Davies, whom we have consulted about her increasingly frequent falls, suddenly tells her one morning in May 2000 that she might have Parkinson's disease. He uses the word 'might', I discover, because there is no clinical test for this disease, and little concrete information regarding its causes or cures. Though his casual pronouncement is a shock, the possibility that Mum has something seriously wrong with her doesn't come upon us as a complete surprise. Nurses and others who have seen Mum during the past year had begun to enquire, innocently enough, whether she already had the disease.

She has the frozen face, one nurse's aide whispers to me, *and the dead eyes.*

Mum has also found it harder and harder to smile. *Look at my face*, she says, staring at herself in her hand-held mirror as she tries to practise her smile. *I can't smile naturally anymore.*

We both examine her various attempts at smiling. Many of them look like the performer's smiles she used to wear in family or social photographs, which we would mock when we were kids. But no matter how much she tries to force her mouth into the kind of smile she has practised for years to acknowledge applause or engender confidence during public speaking engagements, she confesses to me that she now seems to have no control at all over her facial muscles.

Mum once wrote that singing takes a lot of courage. 'Sing and enjoy', she wrote in the Music Teachers' Association's newsletter in March 1989. 'Try for an enormous feeling of love in the singing, then you won't get caught up in the technique. If the sense is right and you have knowledge of the situation, forget about the vocalising and you'll make the right sound.'

I know that this is also the time to try for an enormous feeling of love in every word I speak to her. It's hard to know what to say, though, to someone who wants to die the way that Mum, during the five terrible weeks she stays in hospital after her diagnosis, wants to die. No one can plan for conversations like these. All I can really do is encourage her to keep eating when she refuses the awful hospital food in the hope she might literally fade away. I'm not prepared, though, for how hopeless she feels – not this woman who used to embarrass me sometimes for being so bright, so strong and alive. Her sudden depression enters our bones like poison. As her strength ebbs, I feel the need for mine to rise. I begin to walk to the hospital instead of driving; I lift weights instead of sleeping in. I rise at dawn to stretch and do yoga. I take on my new tasks as a warrior would, and prepare myself for a long and difficult battle.

Her suicidal feelings pass, but their uneasy remnants take hold of us.

Joan: I never really seriously thought about suicide. Well, maybe I thought about dying, but not actually doing it myself. Because I suppose, being a religious person, it's not part of my makeup to do violent things like that. Perhaps that might suit some people more.

Linda: Doing violent things to themselves?

Joan: Yes. They might say 'let's get it all over with'. But if you don't do that of course you suffer a lot more probably. As the years went on, I mixed with other people with many symptoms much worse than mine, and I sympathised with them and their trouble. I learnt of all the troubles which people experience in their lives, which, funnily enough, I never thought would enrich their lives.

Linda: You didn't think it would enrich people's lives to suffer?

Joan: No. But I don't know how many people do suffer. I don't know how many people do have their lives enriched. Perhaps a lot of them are like me.

Linda: And what are you like? What's that?

Joan: Well, my whole life was music, wasn't it? The only people I mixed with were musical people, my students and other teachers. I could have gone on with that but I didn't, because I just lost the will to do it. And I can't think of what I've done since, really, can you?

Cathie has written down for me her own memories of these first few weeks and months following Mum's diagnosis:

Cathie: When a doctor joked that Mum looked like a 'Parkie', I initially was appalled at the lack of apparent care, concern and information that seemed to be available from this profession. I was shocked at the casual way they referred to people in Mum's situation. I expected them to cure my mother and was angry that they did not seem to know how. Like most things in life, you have to try to take some control. So we all started to investigate Parkinson's and found a myriad of information. The challenge it set us as a family was that we all wanted to help and make Mum better. But no one really knew how. We all had different ideas and there were arguments and disagreements for many, many months.

I will wonder during the next few months whether Mr James Parkinson, who first described the as-yet unnamed disease in his 1817 paper 'An Essay on the Shaking Palsy', ever anticipated the dread that people feel when told they have his disease; and, if so, whether he might want to change its name after all, or his own, if only to avoid guilt by association. Although celebrities such as Michael J Fox, Muhammed Ali, the Pope, and my grandmother's favourite violinist, Yehudi Menuhin, have given the disease a profile, it still has not entered the public's consciousness as strongly as cancer and depression have.

After our initial shock has passed, I begin to realise that Dr Davies' casual use of the word 'might' is significant. It really does seem as if no one can confidently diagnose Mum and that a full assessment can only be undertaken over a lengthy period of time. I also find out about 'parkinsonism', a condition which apes the physical symptoms of Parkinson's but which is sometimes caused by the side-effects of certain medications. As Mum has been medicated for over a year now, I don't really want to make the immediate leap from the equivocal 'might have Parkinson's' to the more conclusive 'definitely has Parkinson's' – at least not while there are less dire possibilities still available to us. Mum, on the other hand, seems relieved that her ailment finally has a name. Perhaps she finds it easier to face something that has been labelled rather than something more mysterious; perhaps, for her, Parkinson's is also a more acceptable ailment that a 'nervous breakdown'. So she agrees readily when Dr Davies, after a brief consult with Westminster's resident neurologist, suggests she immediately begin the treatment of the L-dopa medication prescribed to replace the dopamine that is apparently disappearing from her brain.

Dr Davies also suggests we appoint a neurologist to work with him to devise and oversee Mum's course of treatment. We try out a few specialists until we find a 'handsome one', Dr Silver. After running some tests, Dr Silver considers Mum's case to be fairly mild. Relieved, we hear stories about patients who manage the disease for decades, who go on to die peaceful and painless deaths. Soothed by these benign tales, we hold out hope in the face of Mum's dread.

I receive information about the illness from many different places. Mum's friend Marjorie Anderson sends newspaper cuttings and downloaded data from the Internet as well as anecdotal information. 'Beryl Jackson's husband Harry got the disease and spent several fruitful years in a retirement village,' she writes to me in spidery handwriting. 'Then all of sudden he just bent right over and never straightened up.'

Mum now has two doctors at Westminster Hospital – Dr Davies, her general physician, and Dr Silver, her neurologist – as well as the psychiatrist she has seen on a casual basis during the past year or so, who is on holidays during the period when Mum is first 'diagnosed'. Apart from these professionals, we receive information and advice from a variety of sources. A naturopathic acquaintance from Byron Bay sends alternative magazines with suggested treatments: a vegetarian, non-dairy diet with no excessive sugars and lots of meditation and relaxation exercises, but Dr Davies scolds me for having cooked Mum the same food I eat – salads, steamed vegetables, tofu, fish and lentils. They blame her low levels of Vitamin B12 on this diet and order her back on red meat immediately. I see how she thrives on the steak pies and chicken mornay at the hospital; ashamed and confused, I promise to buy chicken breasts and mince to cook for her when she returns home.

I suggest an accompanying course of treatment that includes massage, acupuncture and yoga. The response is a mixture of condescension and annoyance. *Well, it can't actually do her any harm,* a harried nurse tells me when I try to discuss such treatments with her. *But we have a lovely hydrotherapy pool and I strongly encourage your mother to try that.*

So to the pool we go, each day during the last few weeks of her stay in hospital and then once or twice a week when she leaves. Among the overweight geriatric patients and arthritis sufferers, Mum is resplendent, slim and pale in her one-piece costume. To protect her hair, I bring from home the only swimming cap I can find: a gold lamé number which fits comfortably over her curls but, as far as I can tell, would be absolutely useless if her head was ever submerged. It never is, of course. Despite her husband and all of her children being trained swimmers, Mum never learned to swim anything but dog-paddle, which she practises dutifully up and down the small heated pool, carefully avoiding the older, frailer patients who are being held like babies in the water by physios or loved ones.

After the trauma of the disease's naming, Mum seems to enjoy the new variety in her days. We will become therapy junkies, I joke with her as our diary begins to fill with all sorts of new appointments. Soon after her diagnosis, Dr Davies, who is 'the top physician in the hospital' according to Marjorie, as well as Mum's coordinating doctor, presents us with a roster of suggestions regarding Mum's treatment: as Parkinson's disease, or PD as those in the know call it, causes both cognitive and mood disturbance, first on the list is finding a psychiatrist who specialises in dealing with aging neurological patients, in which category Mum now apparently belongs.

There are psychiatrists on staff at the Westminster, for instance, who are aware of the relevant statistics, such as the seventy percent of Parkinson's patients with pre-existing depression who go on to develop anxiety, or the ninety percent with pre-existing anxiety who will develop depression and apathy. We are lucky that psychiatric care qualifies for rebates under Medicare, as well as Mum's private health insurance, because it seems we will frequently be availing ourselves of their services in the future. To me, their fees seem inflated – Mum's first appointment costs one hundred and twenty dollars for fifteen minutes. I have also discovered during the past year that most psychiatrists rely heavily on prescribing drugs, rather than other types of therapies, as a result of their belief that most emotional and mental ailments are caused by chemical imbalances in the brain. Though I respect medicine's ability to repair many ailments and, like my grandmother did, wonder at the 'miracles of science', I am uneasy about this approach and about mainstream medicine's general reliance on drugs to treat emotional problems. None of my fears will prove groundless during the next few years, but I understand I am out of my league here – at this time, I know next to nothing about Parkinson's disease. So all I can do for the moment is try to be a good daughter and dutifully go about the business of booking Mum's appointments and then buying – or procuring, I sometimes joke with her – the drugs that she is now prescribed for anxiety on top of those she is already regularly taking for depression.

Mum's new treatment plan also involves a multi-pronged approach to maintaining those faculties that are considered most likely to degenerate first: in the case of PD, officially categorised as an idiopathic disease – meaning 'having no known cause' – the list of symptoms that may begin to affect her are 'shuffling gait', 'stooped posture', 'muscular rigidity', 'monotonic speech', 'tongue swallowing', 'hypomimia' (frozen, mask-like face), 'micrographia' (small cramped handwriting) and 'drooling'.

To begin our resistance to these degenerations, I make a whole week's worth of appointments – with psychologists, occupational therapists and physiotherapists, most of which are covered by Mum's health insurance. When the bills for these services begin arriving, I sometimes wonder, while thanking our good fortune, how people without cover manage; how they face their ordeal without the team of doctors and therapists that now begins to work on our behalf. Another member of this group is a speech pathologist called Sarah who used to learn singing from Mum. It's humbling for Mum to need the help she used to give professionally, but she takes the role-reversal well. I'm impressed at how she accepts instructions about vocal functions from Sarah, who is deferential, encouraging, and proud – as a mother might be – of Mum's progress.

I wish I could be as humble with Mum's doctors as Mum is with Sarah, but sometimes I can't help myself from asking the kinds of questions that used to annoy Mum so much when I was a child. Mum and I argue in private, as we often do, about her medication, but she's too anxious – and too polite – to directly address her doctors herself. She wants what I suspect she's always said she wanted – a quiet life. I can't stay quiet though, not even on her behalf. Like the 'enfant terrible' my Aunt Lal used to say I was, I just can't stop asking questions.

Mum's new hospital-appointed psychiatrist has me pegged as a troublemaker, I suppose, from the minute I walk through his door and ask: *Wouldn't an anti-depression drug counteract an anti-anxiety drug?*

Away from the hospital we might get on. He might encounter me playing violin somewhere and be moved to tears, as people sometimes are, by the sound of the strings singing. But right now I'm not singing and he is only moved to defend his position: *Not if we get the balance exactly right,* he answers confidently before ushering me out to make way for his next appointment. *It might take a while but that is our aim: to get the balance right.*

Getting the balance right: I will hear this phrase a lot during the next few years. The balance between depression and anxiety. Between highs and lows. Good times and bad times. Between Mum's needs and my needs. I just wish I could get the balance right between our needs and the needs of the medical authorities, wish I could button my lip and proceed gracefully through the hospital corridors, only whispering a sweet song as I go.

Two months after Mum's initial diagnosis, Dr Davies, in consultation with Dr Silver, tries her out on a different, stronger Parkinson's medication. The side-effects – sweating, nausea and headaches – are immediate and she begs me to take her off the drug. We are in her hospital room again when we discuss our plan of action.

I don't think I can do that, Mum, I try to cajole her.

Of course you can. We can do anything we like, she says stubbornly, sitting up in bed with the sheets pulled up high under her chin like a recalcitrant schoolgirl. *It's not a prison here.*

I have to laugh. Mum reminds me so much of me as a child that even she might find it funny if she was not so preoccupied with her problems. I remember once being so angry at being locked out of the lounge room in our holiday house down at the Gold Coast that I smashed my knee through the door, shattering the glass and tearing my knee to bloody shreds. I can't remember what I did to warrant such exclusion, but I do remember the shock on her face as she witnessed just how far I would go – and how much I might hurt myself – in the name of my freedom. Purple with fury, I bent over and screamed at her and Dad for locking me out of the family space, screamed at them to let me back in. She might have forgotten scenes like these, but I never really have. Even with the value of hindsight I have never really understood why I felt such fury as a child; I only know, for sure, that I did. I wonder now whether my sudden fits of anger were a wound for her, a rough scab on what she hoped might be a happy family life. At the time, if she didn't yell back or stand there staring at me, she would just laugh at me, which only made me angrier. Now here we are, so many years later, mirrors of each other and the way we once were.

But things are more serious now. Mum's health and security depend on us finding ways to communicate properly with each other. And with those around us.

I have no idea what you're talking about, Linda, she answers innocently, looking away coyly. *If you don't do anything about it, I'll just refuse to take it.*

She is stubborn, demanding. I put these swings and shifts in mood and attitude down to the medication she's taking. Sometimes I don't recognise her at all and wonder whether what I am witnessing is an aberration or evidence of part of her character that she has managed to hide all these years. Whatever the truth is, I have to adjust quickly to new situations and new sides of my mother. This time, I go along with her and tell the nurses not to give her the drug. I know what I'm asking is against their code of conduct and that only the doctors have the power to change Mum's medication, but I am as adamant as Mum. I have my own problems with authority.

You have to ask the doctor first, Mum's nurse pleads with me.

We can't wait that long, I huff. *It takes days to see the doctors. If they're too busy to come and change it themselves, we just refuse to take it. Mum refuses. She doesn't want it.*

It is the first of many mistakes I will make regarding diplomacy and protocol in the hospital. The words in the phrase 'under a doctor's care' are not there by accident. The hospital hierarchy seems to be both inevitable and problematic. The patient is under, it appears, and the doctor is over and above. Dr Davies, who refuses to speak to me at all after this incident, rings Paul to complain. During this phone call he refers to me as 'a ratbag'. I think he may also have used the word 'scurrilous'.

When I was nine, I won the violin section of the Brisbane Eisteddfod playing 'In a Moonlight Garden' by Dr William Lovelock. It was a slow, simple piece of music and, as usual, Mum accompanied me on the piano. I was competing, as I often did, against older girls who played things like Mozart's

Violin Concerto in E, or *Sicilienne and Rigadaun* by Saint Saens – serious music choices for serious violinists. The adjudicator commented in his written remarks that while I had an unusual flair for interpretation and a melodious feel for the instrument, I needed to hold the violin up higher and that my stooped posture made me look as if I was carrying the weight of the world on my shoulders. Despite my lack of physical grace, he awarded me the first prize anyway and commented on my 'natural instinct for melody'.

She's a nine-year-old girl, my mother hurrumphed as she later proudly displayed my first prize medal to her friends. *Why would she have any weight on her shoulders? She doesn't have a care in the world.*

My aunt Lal, who was married to Dad's brother, Bill, visited soon afterwards. I played 'In a Moonlight Garden' for her, but she was more interested in my increasingly rounded shoulders than she was in the music and taught me some ballet exercises to straighten my back and shoulders. But the violin drooped more and more. Sometimes in my hands it felt as if it weighed a tonne.

You'll thank me in the end, Mum would say as she banged out the notes of 'The Blue Danube' on the keys of her Schirmer upright. *You'll all thank me one day.*

I'll never thank you, I answered her. *Never never never.*

Years later as I began to write about all these things, I played 'The Blue Danube' in a thunderstorm in a small town south of Paris to a woman, the mother of a friend, who was sick and slowly dying. As the rain pelted down – *clackety clack* – on the tin roof of the house, I remember the hours

Mum spent pounding out notes for me to hear – *clackety clack* – on her old piano in that rhythmic thump. The storm brought a strange ominous counterpoint to Strauss's lightness, as if nature itself was playing a duet with me, reminding me of things that survive despite people's best efforts to destroy them. The sound of the violin seemed to ease the woman's physical pain. *Keep playing,* she whispered across to me. *Don't stop. Don't ever stop.*

I took her words to heart. I didn't stop. I kept playing the violin all through the storm, just as my grandmother would have dreamed of doing, even after the lights went out.

VOICE IS THE MUSCLE OF THE SOUL

During the period following Mum's diagnosis, I sometimes took my mini-disc player to her hospital room and asked her if she'd like me to record her voice. 'It doesn't matter what you say,' I encouraged her. 'Say anything that you feel, things you remember, things you worry you might forget. Speak about the things that you love, the things you fear losing.' She was reluctant at first; she associated the microphone with public speaking and having to do things in the proper way. But gradually she relaxed and began to use her voice for things other than singing, instructing students or going about the business of her daily life. As we struggled together during those first despairing weeks, I listened at her bedside while she reached inside herself for the memories and stories that transformed her, for a while at least, into the family chronicler, a position she had always been too busy working to occupy before.

As she spoke I could hear Mum's connection to my sisters in a way that helped me to feel more connected to them as well.

I discovered, for instance, that my sister Janice 'was a bundle of energy from the moment she was born, though there was something else there too; you felt she knew things, understood things about the world way beyond her years. She was like a shiny, bright little button, but even the neighbours called her an "old soul" when they saw her bubbling away in her pram. They thought she was only gurgling, but I could hear, even before she could speak, that she was already singing.'

When she got too old to gurgle, singing made her beautiful just as it did our mother, who often performed vocal duets with Janice, at home or in private recitals or musical gatherings. Later, when Janice's singing talent presented her with career opportunities, Mum sometimes sat for hours at our dining room table putting together Janice's audition scrapbook and she was proud when Janice became the kind of singer who could work professionally in various genres, from opera to musical comedy to a capella, jazz, pop and Australian musical theatre. Janice included Mum in many of these musical adventures and was a vivacious and attentive daughter. Although she had the buoyant personality and energy for performing, she also loved the richness of words and ideas – I have vague memories of her singing Streisand songs while reading Dostoevsky – and after she finished with tours and shows, she found a profession that allowed her to integrate this other passion and became a librarian.

Singing made Cathie beautiful too. She learned how to from Mum – something I would never do – and accompanied her to dozens of vocal workshops and seminars. But she was a natural leader and organiser of groups and studied to become a conductor – of orchestras, jazz and swing bands as well as choirs. Mum would often fly to North Queensland, where Cathie headed up school music departments and directed community choirs and bands, to see and hear these groups perform with her radiant eldest daughter at their helm.

Mum told a story about Cathie, a school band and a triangle:

> It was the end-of-year performance and she had been given the responsibility of playing the triangle in the primary school band. Even as a child she always took her duties very seriously, as you know, and I remember her before the band went on, her little face all lit up, so proud to be involved in her very first concert. Well, when the music started so did Cathie's tears. Oh, it was terrible to watch. She didn't run off or anything like that, she just stood at the back of the band holding the triangle in her hand with tears rolling down her cheeks. After it was over we found her outside. She was distraught. I asked her what happened and she looked up at me and said in the most tragic voice you can imagine: 'They gave me the triangle, Mum, but they forgot to give me the stick to hit it with.' She hadn't asked anyone for the stick or run off to find it because she didn't want to disturb the performance for anyone else. Even now I see that little girl in your sister: she'll stand there not wanting to make a fuss, just so the show can go on.

After nearly three months in and out of hospital Mum is so anxious now she finds it hard to sleep alone at home. The whole family is alarmed, solicitous and everyone is immediately involved. There are no detached silences from any of Mum's children. Paul comes in for regular visits to hospital, Stephen calls from Melbourne where he is now living and working, and Janice phones from London where she works.

A few weeks later Cathie takes time off work in Townsville to fly down to stay with us. She is shaken by Mum's situation and tries to reorganise Mum's therapy regime, encouraging her, as Mum once encouraged us, to work her way through her fears and worries with persistence and diligence. But Mum just wants to be held and protected now. This new dynamic is difficult to adjust to. Cathie and I both now sometimes climb into bed with her when she wakes terrified during the night.

Neither Cathie nor I are prepared to be so suddenly thrown together in crisis mode. She is used to mapping progress through timetables and hard work, while I rely more on the same instincts I use to make music or write a song. I suspect she finds the chaos in our lives unacceptable and within two days of her arrival she is on first-name terms with the President of the Parkinson's Association of Queensland as well as with most of Mum's doctors. I am rattled by our different energies but still marvel at Cathie's efficiency as she makes lists, takes notes and follows things up with the contacts we make while we begin to explore together the world of professional caring, respite centres, hostels and the many non-profit organisations dedicated to helping people with Parkinson's and other neurological diseases.

The old rebel in me is sometimes too ready to question the status quo that Cathie more easily trusts. I recall our earlier struggle to establish our different natures – as well as musical identities – while we grew out into the world. Mum didn't always help things along, sometimes characterising each of us in ways that may have felt easy to her but limiting to both of us. Cathie, two years older, was always the practical daughter, while I had my 'head in the clouds'. Mum's illness seems to challenge these old clichés: now I am the one who is helping at home, while Cathie is out in the world exploring her talents as a teacher, conductor and musician. With our shared concern for Mum's well-being, our former personas are not so easily worn.

One night when Cathie goes out to dinner and I go to a yoga workshop, Mum takes a double dose of her Parkinson's medication. I don't know whether it is an accident or a protest, but she is found delirious in her sheer summer nightie in the middle of the street by a man who lives across the road.

I have no family, Mum tells him when he asks. *I am all alone.*

He drops her off at the emergency ward of the Westminster and leaves a note for us to find when we arrive home later. I come back to an empty house less than two hours after I have left Mum watching television in her room. Panic-stricken and cold with guilt, I call the hospital and discover she has been taken from emergency to the psych ward and that her condition was considered serious enough to call her doctor out from home.

Driving through the night to reach the hospital the world suddenly seems luminal. I sense the anger and protest in

Mum's actions. After a lifetime of getting on with things, now she cannot seem to get on with them at all. I recall also a radio documentary I heard once called *The Voice Is the Muscle of the Soul*. I don't remember much about it at the moment except its title, which I repeat over and over to myself as I drive into the hospital car park.

The voice is the muscle of the soul.

The voice is the muscle of the soul.

I say it softly like a prayer as if by saying it over and over I might call down some help on behalf of my mother.

I have no family, Mum had told the man across the street. *I am all alone.*

I arrive in her room and see her doctor on his knees beside Mum's bed, clasping her hands and saying the Hail Mary.

Hail Mary full of grace

The lord is with thee . . .

Mum's face is shimmering with sweat and her eyes roll around in their sockets. Despite the presence of the nursing staff, her hair and clothes are in disarray and she tugs at the top of her nightie as if she wants to tear it from her body. I shiver. I feel that whatever line Mum has crossed tonight is in front of me now too. I can either walk away, leave her to her god and the ministering of her religious doctor, or I can walk into the room, across the line, and take her other hand.

I don't know if I make a clear decision either way, so I will never know if this is some kind of test that I passed or not. Nor can I say with any certainty: *this is the moment when I knew what I was capable of.* The doctor turns to me and reaches out his hand, gesturing to me to join him in prayer. Mum is too delirious to make any coherent sounds but underneath the rising inflections of the doctor's voice I can hear her moaning as I walk through the doorway. I step slowly towards the harsh halo of light falling down from the fluorescent globe overhead, take my mother's free hand and bow my head in silence, the third player in this hospital tableau which to anyone passing along the corridor might seem resonant of a Vermeer or Rembrandt painting, shadowy and thick with omens.

The next day Cathie is mortified. *All I did was go out to dinner,* she says mournfully, *I thought it would be ok. I feel like we're walking on eggshells, I hear her continue. On tiptoes around her.*

The newly tempestuous nature of Mum's illness comes upon us both as a surprise. We begin to sense something monstrous in our mother in the grip of chemicals and disease.

After Mum's overdose, Cathie and I spend hours together in the car during fiercely hot and humid days urgently checking out more therapy centres and rehabilitation facilities. Our nerves are frayed and disputes often close to the surface. I sense her alarm at what has happened. And sometimes, too, I feel my old sense of inadequacy at how I handle things, how lost I sometimes feel and how much better she is at managing the system than I am.

The night before Cathie is due to fly back north to resume teaching we share a meal at a nearby café. The conversation begins tentatively.

Maybe it's time you moved on, she tells me over tea and buns. *It's no life for you to just be living here with Mum. You should get back to what you were doing.*

What had I been doing? My old life seems a long way away now.

I'm just trying to help, not only Mum but the whole family. It's my way of contributing after years of being away. I feel ashamed of having to explain myself.

There are professionals for this sort of thing, she continues. *People who know what they're doing.*

I feel grateful, actually, that I can do this, I confide in her, *that I can be with Mum right now.*

Her eyes begin to fill with tears and I dislike myself for upsetting her, for not finding the right language to articulate what I mean.

Not all of us have that luxury you know, she tells me, looking down at her empty plate. *Some of us have to work for a living. Some of us* have *mortgages and responsibilities.*

I feel stung by her words, but I don't snap back as I once might have. I know how hard she works and how easy my gypsy life might seem in comparison. Perhaps she feels guilty that she can't be here instead of me. Neither of us says anything more. I think of the little girl with the triangle crying at the back of the school band. And I see what she must see, what perhaps I am meant to see as the sister of that child, as she stands at the back without being able to make a sound because someone has forgotten to hand her the stick: the need to be loyal to her family, to tolerate the different viewpoints of the group and to stand there patiently while someone else is out the front taking a bow.

I try to catch Cathie's eye across the table but she is looking somewhere else. I look away too. Here we are, two sisters, looking in opposite directions, both committed to playing in the same band, but unsure of our new positions within the group. Who should stand at the back now? Who should move to the front? Or do we get through this 'crisis' as we once got through the violin and piano duets we played together as children, when each part balanced out the other? I feel our world reordering itself as we sit there together breathing in the twilight, the dark yellowing glow, the soft scents of dusk. I don't mind our silence; I don't think Cathie does either. We both understand that all good music needs space and time.

At the airport the next day, as Cathie frets and fusses over details to do with her ticket, her luggage, her seat allocation and her meal, I notice how tired she looks. I wonder if she had a sleepless night worrying about Mum and ache for the extra pain I might have caused her. At the departure gate she turns and suddenly hugs me.

We do appreciate everything you are doing, she says, crying close to my ear. I start to cry too, though I wish I could sing instead of weep, there in the airport; we are still our mother's daughters and music is what we understand, perhaps better than words.

You know I'm only a phone call away, she shouts back to me as she leaves for the tarmac. As I watch her slim, solid body striding purposefully – 'so much like your grandmother', Mum used to say, 'your beautiful, vibrant sister' – to the plane, I am overwhelmed by concern for her, for Mum, for the threads of history that weave us all together. I stand there looking at her disappear, suddenly wondering how far away a phone call actually is, or whether, if I did try to call, there would be a proper device to measure such things.

Later, Cathie shares with me her recollection of her last grand singing adventure with Mum and how she feels it might have impacted on the onset of Mum's illness.

Cathie: My first encounter with Mum's Parkinson's was probably when we were travelling together overseas in mid-1998. She met up with me in Singapore where I had a vocal jazz group performing at the Singapore Arts Festival. I wasn't aware at the time that there was anything wrong with Mum and as I did not want her to miss anything, I don't think I gave her enough time to rest after the long trips. We did many long journeys during the following five weeks which took us to various parts of Canada, America and back to Australia. We had enrolled in three summer schools in the US and in hindsight I realise it was just too much for Mum. I have to admit that, at times, I was not very understanding. She did not sleep well at all and this would probably have aggravated everything. But I just didn't know what was happening to her then. We'd travelled together a lot in the past and always had a wonderful time.

After Cathie leaves, Mum stays at Westminster Hospital on and off for several weeks while her doctors adjust her medication again. The degree of Mum's anxiety appears to puzzle everybody and we are told that her terrors and depression are not normally associated with Parkinson's. But I am beginning to understand that nobody really knows what's happening to Mum. Or what to do about it. And also that the drugs Mum is now taking would have an impact on any woman who has lived without any kind of medication for most of her life. I dream sometimes of arriving at the hospital in the middle of the night, bundling her into the car and driving off somewhere together where we could face her difficulties in a more natural way, through tears and laughter, shared cups of tea around the kitchen table – where she often tackled the problems of children, friends, relatives and students – and also, perhaps, through music and song.

Her psychiatrist, though, a man who perhaps has no time in his busy schedule to sing or cry or share cups of tea around a table, looks for explanations that he is trained to understand and name. *It might be something separate altogether,* he muses to me. *We're just trying to get to the bottom of it. Did she suffer some kind of anxiety or trauma in her childhood?*

What can I say here? I wonder. What *should* I say here? Should I inform him about the funny story Mum used to tell about running down the street as a child after her best friend Joanie Wilson, the 'other Joan', wielding an axe? Could this story be open to misinterpretation? Would he read something sinister into an event that Mum used to think, as we all did, was hilarious? Or should I tell him about the road trip we once made down to Sydney in the family Kingswood to see Dad's brother, Bill, when there were seven of us in the car, five of us under fourteen? How Mum packed for days to get us ready; how Dad drove so sedately, stopping for solitary walks away from the car and its inhabitants only when the noise and the fighting got too much for him? How somewhere along the Pacific Highway our luggage flew off the roof rack and scattered for miles across the bitumen; how our Uncle Bill was so irritated about having us 'ragamuffin kids' to stay at his house at Hunters Hill that he followed us from room to room turning off light switches as he went and every day stood grumbling outside the bathroom timing our showers – and Mum's too? Should I tell him that Mum referred to the aftermath of that family trip as a 'kind of trauma'? Or that she had briefly agreed when, after struggling with fatigue and stress upon her return to her duties as mother, wife, singer and teacher, her doctor gave her 'a little something' to help soothe her nerves? Should I then add that, in a matter of weeks, whatever was bothering her passed and she 'got on with things' as she always had?

I decide against such disclosure. It hardly seems relevant now. I am growing wary of how stories – full of emotion, primal secrets and the effort of loving and living – can sometimes be reinterpreted as symptoms of madness or disease. So I wrap my silence around my mother and hold her history inside me until it can be spoken and heard in context.

The psych ward is becoming Mum's second home. I visit daily, clinging to habits now as the familiar path disappears beneath my feet. The habit of duty. The habit of service. I dig deep to find these things in myself. They don't spring yet from my heart or from love, only from some profound genetic memory.

I arrive at Ward 6B with flowers. The nurses at reception smile uneasily when they see me. They both enjoy and dread me now – they enjoy the variety and colours of the flowers I bring, but dread the questions I need answers to.

How's Mum today? I ask a nurse, whose badge identifies her as Hilary, and whom I have not met before.

Much the same, she answers politely.

Did she sleep ok? Last night, I mean, I press her.

I wasn't here last night. You'll have to ask the nurse who was on night shift.

I sense the ground shifting between us, sense myself walking over from the no-(wo)man's land that the hospital prefers relatives of patients to occupy to the territory where my mother now lives. I don't really want this to happen. I have not been on the side of my mother ever before in my life. I do not really even believe in sides, but this seems to be no time for staying neutral. Lines have been drawn and I am about to cross over to somewhere dark and primal.

What about her chart? I fix my eyes on the paperwork neatly lined up on her side of the desk. *What does it say on her chart?*

You'll have to wait and ask the doctor, she says firmly.

I see I am bothering her, but I continue: *I thought the new medication was supposed to make her less anxious,* I continue. *She was getting so scared in the night that sometimes we had to get into bed with her to help her sleep.*

Another nurse, whose badge tells me her name is Sister Robinson, joins in: *Oh, that's highly inappropriate,* she tells me politely. *For you to be sleeping in the same bed as your mother.*

Hilary and Sister Robinson stand shoulder to shoulder as they face me behind the safety of the nurses' desk. I stand shoulder to shoulder with nothing but weary indignity. I protest now almost automatically. I hardly trust any of my old responses anymore.

She wakes up in the middle of the night. Crying. Unable to sleep, I tell her. *So one of us gets in with her, just to calm her down.*

A word of advice, Sister Robinson scolds me. *Stay out of your mother's bed. It probably hurts more than it helps. Both of you.*

Suddenly I want to tell this reasonable, stressed, professional woman with her clinical charts and neat rows of medicine bottles arranged on the ledge behind her that Mum and I seem to have left the land of right and wrong. We have left the land of orderly behaviour. We have pushed off together on our little boat and are now lost at sea trying to find a safe shore on which to land. Polite, civilised, landlocked society has no power where we exist now; the wilder, tumultuous laws of the ocean claim us, not human laws.

It's quite normal, really, Hilary says soothingly as Sister Robinson leaves to see to another patient.

What's normal? I ask, almost in tears.

Everything you're going through, she says gently. *The attachment. The worry.*

No, I say wearily. *I mean, what is normal? What is the definition of normal?*

She rests her hand on my shoulder as she speaks, glancing over her shoulder to see if there are any witnesses to our conversation: *That's not really for me to say. Look, it's hard to be detached in your situation. Sometimes it's good to just talk things over with someone who might offer a more objective point of view. Do you have anyone to talk to?*

I want to cry. I don't want to yell or scream or make things difficult. I just want to cry.

I don't know what to do anymore, I whisper, unable to move for the shame I feel at not knowing when my mother, my father and all my friends and lovers have told me my whole life how clever I am, when they have loved me always for how much I did know.

Is there anyone? she asks again warmly.

I think of what my mother said to the man who found her in her nightdress in the middle of the street: *I am all alone. I have no family.* I think of all the people whose lives I have passed through, the friends, the lovers, the relatives, the strangers, the ancestors, known and unknown. Is there anyone among them, I wonder, whom we could turn to now? Or, if not a person, then some clue buried in our history?

I still can't answer Hilary's question as I stare at her. She doesn't mirror my confusion; there is nothing but kindness in her eyes as she propels me out of the ward down towards the nearby café.

Why don't you go and have a cup of tea at the cafeteria, she says maternally, guiding me as if I was her child. *Your mum's sleeping at the moment. We'll wake her up for morning tea and have a chat with her about her rights as a patient, if you like.*

I don't know what I like or don't like anymore. I feel upended. I bite my tongue and remind myself in future to choose my words as carefully as I wish the nurses would choose theirs. In hospital, I am discovering, language can normalise, demonise, trivialise and brand you as insane. But I say nothing of this to Hilary. If there's one thing I'm learning it's that it's best not to argue with kindness. I am discovering how precious it is, as we arrive at the café where Hilary buys me a cup of lukewarm tea and an Arnott's biscuit to cheer me up.

ONE DAY WHEN WE WERE YOUNG

But still the fates will leave me my voice
And by my voice I shall be known.

Ovid, *Metamorphoses*

We used to give up Arnott's biscuits for Lent. Lollies too. Grandma used to tell me that I would have to give up something in order to have something else so she especially approved of the sacrifices I made every Lent when I struck my own private bargain with God the Father for the sake of my miserable soul. If I gave up eating chocolate frogs and musk sticks for four weeks before Easter, for instance, I would be able to eat all the chocolate eggs I wanted on Resurrection Sunday, the day that our Lord Jesus Christ, God the Son, rose from the dead and walked out of his dark tomb into the light. It would also help save me from eternal damnation, not to mention the fires of Hell. The Catholic Church was full of fire and souls, the dark and the light. The fear of the dark, the absence of light.

Light could choke you though. Once I was carried out of the church after fainting from inhaling too much candlelight. Or so I believed. *Just hold your breath until help gets here,* I heard Grandma whisper. Looking upwards as I lay on the church floor I imagined she was already in heaven and that I had been unable or – worse – not permitted to make the ascent. Her face was framed by angel wings and the robes of the saints who lined the walls of the church as she told me over and over not to breathe too deeply or I might pass out again. Words like 'toxic fumes' were unheard of then. Either way I learned early that not breathing could protect you. Not breathing made your body into a kind of armour. If you made your body tight and strong you would not breathe in too much light. Or too much pain.

I once asked Grandma if she felt sad when my grandfather died – long before I was born – and left her a relatively young widow at the age of fifty-two. She didn't even hesitate as she leaned in towards me and said with great deliberation: *I didn't feel sad. I felt released.* Except for a man called Fred, whom she met at a place called Land's End sometime during the overseas trip she took when she was seventy-three, I never saw Grandma arm-in-arm with any man. *Watch out for men,* she would tell me, *they'll just take all your money.*

Perhaps Grandma gave up men so she would never have to give up on the violin. From the very first violin she bought it was a love that endured long after she had decided that men 'just weigh on you and hold you back'. She believed in the saints of the Catholic Church and the gods of music and it was to them she gave her love and devotion even before her future husband Albert Cottrell and his sisters Minnie, Florrie and Dot came into her life. Using her business skills, her ability to work hard at menial jobs, and her delight in the small triumphs of her family, she did her duty to her church and her family. She endured. But when she boarded the *Fairstar* to travel the world at the age of seventy-three, liberated finally from her life of service and devotion, she carried only a violin and a small suitcase with her up the ramp. Her instrument, a perfect copy of an old Stradivarius, would never travel cargo. Like a small, perfectly formed lover, it would always share her cabin.

Grandma had breathed just deep enough to put down roots, to be independent. Breathing deep enough to catch the breath inside and stretch it out in her belly like a trampoline on which the voice could spring and ascend higher and higher never occurred to her and she must have heard her daughter, Joan, sing in her high soprano voice for the first time with a kind of wonder. Joan would be a typist, of course, a secretary with job security until she married – that was the plan. After that, God – and my mother's womb – would determine the rest.

But you could not plan for magic. Or love. That is what she learned from her daughter. And from Yehudi Menuhin, whose gifts had come upon him, she had read, like a mystery; beautiful Yehudi, little Mister Menuhin, who slept with his violin at the height of his prodigious flowering, unlike my grandmother, who always placed it carefully in its case after playing it late into the evening. She couldn't imagine sharing a bed with either a violin or, after her husband died, a man. It was not that she was afraid of being broken – she knew how to hold the breath to stomach things – but that she might stop breathing altogether from fear that her violin, her love, might itself be broken, and that she, not it, might do the breaking.

Good country folk didn't play music – or sing – for a living. They worked the land, took in sewing and boarders, they mended things, and endured like the trees that sometimes turned to ash during the bushfire season. After they became grandmothers, the women visited family all across the country to make sure their children – and their children's children – went to church. They did their duty and wrote letters to relatives. They enquired after their grandchildren's school grades and music lessons and invited leftover relatives to stay for the holidays. They might suck in their bellies deep enough to sing a lullaby to a sleeping baby, a hymn at a funeral, or an Irish folk tune around an old pianola, but after their childbearing years, their soft round bellies held no other mysteries. They left the matter of mysteries up to their priests, prayed for salvation, and waited for heaven.

Grandma, though, knew that there was a heaven on earth. She had heard it singing through the strings of a violin. It caught her breath in a little gasp. Like heartbreak. Like love. She understood why I loved Michael Franklin. She had only ever loved a violinist in her dreams. It was up to me, I suppose, to love one for real.

There is a picture I still have of my two sisters and me sitting at a piano beside our mother. Our little fingers are curved over the piano keys and Mum's face is unlined, fair and beautiful as she smiles serenely at the camera. A photographer from the *Courier Mail* had come around especially to photograph

Mum, who was just beginning to earn recognition and roles with touring opera companies from overseas. There had been other accomplishments before she married Dad. Winner of special awards for typing, first aid and tennis, the Queensland finals of the Mobil Quest singing competition, then a finalist in the nationals, a commendation from the famous Australian tenor Donald Smith, as well as a chuck under the chin for being so young and pretty. Later, with two young babies in tow, she was invited to sing in the chorus of the Sadler's Wells Opera Company when they played in Queensland – as well as a special request to join their national tour, an opportunity she turned down because of a new pregnancy and Dad's concern.

There are other photographs in Mum's house that chronicle the period in her life when she was at the height of her young woman's beauty. These photos celebrate her days of dancing at Cloudland. She loved going to Cloudland, but this, however, did not stop her voting for the man – Premier Johannes Bjelke-Petersen – who ordered the early morning destruction of this cherished Brisbane landmark. These photos show Mum in a variety of lovely gowns sitting next to an equally various assortment of young men. Friends of her brother Neville Cottrell, young Rugby Union star and future Wallaby captain, these young men had names like Kevvie, Dezzie, Wally and Brian. The dances were always innocent; if any secretly drunk boy let his lust get the better of him, Nevvie was there to keep an eye on her and if necessary perhaps step in and warn the unfortunate culprit that if 'you lay another hand on my sister there'll be another laying on of hands outside'. There were gatekeepers even at Cloudland, surely as close to heaven as a girl could get in those days.

By the end of 2000 Mum finds it increasingly difficult to sing and play the piano. The muscles in her tongue have become frozen by the Parkinson's, and her medication makes her rasp and wheeze. Breathing will not come as easily as it once did and she now faces life without the things that give her joy.

Joan: It was a tragedy for me. Not only did I lose the piano, the singing, and the teaching, I found out that what I thought I could do, I can't do anymore. I just can't do it. For instance, the other day I walked down to the beach, singing all the way . . .

Linda: But you said you couldn't sing.

Joan: Well, it's hardly what I would have called singing before.

Linda: That must have been nice.

Joan: It was really good. I didn't care who heard me, didn't care who heard how awful I sounded. And then I sat down on the benches in the shade. Still singing. It was a lovely day.

Linda: What were you singing, Mum?

Joan: I sang 'One Day When We Were Young'.

Linda: Oh, you used to sing that with Dad, didn't you?

Joan: Yes, I sang it to him on our wedding day.

Joan starts to sing:

You told me you loved me
That gorgeous day in May.

He loved me singing, your father. Just loved it.

Book Two

LEARNING HOW TO BREATHE

OUR FATHER WHOSE ART WAS HEAVEN

My father, born Arthur ('bear-like man') Gerard ('brave man with spear') Neil, but known throughout his married life as Ben, loved telling stories. The story was his song, and his voice, quiet, mellifluous, lilting, not typically Australian, was his instrument. One of his favourite stories was of how he met my mother. I remember this story more clearly than I remember any other story that I read or listened to.

It begins like this: one day in Brisbane, my mother, who has golden hair and rosy cheeks, is sitting on the banks of the West End side of the Brisbane River. It is a silvery spring day and she is dragging her nets out into the water. She loves the solitude of prawning, even though she is only twelve, and her brother is up at the house making a racket with his footie mates. Dad, who looks like a young Montgomery Clift, is on his way to Mum's house to tutor this rowdy brother. He stops and talks to the pretty child who tells him about prawning, about throwing the nets out wide and dragging them in slowly, about waiting, about the wash of the waves from the ferries that chug between the banks of the river. As the beautiful man smiles, the sun glints off his perfect teeth, and whatever serendipity existed in the skies above West End that day beamed down on my future parents.

Dad had a habit of embellishing all his narratives so I can't say that I particularly believe in the story he used to tell about his first meeting with my mother. But I remember it because it was told to me. I remember it because of how it was told to me, simply, poetically, musically, with a reverence for its details. There were always specific words used to describe things; for instance, Mum's prawning net was always 'handwoven' and Dad's hair always 'crinkled in sooty black waves', as if the story's details could prove, or at least preserve, its veracity. And despite the fact that my parents' relationship was scarred by difficulties, the story of the beginning of their romance still lives as a strange heightened fiction.

Mum told Paul that when Dad came to visit again years after they all first met, Grandma said: 'You'd do well to hold on to that one, Joan.'

Paul: Mum always reckoned Gran was sweet on Dad, long before they all met up again. He was actually much closer in age to Grandma than to Mum. You've got to remember that the first time Mum and Dad met, Mum was a twelve-year-old up to her knees in mud with her skirts all pulled up. Dad was her brother's teacher. If you'd seen them all – Mum, Dad, Grandma – that day Mum and Dad first met, you'd never have thought 'oh, he'll end up marrying that woman's daughter'. But he did. And you know it might seem unusual, but there are a million stories like that out there. People do all sorts of unexpected things.

According to Kym, Paul's wife, Dad's sense of humour and his stories were 'really out there'. *Paul is like that too. He tells these funny stories,* Kym divulges to me, *that sound incredibly truthful and then you'll see the expression on his face and you'll suddenly realise he's been having you on the whole time. It's like part of your genetic code – the storytelling.*

I wish I could say the storytelling was the Irish in my father, but he was born in Manchester, England, had Celtic ancestry, and arrived in Australia by boat when he was eleven. At thirteen he was offered a scholarship by the Christian Brothers. He officially entered the order at sixteen and was known from the day he took his full vows as Brother Benedict, the name he later retained as the shortened, secular 'Ben'. Towards the end of nearly thirty years as a Christian Brother he was appointed head of the Strathfield seminary in Sydney and became, in effect, the head of all the young religious men in Australia, until he walked out one evening, leaving his charred dinner burning in a saucepan.

According to Aunty Kath, the wife of Dad's brother, Charlie, Dad then spent six months walking the cliffs from Bondi to Bronte wondering about his place in the world, and the breakdown he had as he entered secular life would not be his last. Dad never mentioned to me that he had already lived nearly a lifetime before he began his other life with us. I only found out about his other life by accident at the age of twelve when I discovered an old black and white photograph of a vaguely familiar dark-haired man in a robe and collar. It took me a while to realise that this handsome young man with the movie star profile and sensual lips was my father.

Joan: He never talked much about it, even to me. All he said once was that he used to have issues with how the young men were treated. How they were made to sleep outside on the verandas even in winter – apparently to build up their character. I don't really know what else he saw going on in there, but he never spoke about it. I think he just felt he couldn't support them treating the boys how they did. I guess he remembered how it was for him, taken away from your family and thrown into the cold.

Aunty Kath told me that in those days the Catholic Church was terrible to people who left. There was no follow-up and no support as the ex-religious person tried to reintegrate themselves into the world. She told me they gave Dad nothing but a blue suit for all his years of service. He stayed with her and Uncle Charlie at Bondi after he left because he had nowhere else to go. Afterwards, there was a to-do with the authorities in Rome, because he'd been one of the top-ranking brothers in Australia. There was some question about his mental state. Of course, according to Kath, not even his mother spoke directly to him about what was probably perceived as his 'religious failing'. 'Those old English migrant matriarchs were as hard as nails. They had it all worked out for their children,' Kath told me. When Dad walked out on his vocation, his mother took it as her own personal failure. The Catholics often gave one of their children to the Church as a trade-off for their place in heaven. Perhaps she wondered if that place was still secure.

Arthur Gerard had been the most intelligent of her children, so he was marked out for the scholarship that came with a religious life. One of his other brothers, my uncle Bill, was a young scrapper so he went into business. And according to Kath, 'Poor old Charlie got offered the same scholarship as your father but his mother knocked it back and said he had to stay behind and help his father milk the cows. I don't think Charlie ever got over that. He got into the drink and never got off it.'

Kath once showed me a photograph of the youngest son, Frank, a big-boned smirking boy leaning back on his motorbike like a movie star, his leather jacket gleaming as brightly as the Brylcreem in his hair. Kath called him 'the cocky one': 'It probably killed the mother when Frank died in the bike accident, but if you were looking down on it from up there in heaven you could have seen it coming because those types can't last the way they are. You could have seen that one was marked for an early exit. I never heard her mention him once after he was gone. It was as if she just shut the door on him and never opened it again.'

The fate of my father's family can be told in shorthand: one brother an alcoholic, one a businessman, one 'wild boy' dead in his twenties, one 'fragile' sister, Edith, dead before the age of forty, and one 'normal' sister, Flora, who lived quietly and without incident in North Ryde for the rest of her life.

And my father, a beautiful ex-religious man who scored the ultimate prize in the outside world: a blonde, devout and devoted young wife.

After a honeymoon period that perhaps Dad wished had gone on forever, there we were, the five of us, one after the other, not exactly tumbling out, but born after dignified periods of time during which my father would perhaps woo my mother all over again. The offspring of an ex-religious parent are sometimes referred to as actualised prayer. In Dad's case, the word really was made flesh five times. There is another school of thought, though, that would have called us penance for our father's sins made flesh.

Throughout 2000, Cathie continues to visit regularly. During each stay, we both understand better how to pool our strengths and tolerate our weaknesses, how to step forward or back depending on what is needed at the time. She is eager to participate with me as I collect and record family stories, and her memories of Dad in particular are acute, detailed and full of affection. We're drinking tea together at the kitchen table one afternoon late in 2000 when I record one of her stories about sitting at the same table talking to Dad ten years earlier. Her brilliant blue eyes water as she speaks.

Cathie: He was talking about someone we knew when we were kids. It was quite a long, in-depth story. Of course, I was just fascinated. I really believed that it had happened. Then, after about twenty minutes I looked him in the eye and said: 'You're having me on, aren't you?' The whole thing had been a complete and utter fantasy, but he'd interwoven enough facts into the story to make me believe it was true. He takes you on a long journey where you think you know where you're going – but then you find out you really had no idea at all.

Nothing about our father was quite what it seemed. Another peculiar story involves the matter of Dad's two birthdays, as well as his sometimes confusing abundance of names.

Cathie: We always thought Dad's birthday was November 9. When I applied for my British passport, I had to get a copy of his birth certificate and when it arrived we discovered that it had November 14 recorded as Dad's birthday. His own parents must have forgotten exactly when he was born. And his name was recorded as Arthur Gerard Neil. I remembered then the time we went to Sydney to see Uncle Bill after he had a brain clot. All our cousins were calling Dad 'Uncle Gerard'. And Uncle Bill and Aunt Lal called him 'Gerard' too, or even, sometimes, 'Arthur'. I was totally confused and I had no idea who anyone was talking to because I had only ever heard Dad referred to as 'Ben'. That was when Mum told me he had been a Christian Brother and had taken as his religious name 'Benedict'. Even after he left the Brothers he always signed his name 'Gerard Benedict Neil', out of respect, perhaps, for his years in the brotherhood and to honour and recognise, I suppose, his two lives.

During our exchanges we also remark, not for the first or last time, on the different nature of our memories. When we swap stories, which we often do during her visits, Cathie is lively, emotional and readily moved, while I ponder and puzzle more. Cathie remembers Dad's fondness for inventing tales and confusing his audience, for instance, but she doesn't worry or wear away at the benign surfaces of his inventions as I do. She doesn't wonder what lies beneath his fondness for tricks and games or the secret narratives, those that were untold, of his other life.

In an old photograph Dad's younger sister, Edith, is as beautiful as my father, who is standing beside her. She is smiling brightly; he is not. He has a dimple in his chin – something I don't recall him having when his face filled out with age – and a side part in his curly black hair and he wears a black suit with a white clerical collar. Edith has a centre part and has flowers at the top of the ruffle that cascades down the front of her dress, which, by the look of the creases in its fabric, must have been made from cotton or linen. They could be twins with their sensual mouths, dark-eyed gazes and similar high, wide foreheads, which are white, unmarked and 'full of brains' – 'too many brains', as Grandma would remark while shaking her head mournfully. The difference between this brother and sister is indicated only by the tiny markings of stress around Edith's eyes, and the particular shine in them. I have looked at this photograph many times and seen in my 'poor Aunt Edith' a woman who perhaps hungered for touch, for adventures that her need for survival denied her, who perhaps escaped into a fantasy world of hairdos, fine clothes, and makeup when real life proved disappointing for her.

When Edith died one day from a combination of diet pills and sedatives, it was called 'an accidental death'. Suicide was a mortal sin, according to the Church, and so if her passing was mentioned at all it was as a terrible, unforeseeable accident. For years Mum was under the impression that Edith had died a natural death, although what death, she sometimes asked herself, could be natural in a childless woman not yet forty who had hardly worked since her marriage and who had no identifiable disease.

It pulls at me like an ache to look at this picture of a woman I didn't know who took her own life. Did she use up all her breath? Or did she no longer believe that release was possible? In the photograph, her piercing gaze seems to search for something outside of herself, in the distance, in her imagination or her increasingly fevered mind, but never inside her body.

Her widower, Norm, was somehow blamed for her suicide and shunned by the family. Mum was expected to boycott him too, but a few years later she went, without Dad, to visit Norm and his new wife. He remained wistful, Mum told me, but happy to receive her, this unexpected reminder of old trauma. His new wide-hipped wife bore him children and he had settled, happily enough, in a quiet Sydney suburb. Apparently he was never referred to again by Edith's mother, old Ma Neil, who also never spoke to anyone about her losses. Perhaps her priest knew of her grief for the two children she had buried, but like a pragmatic Catholic she had borne enough children to have a few spare to support her in her old age and so she moved on quickly to the remaining few to help her reach the paradise she prayed every Sunday to be allowed to enter.

IT'S A GREAT LIFE IF YOU DON'T WEAKEN

Joan: I don't understand women saying they don't like having their babies. I loved all my babies and I loved being a mother. Of course, your grandmother always came after each new baby and helped. There wasn't a lot of time and I admit that some of you might have benefited from having more one-on-one attention. But in those days you just got on with things and didn't think too much about it all. I'm not sure even now whether there's any use in thinking too much. I remember your grandmother used to worry about you and all your brains. *It's better to be a clod in this world,* she used to say. *Better to be a clod and just plod along.* And in many ways, I think she was right. I was never very bright but I knew how to work hard. If I was really smart, perhaps I wouldn't have been so happy with the things I had. You learn to appreciate the little things around you when your mind is occupied and not too restless and curious about the rest of the world.

One of Mum's favourite sayings was: 'It's a great life if you don't weaken.' I heard Grandma say these words many times as well. They impressed upon me that the ability to endure was one of the most desirable assets in life. Mum told me that despite her five babies she never once suffered from post-natal depression, but I know that she endured a lot for the sake of her marriage and her children. The mantra of strength and tenacity was a constant throughout my childhood. Difficult things were never considered a problem. They were 'challenges to be faced' and hopefully – with the help of God – you came through them with a little more wisdom than you had before they began.

For my poor, uneducated ancestors, tenacity was a necessity. Survival depended on it. You endured things so that the next generation might have a little more, know a little more, understand a little more. My grandmother bought her houses, the ones that became our homes, in swamps and wasteland, in the hope they would eventually be worth something.

Music was the balm for these women. Something spiritual. To teach music was to pass on this balm. For Mum, teaching was also a kind of frontier activity; it was not bequeathed to her as a profession by her working-class parents or poor rural ancestors. She came across it like a vast brown land, full of secrets and possibilities, if she could only find the courage to voyage through it and discover its riches.

Dad had his own way of keeping his spirits up. His love of the water was a kind of leitmotif in his life. On Mum and Dad's honeymoon they sailed up the Hawkesbury River and stayed for a week in a houseboat near Gosford. Thirty-five years later

Dad fell over and died while taking a shower at home. He'd had what my country relatives might have referred to as 'a good innings'. According to his doctors, the massive stroke, the first of three, that he had had a few years before would have killed a man who was less fit, who hadn't been churning up and down the pool every day as Dad had. It certainly would have struck down a man who did not love to swim, who did not love the water as much as my father did.

'My back's killing me today', he wrote in a letter to Cathie in 1985. 'But I've been in great form up till now and tomorrow I'll be fit again because I churned through many laps of the swimming pool for therapeutic reasons. I've been swimming twice a day trying to keep fit and well in spite of enormous obstacles. I remember swimming in tiled pools in England. I must have been swimming since the cradle.'

My father's words seem rich with clues. I detect in the word 'churned' the effort he makes daily to aid his own recovery. I wonder at the choice of the phrase 'therapeutic reasons'. Does he mean this in just the physical sense? Or are there other issues at stake here? And the enormous obstacles of which he writes – could these just be about his sciatic nerves or other kind of nerves as well, the ones that determine his peace of mind, the ones that give him courage? Are there mental obstacles as well as bodily ones? Are there other things killing him besides his back?

Recovering from his second stroke he swam a kilometre a day up at the university pool while Mum walked around the river road saying her prayers and watching the tiny chug-a-lug ferries crisscross the river. It is also part of our family folklore that swimming was how Dad cured himself of the sciatica that had him bedridden for months after he retired. Numerous medical professionals pronounced his condition incurable and advised a complicated spine operation that did not have a hundred percent success rate, but which was his only hope of ever moving freely again. Dad decided to risk the chance of complete immobility (though perhaps, after a lifetime of hard work, his body just wanted a long rest) and chose not to have the operation. Instead he stayed in bed or walked with a stick for months, waiting out his recovery, waiting, perhaps, for a miracle, a miracle that eventually arrived in the form of a young female physiotherapist who suggested Dad go to the pool and do what he really loved to do; when he began to swim again, he slowly began to walk again.

Dad's inability to move without suffering became a kind of collective wound in the whole family. His stoicism was our shared blessing too, though it was not unexpected. He was, after all, a religious man who loved poetry and therefore understood the usefulness of metaphor. Perhaps he knew that wounds, especially to the hip – as God in the guise of an angel gave to Jacob in the Old Testament – were also spiritual gifts. He swam his way to recovery with humour and only a rare word of complaint. His acceptance of pain gave all of us a sense of the possibility of life and its random and hopeful miracles.

Mum spends the next five months in and out of hospital, which I still call her 'second home'. Unable to carry her own weight, she collapses regularly now and prepares herself for a life of immobility. A test reveals that she is deficient in salt. I assume it is because I have not used enough salt in her meals, but it turns out that the salt deficiency has been induced by a blood pressure tablet which her physician prescribed for her months earlier.

The tablet is removed from her medication and suddenly Mum is mobile again. An interlude of joy ensues. Each moment is like a celebration. She attempts things she could hardly manage when she was well and begins to walk every day up and down the steep hill outside the hospital, swinging her arms in wide arcs until she literally falls into bed with fatigue. This falling, though, is a gift to us as well, especially after the dread of the previous months, and when her medication is stable she is discharged once again into my care.

She arrives home like a newborn. I watch her wander around the house as if she is from another planet, touching things, fingering walls, sniffing the air, unsettled, lost, trying to get her bearings not just of the physical environment but of the sensory one as well.

Joan: The joy of that short time that I could play the piano again was a rich experience, and it went on for a few weeks and then I couldn't do it again. It was very sad.

Linda: What about the singing? I hear that you sing up and down the corridors, Mum.

Joan: They're all telling me now, someone just said today to me, about me singing, now what was it she said? She said, 'Oh, you've got a beautiful voice.' At dinnertime. She said, 'You've got a beautiful voice. Why don't you let us have more of it? Sing out. Loud.'

SEPTEMBER SONGS

From the time I arrive back home in 1998, Mum and I are regularly approached by estate agents who want to 'help in any way we can' to make our 'burden' easier. The 'burden', apparently, is the ownership of a large house in a prime location for townhouse development. During the first few years of the new century it often feels as if estate agents in the area are like circling sharks, waiting for aging and often exhausted homeowners to finally give in, surrender their 'burden', sell up and move on.

To encourage this process, cards are left in letterboxes, notes stuck on car windscreens, and leaflets pushed under front and back doors. Any hint on our part that we are thinking of selling 'sometime in the future' accelerates the wooing process. Meetings are arranged and preliminary offers made. I am unfamiliar with these bartering rituals and treat the visits like social occasions. Mum is gracious too. When agents drop by 'just for a chat', I serve fruit buns on our best china plates and Mum makes cups of tea. We are polite, amenable and promise to 'think about' any offers, but when we decide not to accept what we are told are 'extremely reasonable tenders that might not be made again', we begin to sense a hint of intimidation. My response to subsequent approaches becomes increasingly frosty, especially after friends and relatives tell us to bide our time and that we are 'sitting on a gold mine'.

Mum's frequent stays in hospital cause only brief pauses in the process. When I inform one agent that we cannot discuss selling while Mum is sick, he arrives at the front door late one night with flowers and a gift basket 'as a sign of my respect'. I refuse his gifts, but the crusade to acquire our property continues. It is, we discover, the blessing and the curse of having a home in an area that Grandma once described as 'swampland' but is now referred to as an 'upmarket, rapidly-appreciating, investment-friendly developers' dream locale'. Mum is sanguine about the need to sell. She knows the energy she requires to maintain her home is slowly slipping away from her. After an initial burst of packing up bags of old clothes, taking them to second-hand shops and selling off many of the old books that are no longer read or needed, I also become exhausted by the sheer size and effort of maintaining things. I was never much good at housekeeping either, and regularly hire cleaners to help keep some order in the place. I know also that as I commit more to my connection to Mum I am also growing less capable of moving out and moving on as easily as I used to. We have a relationship now, as mother and daughter, two women, two people going through something together, for better or for worse.

In early September 2001, I see Raphael at an organic fruit and vegetable market in West End. He is picking out mangoes at a stall and I am at another stall selecting oranges and mandarins. He is a lot thinner and browner than when I last saw him; he looks as if he has been fasting and working a lot in the sun. I remember then how we used to laugh about his colouring; how he used to take pride in suggesting he might have some Indigenous blood, or some Greek perhaps, as a way of explaining the way he went dark so quickly in the sun. We must have looked a peculiar sight when we were at the beach: me with my sun-damaged white skin, huge hat, big black sunglasses and long-sleeved shirt, him with his broad brown chest and long body. He'd liked the contrast, thought we looked good together. But I'd always found the heat too fierce at the beach, where he loved to be, and shied away from the sun.

He looks like a long, brown stick insect, as if the solid man I knew had been hollowed out and scraped clean. He's probably been on a juice fast. Detoxing. I think back suddenly on our days together by the sea as if they were a dream.

I just wasn't ready for it, I had told him. 'Not ready for love?' he had queried. 'I don't understand. When it comes to you all you need to do is to hold out your arms and receive it.'

I don't approach him, ashamed that I left him so thoughtlessly to return to Brisbane, especially after he had welcomed me into his life when I had arrived exhausted in

Byron Bay after five years plugged into amplifiers in Sydney. He shared more than a home with me as I began to explore more acoustic music in Byron: if love and music go together he was as robust as the sound of my un-electrified violin. I recall our intimacy, his love for the nature around us and the nature in me. Embarrassed by the rush of remembered physicality, I turn away, hoping to avoid an encounter with him, but he sees me. He calls across, holding a ripe golden mango in each of his large brown hands. *How are you?*

Ok . . . Ok. I stutter. *And you?*

Just then, as a kind of answer to my question, an equally long stick insect of a young woman steps out from behind him, carrying on her hip a tiny version of herself.

We're all doing fine, he calls out.

He squints at me quizzically as the young woman rocks her child on her hip. He's not wearing sunglasses, as usual; and, as usual, I am. I am glad he cannot see my eyes. Cannot see the sudden burn of loss well up and trickle down onto my cheeks.

It's not as if I am shocked to see him with someone. He has been considerate enough to tell me during the intermittent phone calls he made to me during the last few years. I know that he moved in with someone young, a single mother, but seeing him in the flesh makes me 'know' it in a different, more visceral way.

Mum met Raphael just once when he visited us both in Brisbane; she thought we were completely unsuited.

'He wasn't smart enough for you,' she said after he had left. I didn't want to hear it. Didn't want to be boxed as the 'clever girl' I'd been at school when I'd thought that I would be alone forever. She was wrong though. Raphael was smarter about some things than either Mum or me. I didn't want to defend him, not in my mother's lounge room. I didn't want to tie the threads of my old life to this new life.

But it was obvious when I saw him standing in Mum's house that we were just too different – that I was, despite my rebellion and drive, still my parents' daughter. Raphael had seemed too large then, too full of life. In front of this glowing, sensual man, I'd been ashamed of the sickness around me. But I hadn't turned away from him for the sake of my sick mother, although perhaps he thought that I had. It was not a sacrifice I was making for my mother, to turn away from this beautiful man. It was something less obvious than that, more internal. Sometimes you find what you need in the most unexpected places; not on beaches, or in beds with beautiful lovers, but somewhere nondescript and ordinary.

'You don't have to do this. You can choose happiness over this if you really want to,' Raphael said to me at the Roma Street bus station where I had driven him at the end of his visit. I had been deliberately obtuse then and avoided the real implication of his statement. I resisted the temptation to ask him exactly what he meant by that word, happiness. Instead, I chatted casually as we walked together to the bus which would take him back to Byron Bay.

'Oh, I don't mind driving you. Seeing you off. After everything you did for me. And it's been so good to see you.'

Raphael didn't push me; didn't hold me to him or make me remember our intimacy, although I could feel he wanted to. He gave me my freedom right up until the end, just as he had always promised he would. I didn't even cry, not once, when we parted. I'd held those tears for this moment, surrounded by toxin-free fruit opposite a toxin-free man under an old fig tree at West End, the suburb where my mother had grown up, across the river from the suburb where I had grown up.

You look good, he calls out then over the dusty space across which neither of us will walk to greet each other, while the young woman and child wrap themselves around him. I wonder if I do.

So do you. Just great. He smiles at me, and even though he hasn't walked across the space to greet me, I can feel his smile as if it has broken across my own face. I can feel his smile enter me through the pores of my skin. I watch him turn and walk away, his arm around the pair of beautiful girls, and I suddenly wonder why, when love comes to some of us, we still think it is a puzzle that needs to be solved. To Raphael, love was a reason to rejoice and celebrate, while to me it was a reason to ponder and question. It isn't that I want Raphael with me now; I know I would grieve to pass on to him the suffering of my mother's suffering. He would grieve for my struggle and my struggle needs to find its own nature, its own reason and its own ending.

I feel the soft shadows of the fig tree quiver above me as the late morning crowds suddenly seem to converge at that moment. As I watch him disappear from view I don't know whether to cry or to smile. I waver on that in-between point that seems to fill you up from deep inside, when everything seems absolutely right and absolutely wrong with the world at exactly the same time.

Mum's second grandchild, Kel Neil, isn't even one month old when the Twin Towers of the World Trade Center in New York collapse on 11 September 2001. We have welcomed him into the world with much ado, a blond, beautiful and precious boy who looks a lot like Mum did as a child. So Paul now has two children: one dark, one light; Finn like Dad, Kel like Mum. Mum is less involved with this birth than Finn's, yet the new baby enters our lives again like the arrival of new possibilities. Although we are giddy with joy, I regret that I don't write songs to celebrate this new life as I did with Finn. The business of Mum's illness has taken up more and more of my life – and hers as well – and songs do not come as easily now as they once did.

On 12 September, I scrape my car on a concrete pillar while backing out of a parking space at Toowong Village Shopping Centre. Mum is back in the psych ward of Westminster Hospital again and I have gone to Kmart to buy her some new nighties. She is unaware of the events which have taken place in New York and phoned early in the morning with a list of things she needed me to get for her.

Mum's hospital room is full of light that day; early spring is usually beautiful in Brisbane, but perhaps also, after a night of horror, I am looking especially hard for pockets of brightness. I remember staring at two butcherbirds singing outside and then trying to open the window to let their music fill the room. I also spend a longer than usual amount of time holding Mum's hand.

Mum is vague about the attacks in New York. I tell her what has happened and she mentions she has seen a newspaper headline that morning. But I know that the events of the world have become further and further removed from her concerns as the terror explodes in her inner world. We speak a little about the city of New York, which she had visited just before she first became ill.

What I remember most about New York, she tells me, *was all those beautiful black people everywhere. And so polite and well dressed. Put a lot of us back home to shame. Now, they truly look like God's creatures to me. And the magnificent singing! Jessie Norman singing Mozart's 'Hallelujah'. What a highlight that was!*

THE KEYS OF HEAVEN

In 1989 my father wrote:

> I went to the pool for a swim yesterday morning. It was 17 degrees. So with a pain under my scapula I pondered on (1) would a swim relieve my pain or (2) would a swim exacerbate it? So I sat in the car and listened to Furlonger on the International Situation, Dr Hackett on the Body Programme and a pleasant exchange of messages and music between England and Australia. I can listen well still, even with all my pain, with attention and discrimination and pleasure.

There is a picture of Dad in a swimming pool taken when he was nearly eighty. He is smiling in the photograph and wears tiny dark blue Speedos and a red swimming cap on his head. As Dad beams up at the camera, his eyes are lit by the sun on the water. The impression is one of overwhelming light – in the pale blue water around him and in his face; he seems as vital and energised as a boy. *He had such a healthy body for a man of his age*, Kym tells me. *And then I think of him when he was sick after the strokes when Paul was looking after him. He was so frail, but such a good patient.* His incapacity opened him up and made him more vulnerable. *He couldn't get enough hugs and he was always crying at something he'd seen on the television. I think the fact that he had kids later meant he didn't have the drive, the ego or ambitions of a younger man. Paul's like that too: just interested in his kids.*

When Kym met Dad he was already retired and over the worst of his sciatica. While I remember a man flailing against his loss of work and authority with sometimes mordant humour, she remembers a man who eventually knew how to soften. She tells me in an interview:

> When I said goodbye after the second meeting I had with your dad, I went to give him a hug and he put his hands really straight and stiff down at his sides and he wouldn't let me touch him. No way. He wasn't having any of that physical affection. I'll never forget one day I came and at the end of the visit I kissed your dad, and then he actually gave me a hug. Paul told me that he'd never seen your dad do that to anyone before because you weren't a very affectionate family and definitely the boys never hugged each other or your father for that matter. So that was our thing. He used to pretend he didn't want to kiss me goodbye and then he'd give me a hug. I thought it was a sort of breakthrough because your dad used to put up these barriers.

I knew about these barriers, knew about things I wasn't supposed to know. One night, as a teenager, I discovered my father crying on the back stairs. When he saw me, he got up and walked into the darkness of our back yard.

'Where are you going, Dad?' I called out.

'Down the back to lick my wounds.' His voice sounded strangled. It was the first time in my life I'd heard what a person's pain sounded like: the tightness of the throat, the thick furrowing of sound.

'Dad?' I called out. 'Dad?'

It was a question, though I was inarticulate too. If he answered, what would I ask him? To read to me? To sing? To tell a funny story?

'Dad, where are you going? Where are you going?' I called out to him.

'Somewhere I'm wanted,' he cried back at me, his voice strained and tight.

'We want you, Dad. We need you.' I wish I had called out these words. But I didn't know the language then for the enormity and the delicacy of what was happening around me.

But I knew too much about things I shouldn't have known. So I learnt to keep silent. I didn't speak to anyone about these things. I never told anyone that my father was driving off late at night; that sometimes I sat out on the footpath until he returned home; that underneath my bedroom was the small room filled with books where Dad now slept on a single bed. That on many nights I heard my parents arguing.

Later I would understand about taking off in the car at night and driving around the streets in the dark. I used to do it a lot after moving out of home, when the stresses and noises of shared households became too much for me. And what was our residence at Warren Street, I used to think, but one giant, rambunctious shared household, the kind of dwelling that would only ever be allowed to legally house four or at the most five rent-paying students, but which usually held at the very least seven and sometimes more family members and sundry friends and relatives. No wonder Dad needed to get away. I also discovered the joys of the fold-out single bed when I would camp in the lounge rooms and corridors of friends' houses while passing through their towns and cities on music tours. The creaky camp bed, 'somewhere to crash', was an artefact of freedom, of portability, of the secret musical diaspora that all touring musicians and gypsy fiddlers knew about.

I became a solitary walker too, just like Dad, who walked his way back to health after his post-seminary crisis and many times after that. He gave us all the habit of walking. I loved, as perhaps he did, the way my brain felt as I strode along the streets, the journey my thoughts could take, the mysteries that could be encountered as I voyaged all around the world and back again without my body ever leaving the neighbourhood.

I've done my fair share of arguing too, along with screaming, crying, accusing, begging, pleading and ignoring – in music as well as in life, although sometimes the two things seemed inseparable. I usually found it physically as well as emotionally distressing, as I am sure my father did, and a poor substitute, often, for the kindness of restraint and silence.

'Last Friday,' he wrote cryptically during that time in another one of his numerous letters to Cathie, 'I went to a battered husbands' club, a seminar for handicapped people (this is handicapped people's year) and according to Chinese Mythology it is the Year of the Rooster. So now I'm looking for a Handicapped Rooster's Club too.'

Cathie: Dad was not a typical male by any means, but I still think he had to deal with major changes in his life when he retired. He was at home, Mum's domain, and she had her systems worked out. She was just coming into her prime and suddenly Dad was there in the mix. For a while he did some work for Meals on Wheels. And the boys definitely helped. He loved being with them. But they were at school most of the day. What should he do till they came home? And even then they mightn't want to be hanging around with their father.

I don't think any of us really knows how hard it was for Dad. We could probably never imagine what it was like for him to leave the Church and have to start again; to be an older father with a young family; then to be finished with work while he was still educating all his kids. Retiring was just another change in a long line of them . . . It was hard for Mum too.

Joan: After five kids I was tired. I thought five was enough. Your father still believed all the teachings of the Catholic Church. I guess after all his years in the Brothers he couldn't be flexible about stuff like that. He was very old-fashioned that way. I guess because he was so much older he was just a little set in his ways and he couldn't change his mind.

Linda: So it was just a matter of not wanting any more kids?

Joan: Well, there were other things too. There's never just one person at fault when things go wrong in a marriage. I was busy with all my study and my teaching. It wasn't easy for him. He was inexperienced, your father. He was a very attractive, charming man, but you've got to remember I was his first love and he was nearly fifty when we married. But I was always faithful to your father. Always.

One day a few years earlier in a queue in the Newtown post office I had run into the daughters of Mum's best friend, Rita Booth, whose husband was at one time the manager of Myer where my sisters and I worked during the Christmas holidays. Daisy and Mia seemed embarrassed when the talk turned to Dad; eventually they told me that he had 'been with our mother' in the months before she died of cancer. Their euphemistic revelation knocked me sideways. I didn't know what they meant by 'been with our mother' and I didn't really want to know. I always imagined that, being Dad, he just visited. And spoke quietly to a dying woman in need of help. I never mentioned to Mum what I heard in the Newtown post office. Eventually, though, deep into her illness, she divulges more to me.

Joan: On the day of Rita's funeral, your father was driving a yellow Mazda, which I knew was hers and which he'd told me she'd lent to him. In the glove box I discovered some registration papers, which said the car was his. She'd given him the car, signed it over to him. I didn't think anything of it really. I knew he'd been helping her. Her husband had just died of cancer and she was dying too. She also had a troublesome son who used to come over and threaten her and try and get money from her. So of course she needed support. Poor Rita, she had so much to put up with. But I suddenly just felt angry with your father. Angry that he hadn't told me about the car.

She was *my* friend. My best friend. He knew that. She knew it too. Then he asked me if I really thought I should go to the funeral. I was so furious and so upset about Rita's funeral I said to him: 'I am going to go and see my dear friend off and afterwards . . . afterwards we'll see what we'll do.'

So we went to the funeral. And oh, it felt like my heart was breaking . . . in so many ways. But I did what was right. I said my prayers over Rita's casket.

Afterwards I asked your father: 'What did you two do together?'

You know what he said? Rita had had cancer the whole time. He just looked at me with the saddest look on his face and said: 'Mostly I just helped her breathe.' I could feel my heart was breaking . . . at the thought of that poor woman . . . being held by someone while she was trying to breathe. That was probably all he did, you know . . . your father. Just helped her breathe. He was a very caring man and when I got too busy perhaps he looked around for someone to care for. And, in a way, thank god I *was* busy and he was there . . . for her sake.

Linda: Were you angry with your friend, Mum? Were you angry with Rita?

Joan: You know, the funny thing is, I never was. She had the most awful life. I mean, she was terribly well off, but in all the years I knew her husband before he died I never heard him say one nice thing to her. All he ever did was criticise her. And of course your father adored me. Always said lovely things to me. No, I wasn't mad with her. I just thought, well, at least she got a little love, a little tenderness before she died. It's funny, isn't it? I mean, it took me a long time to forgive your father . . . for not telling me about the car . . . a long, long time. But Rita . . . no . . . I was never even angry with her.

'Energy in the voice is mental,' Mum wrote in September 1994 for the Music Teachers' Association Newsletter. 'Use your imagination and let the poetry lead you to the music. And the music will lead you back to the poetry.'

The balance of poetry and music appears in its most exquisite form in the songs of Franz Schubert in which the craft of the accompanist provides a counterpoint to the skill of the singer. In the art of the Lied, the art of the song, the singer sings a duet with the pianist. In the Lied, the piano does not just accompany the song, it supports, harmonises, interweaves. In Schubert's 'The Trout', for instance, the piano's rippling arpeggios create the cascading water in which the fish leaps and swims. In this Lied, the pianist is an equal partner to the singer.

To the pianist, Mum once wrote: 'Create the mood of happiness, wonder, sadness at the piano. Use the piano as a wonderfully rich instrument to bring out all the musical changes. Don't be too shy at the piano. Lied is a duet. You are an equal partner and must give the singer continual support.'

The piano and the voice. Swimming and reading. The physical and the intellect. The duality that appeared to exist in the outside world didn't seem to matter to Dad at all. His idea always seemed to be that opposites not only attract, but also support each other. As Mum passes through what she refers to as her own 'dark night of the soul', he always seems to be with us. I listen to his song in the stories and words I hear about him – from Mum, from my siblings, and from friends. Sometimes it feels as if I am somewhere in the middle of them both, my mother and my father, learning how not to take sides, how not to make the obvious choices, how to find that perfect balance between sorrow and joy, rhythm and melody, music and words.

As well as teaching me to swim, Dad taught me to read. Even before I started school I was already reading small story books and later Dad took me on weekly trips to the Toowong Municipal Library. Cathie remembers that every day after he arrived home from work our father would take his three daughters out walking around the university near the river. Cathie and I would walk hand-in-hand, Janice gurgling in the pram, while Dad read us French and Latin poetry. Cathie also remembers – although sometimes I wonder why I cannot – that in the mornings he used to read to us French story books. 'We just thought it was normal,' she says. 'Latin and French in the Brisbane suburbs.'

Dad got me onto the meatier stuff when I was still quite young. I was about eight when he first read me Yeats. After Yeats there was Keats, Donne, Coleridge, Wordsworth, and other poets who appeared in Dad's old edition of *Great English Poets of the World*. Dad loved Latin too – the dead language not the dance, I would explain to my school friends – loved, as I did, the way it rolled off the tongue, the musical logic of its declensions.

scribere
scribe
scribementum
scribementa
scribemento
scribementis

On holidays at the Gold Coast he would read Virgil and Cicero in his spare moments between doing cryptic crosswords, repairing the inner tubes of our second-hand bikes, and ferrying us to and from the waters of Palm Beach, Currumbin or Burleigh Heads in the less fierce heat of the mornings and evenings. We would play tennis in the back yard, football on the street, cricket on the beach, and play and sing music in the lounge room. I would lead neighbourhood kids on bike journeys to Surfers Paradise and back, and when we returned Dad would bundle us into the car for our sometimes daily holiday trips to the Burleigh Heads library where I read authors from the teenage section when I was still a child and authors from the adult section when I was still a teenager. Dad always encouraged me to extend my vocabulary, just as he always encouraged me to ride the Gold Coast waves without a boogie board, to trust the feel of my own body through the water, to trust that my brain could understand things long before my experience had caught up with it.

My love of reading sometimes caused running battles between me and Mum who, as well as being our cook, cleaner, medico and entertainment coordinator, was also the family's official censor. She had her work cut out with me – I read everything I could get my hands on: fairytales, adventure stories, pirate yarns, forensic medicine cases, detective novels and murder mysteries full of blood and gore set in the gloomy shadows of urban underworlds. Dad never discouraged me; as well as driving sometimes twice a week to the local library he often helped me carry to the car the teetering piles of books that, even during school nights when I should have been asleep, became conduits into other worlds for my imagination.

Mum tried her best to protect me from the kind of feverish overstimulation she feared might ruin my mind by encouraging me to keep up my violin practice. The discipline, she said, was good for my heart and my body. She was right, but I didn't want to give up words for the sake of music. I needed them both. Mum wasn't convinced, though. Subsequently, articles about grisly murders or sex crimes were secretly removed from the Sunday papers before I could get to them, books I was halfway through suddenly taken from me and hidden, paperbacks grabbed out of my hands. Even the Cornflakes packets on the kitchen table at breakfast were not safe from my inquisitive eyes; I lingered longer than I should have over recipes and even before I could recite by memory the Ten Commandments I could itemise the ingredients for Cornflake crackles, which were never as popular, in our house anyway, as the more traditional chocolate crackles made from cocoa, lard, icing sugar, coconut and Rice Bubbles – I knew this recipe by heart too.

Mum may have been mildly amused by our contest, but she reached her limit when, with Dad's approval, I took out from the Burleigh Heads library during one of our summer holidays a book with the memorable title *My Darling My Hamburger*, which featured teenage sex, abortion, contraceptives and youth suicide. The book became infamous in our home when Mum forcibly removed it from my room. Later Mum and I will laugh together as we remember the battle that ensued: how I scoured the house for the book, in cupboards, siblings' rooms, crockery drawers and kitchen dressers; how cunning Mum was when she began to transfer it from one hiding place to another as if it was a fugitive prisoner-of-war; the manoeuvres that went on for days until, exhausted by the sheer effort of daily life seeing to her house, husband, teaching and kids, Mum eventually forgot to move it and I found *My Darling My Hamburger* one night, frozen solid behind a leg of lamb in the freezer, after which it was thawed, towel-dried, finished and refrozen by dinnertime next evening.

Dad liked a good comedy and adored elegant, deeply felt verse, but he never talked much about his feelings. It was only later, after suffering three strokes, that he became more affectionate, began to cry at sad stories on the television and feel anxious when Mum didn't come home on time. He would wait outside the house then, peering down the street until she appeared around the corner. It was his generation of men, Mum would explain, who never spoke of such things, and although his practical jokes illustrated his absurdist life view, it was through his favourite poetry that I felt who my father might be. Intellectually, I rarely had any idea what the poems were about, but the tone, the sound, the melancholy transferred their meaning and shady impressions of my father to me.

There is a dark
Inscrutable workmanship which reconciles
Discordant elements, makes them cling together
In one society

While clearing out the old rooms underneath the house, I discover a small, finely ruled exercise book containing his notes on *King Lear,* a text he used to teach regularly to his senior English students. 'A character study in jealousy and the pettiness of power', he wrote. 'And what is the flaw in a man who would turn against his own daughter for the sake of ego and vanity?'

I peruse the book for hours, fascinated by the spidery writing commenting on his favourite Shakespearean play. What am I looking for as I scan it keenly? Signs? Clues? Insight? I wonder why I still wonder so intensely after all this time about my father's real nature, as if his character is still a dark shadowy puzzle that needs to be brought into the light in order to be solved.

Joan: I never would have left your father. Catholics don't believe in divorce. You've got to remember he was from a different generation and he had to adjust to a lot of things. But he had a lot of qualities you'd never find in another man. I mean, he washed up *every* night of our married life until he had his stroke and even then he'd try to shoo me away from the sink, shuffle over towards me and tell me he was the only one in our household who ever knew how to wash the dishes properly. He was right, I suppose. I was never terribly interested in housework. I mean you *had* to do it, didn't you? But no one could ever make you enjoy it. So in many ways he was ahead of his time. I mean, these days people would call that a feminist, wouldn't they? A man who did the washing up and put the clothes on the line? Though the less said about his cooking the better.

During happy times, Mum and Dad used to sing together at home. Their favourite song was a duet called 'The Keys of Heaven'. Mum's voice was sweet, high and effortless, but I remember my father singing as if he was pulling his voice out from somewhere deep inside his body.

Will you give me the keys of heaven?
Will you give me the keys to your heart?

Madam, will you walk?
Madam, will you talk?
Madam, will you walk and talk with me?

Dad had what Mum called a fine mid-range baritone and he loved to play the part of Mum's lover when they sang duets. This involved him clasping her hands close to his heart and looking soulfully into her eyes as he sang, something that used to embarrass me deeply. Perhaps their love of singing together, the pleasure of harmonising their emotions through music, made their marriage endure despite their difficulties. When Mum sang back to him it was perhaps the best way she knew how to answer his call of love.

I will give you the keys of heaven,
I will give you the keys to my heart,
Yes sir, I will walk,
Yes sir, I will talk,
Yes sir, I will walk and talk with you.

Joan: They were difficult years. Sometimes I didn't know how I would get through them. But that's what marriage was in those days. You endured things, even after they became terrible and difficult. Oh, I know it's not fashionable now, but I have to tell you that after years of praying, one day I felt released and I forgave your father. I opened my heart to him and gradually we became – first friends, and then husband and wife again. And it was softer, more precious than when we first loved each other. We'd come

> through something dark and horrible and afterwards there was . . . just a lot of light.

'Your cards and letter tell me that you are in a happier mood,' Dad wrote to Cathie in a letter at the end of that time. 'I am also better all the time. I guessed that you were passing through emotional trauma, but now the trauma is, to some extent at least, over. Stay that way. Keep travelling. Keep being happy, we all send our love.'

FIDDLING IN THE UNDERWORLD

In one of her articles for the Music Teachers' Association, Mum advised her readers to 'encourage your students to take any and every opportunity to take the music out of the practice rooms and into the real world'.

I joke with her later that I followed her advice, right down to the gritty details, when I took my music out of the practice rooms, the concert and recital halls, and onto the streets of Sydney. It was really her fault, I tell her, that I went crazy for a while, that I went wild as I took any and every opportunity to make my dreams of music real.

For instance, busking. The hardest thing about busking is choosing the spot, *marking your territory*, my friend Busker Joe used to call it, except we're too civilised to cock a leg and piss on the footpath. Still, there were always a few moments of terror between putting your violin case down and opening it up, when you didn't really want to do it, except you'd set yourself goals – *yes, Prime Minister, even buskers have goals* – well *a* goal anyway, of at least an hour a day, clocking in and clocking out, usually during peak hours, as if there was some unseen boss checking out your work ethic.

Back in Mum's house, it seems like a dream now, this wild musical life I'd had in Sydney when I'd played with famous people and heard my violin on the radio. Though I rarely refer to it, I am neither proud nor ashamed of it. It was something I did then, just as looking after Mum is something I am doing now.

Since I've been, in Mum's words, 'back in the fold', playing violin for Mum's friends at weddings and funerals, it is even the source of funny stories. *Oh yes, Linda played on the streets for a while,* Mum might offer a visitor, as if she is passing unusually shaped biscuits around the table. *Oh really,* they might reply, reaching out in curiosity like they might really take a nibble out of me. *How interesting*! I tell stories as they sip their tea. My stories encourage their stories: about nephews and nieces, friends of cousins, relatives of accountants who also busked 'for pocket money' to pay for overseas trips, to pay off bills, to pay for rent. My Irish roots explain a lot, I sometimes think, as I observe this secret admiration for private enterprise, this bypassing of the system, this playing of music for the people and not for the elite. Many professional classical musicians refer to busking as begging, but for me it was a kind of badge of honour. I knew that it taught me courage and restored to me the faith in the wild, spontaneous and real that my years of discipline and study had suppressed in me. I also knew that my training and discipline were always at the back of my creative adventures in Sydney. It was the synthesis of these things – the highbrow, the lowbrow, the no-brows-at-all – that gave me work habits even in the middle of the chaos around me.

Mum and Dad raised me to be a nice girl, but I don't think I would have qualified as a nice girl when I played my violin on the footpaths of Sydney. I suppose they thought I'd gone mad when I took to playing music on the streets and in bands, especially since they had been relieved that after dropping out of law I had finished a music degree at university. They probably expected me to settle into a life of teaching and professional music-making in an establishment that had seemingly opened its door to me. But the professors I needed now were somewhere different – they were playing on footpaths and in bars, on street corners and in arcades. I wanted to learn to play the violin differently and to find a new way of life to go along with it. I wanted something raw to enter the sound I'd learned to refine in the temples of music and a new energy in my body and mind as well.

I couldn't articulate these things at the time, but my passion to explore overrode all the fears that, as a daughter of good parents, I naturally had. The nicest thing I did for Mum and Dad, though, was that I was living in another city when I leapt into the unknown over barriers of classical music and went down into the wild and the dark where I would hear for the first time the sound of my own music.

I picked the grungiest part of the city to begin my musical journey. Kings Cross. I made a lot of money at the Cross, but no one wanted to hear anything original. If I played my own music I always ended the day penniless, so I stuck to Vivaldi and Mozart if I wanted to rake in the money from the yuppies in Elizabeth Bay and Potts Point walking to their high rise apartments from the train station. Classical music – paying for classical music – made them feel separate from the prostitutes and desperados who sold junk and banged on tin cans with old spoons, like an old guy called Gilbert who always played six doors up from me, right outside The Pink Pussycat.

Eventually the Cross just got too hard on my own. It was great for a while gathering an audience around me as I made my way through the greatest hits of the classical repertoire. I even enjoyed the added bonus sometimes of getting fifty bucks chucked in my case for having 'the best legs in the Cross'. But things turned weird one day when a man called Mario, who said he was a record producer, lured me to his hotel room to talk about 'a deal' and then tried to take all my clothes off. I fled down the fire escape and the next day moved my operation to the Central Station tunnel at peak hour, where the clientele was anonymous, regular and cashed up, and the acoustics were absolute heaven.

Moving from the street to the tunnel felt sometimes as if I was burrowing down further into a musical underworld, as if the heart I was trying to discover was truly filled with darkness. Some days it felt like things couldn't get any worse, that I really had gone mad, that I really was crazy for music: when I'd been playing for hours and all I had in my case was twenty cents. When my face would be red from shame and hunger because I couldn't afford anything to eat. When I'd feel like smashing the violin, giving up and going home, back to where I came from, where I would do what was expected of me, where I would play other people's music, and teach other people to do the same thing. Times when I thought I couldn't stand to play another note of Mozart or Vitelli or Corelli or Locatelli. Times when in sheer bloody frustration I'd rip into some big, fat, juicy sound just to keep myself warm, because a musician knows that music can hang there in the high space of the tunnel and warm you like the sun. There'd be nothing like those times. I could never be lonely enough, cold enough, hungry enough to give up those moments when all the resonance harmonises and even the mosaics on the wall seem to shimmer with the vibrations of the violin. When I could feel – not just hear – the sound I was making. When the sound of the music seemed to heat me up from the inside.

This was when my dream of making music began to feel real, bit by bit, those moments when I was enveloped in sound, as if I was standing in a womb of music waiting to be reborn.

I wish I'd been able to find the words to tell this story to Dad, but we didn't really communicate often during that time, although Mum still sent me regular letters and cards on which Dad would add a few dutiful lines at the end. I didn't tell Mum much either. I know she fretted about me, but thought I was smart enough to turn things around if I wanted to. I think Dad took my situation personally, though, and I resented his disappointment in me. When I visited then, I was ashamed and defiant, unable to articulate to him, or even to myself, why I was doing what I was doing, when he had educated me to live in other ways. I was stubborn too. I began to look, in my mother's words, 'blowsy'. It probably broke Dad's heart to see me go wild. I knew that my underground life was only part of a longer journey for me and that I would have to find my way back to some middle ground. But I couldn't turn back. Even if I wanted to, I didn't know how. Perhaps I really was – as Grandma once accused me of being – 'as stubborn as sin' and 'headed straight for hell'.

But if I'd known then the right words, if I'd understood the use of a good metaphor, Dad might have understood exactly what I was doing – if I'd been able to tell him that I wasn't wasting myself or whatever gift I had for life or music. That I was only fiddling in the underworld and I had to keep going until I found the light.

They came with plates of pikelets and sandwiches, fairy cakes and lamingtons, clutching sheet music of songs from operettas and musical comedy. They carried handbags stuffed with accoutrements to enhance their performances that day: false eyelashes, black plastic compacts rimmed in gold and filled with powder for the face, rouge for the cheeks and false curls for a performance of 'Three Little Maids from School' from *The Mikado*, white pancake makeup for a rendition of 'One Fine Day' from *Madam Butterfly*, a black lace fan used as a prop while singing a flirtatious aria from *The Merry Widow*. There were pearls for *The Pearl Fishers*. There was a red plastic rose to be thrown dramatically onto the floor while a big-boned mezzo soprano sang the 'Habanera' from *Carmen*. There was a black babushka worn by my mother as she sang 'Mother You Know the Story' from *Cavalleria Rusticana*. There were saucers of cream for the 'Cat Duet' and later, without props, four-handed versions of 'Granada' and 'The Can Can' from *Orpheus in the Underworld*. Before lunch, my sister Cathie would play such a bustling version of Mozart's 'Alla Turka' that the piano keys clicked and rattled as if we were not really crowded into a tiny lounge room in a Brisbane suburb, but stuffed together, sweating and breathless, in an old cart careering along a road to Istanbul. Then, after food, there were tentative performances of old violin light classics like 'Melody in F' by Arthur Rubenstein and 'Intermezzo' from *Cavalleria Rusticana*, which I played reluctantly with bowed shoulders and drooping head while Mum yelled at me to *Play up! Play louder*!

I might have forgotten now other specific sounds from Mum's annual Musical Day, but I can still remember an invisible sound, or, more accurately, I remember the sound of invisible energy: of these women coming to life, moment by moment, as they sang, listened, clapped and laughed along in delight at their sharing of this music and song.

Men rarely, if ever, made an appearance; it was a day of secret women's business before we ever knew what that phrase meant. Husbands were seen dropping off their wives in our driveway, or occasionally helping them carry the trays of cakes and sandwiches and the piles of sheet music that would make up the day's performance repertoire. Sometimes, late in the day, one would venture as far as our back door and peer in through the flyscreen looking for his wife, hardly daring to enter what must have seemed from the outside to be an overwhelming world of laughing, singing women.

As well as the muscles in her throat, the muscles in Mum's eyes now begin to cause her trouble. She responds to this with alarm. Apart from the fear of losing her voice, she is now terrified of going blind. Unable to reach her doctors to voice her concerns in person, Mum begins the habit of writing little notes and letters on scraps of paper which she then might hand to the doctor when she arrives. Many of them are forgotten, though, between the time when they are written and the time the doctor arrives. She writes politely and goes into detail like a supplicant in a legal case.

> Dear Doctor,
>
> Regarding my eyes during the night: after I wake and can't get to sleep again owing to the flickering of my eyes, the same thing happened last night. I continually flickered my light [sic] for the night nurse (a tall gentleman) and told him what was happening and that I couldn't sleep because of my eyes. He first gave me Xanax, then camomile tea and we were talking about how often this had happened. After several calls I suggested he give me a Madopar early (at about 4.30 I think) then he went and within about eight minutes or so I must have gone to sleep till about a quarter to seven. I'm sure he will verify this.
>
> I'm hoping something can be looked into about my eyes and hopefully something can be done as it is becoming a real problem for me.
>
> Yours sincerely
> Joan Neil

Pricilla Leighton, an old vocal student of Mum's, wasn't around for her musical days, but she is a regular visitor during the first years of Mum's illness. *Your mother was my rock,* Pricilla tells me. *She got me through my bad times. She was always someone you could rely on. To drop in for a cup of tea. To tell your problems to. And I don't just mean musical ones. I thought she would have handled this better. The way she expected me to handle my problems.*

There sometimes seems nothing to say to comments like these so I adopt the habit of getting the violin out when Pricilla visits. Music diverts Mum – and Pricilla as well – from feeling embarrassed by her worsening condition. Sometimes I have the same feeling I used to as a child: a performing seal trundled out for Mum's friends at concerts and recitals. But music is a gift I feel increasingly grateful for and I now play happily for Mum and whoever visits her. I even take requests.

Play that gypsy piece for us, will you, Linda? Pricilla calls out to me during one of her last visits to the house. *The one you used to play on the street. You with your wild, wild heart.*

There is a beautiful symmetry, a sense of return, when I relive my busking days in Mum's house, the place where I first heard and learnt to play these gypsy tunes. Now we are not one, but three women going feral in the suburbs, the way I went feral on the streets. I prowl around the corridors with my fiddle the way I used to prowl the footpaths of the Cross, scraping my violin strings as if they are made of raw metal. Pricilla, an occupational therapist who dreams in her time off of one day escaping the confines of her million-dollar house up the road and singing in the great opera houses of the world, is delighted.

It feels good to bring delight back into my mother's house; delight can wipe out the shadows of the past. It shimmies like a glittering sequinned woman through the denseness of depression. It is, like the music of buskers, full of gesture and affect. It is a showgirl, a peach. It does no damage. And it gives a point to my fall away from my mother. It gives meaning to my days on the streets. Sometimes now when I am playing my crazy fiddle and Pricilla is clapping wildly I feel as if the present is linked all the way back to some distant past, before words, before language, when people danced and screamed to express their stories, when sorrow could be told through sound, and passion relayed through rhythm and dance. Sometimes it seems as if this delight and laughter is the final transformation of all my mad adventures, the looping back of my own fall, to find upon my return among the cracked cups and dusty linoleum of my mother's kitchen, the real grace of music.

THE ASYLUM SEEKERS

In Santuzza's aria 'Voi lo Sapete' from the opera *Cavalleria Rusticana,* which Mum often sang around the house when I was a child, a young peasant girl confesses to her mother her despair at her faithless lover.

Mother you know the story,
That evil one,
for all my rightful pleasure,
burns now with jealousy.
Me she has outraged!
Despoiled of my honour
I live on –

Mum never had the build, the voice or the passion for Wagner and was never meant to be a Valkyrie or a Gotterdamerung. Grand opera didn't suit her style either. Though she admired Dame Joan Sutherland, she never attempted the coloratura roles for which Sutherland was famous, the Normas and the Lucia d' Lammermoors. She preferred the energy and emotion of a Puccini opera, as well as the refinement of a beautiful Mozart aria to the madness and drama of a Lucia. Being the younger wife of an older man, she was always, in his eyes anyway, young, beautiful and girlish, and so she was physically well suited to sing Santuzza's lament.

Before I was old enough to properly understand the difference between make-believe and reality, I could have sworn that real despair was tearing my mother's heart as she clutched at her breast. What did she draw on, I wondered, to find such wretchedness with which to sing? She tells me later:

> You don't necessarily have to live through something to understand it. To sing opera – to enact an aria – you have to go further than just finding the splendour of the voice. You have to understand the story and, if necessary, let the voice crack and break. You have to be willing to surrender perfection, to find the light and the shade, to be brave enough to produce a sound that might be technically flawed for the sake of the real art of the song.

In late 2001, a boat carrying asylum seekers is discovered in difficulties off the coast of Western Australia. Mum and I watch the footage of the boat and the refugees in the television room of Woodlands Hospital where Mum is staying for observation while she undergoes further adjustments to her antidepressant medication. There is a scandal about photographs that purportedly show some of the asylum seekers throwing their children overboard.

As her inner world continues in chaos, Mum is increasingly vague about outside events. She manages a few comments, though, on the children who have supposedly been hurled into the sea: *I don't think any parent would do that,* she says. *And if they did it can only be because the parents thought they would be safer in the sea.* She trails off, before continuing quizzically: *You wouldn't think they would be safer in the sea. But sometimes your perspective suddenly changes and everything you believed in is turned upside down.*

A week after this incident, Mum's legs are so stiff she can't get out of bed. She asks her nurse for a wheelchair to help her get to the toilet. After examining Mum's legs, the nurse tells Mum she is fine and to get out of bed and walk to the toilet herself. Unable to stand on her own, Mum falls to the floor and is accused of malingering. The head nurse, who is called to sort things out, will have none of Mum's 'play-acting' and says she will not 'placate such attention-seeking behaviour'.

As I arrive for my daily visit, I am able to hear the head nurse from down the corridor. *Get up, Joan,* she growls. *I know you can walk by yourself. We're not going to waste a wheelchair on you.* I hurry towards Mum's room where I see a large woman, whose name tag reads 'Nola', trying to pull Mum up onto the bed. Mum is yelping in pain as she struggles against Nola's greater weight. My natural instinct is to physically confront Nola, but our frequent hospital visits have made me wary of those who hold the power. I feel like a traitor collaborating with an enemy, but for the moment I don't dare confront

Nola – this careless, ignorant woman is our passage out of here.

I coax Nola's hand from my mother's arm and whisper: *Can we just humour Mum, please?*

As I release her grip on Mum's arm, I ask her meekly to call an ambulance to take us to Westminster Hospital so we can have Mum's knee seen too. It might be a wasted trip, as Nola suggests, but right now it might be the only way to get Mum out of here.

I can tell you now, love, Nola spits at me as she throws down her hands in disgust and walks out of the room, *it'll just be a waste of time and a wasted trip for the ambos.*

I understand what she's telling me. I understand also that sometimes Mum's feelings of helplessness reveal themselves in these passive-aggressive encounters with people like Nola. But such analysis is for another time and I'm in no position to argue the point. Mum is crying. *Please, Linda. Please,* she gasps at me. *Why is this happening? Why is this happening to us? Do you know? Can someone tell me?*

These are existential questions, as far as I am concerned. Even though all through my childhood Mum called me the impractical one, I am at this moment way too practical to answer any of them, on either a philosophical or literal level. Right now the hospital seems to be a war zone and I am going to do what I have to do – collude, lie, make peace with the enemy – to get Mum the hell out of here.

I look up and down the corridor for another nurse and eventually find one who is willing to be persuaded to ring an ambulance to take us to Westminster Hospital. That's the plan anyway. Nothing is simple though: we have to wait for the ambulance for over an hour, during which time Nola theatrically stamps past our room several times snorting her disapproval. The ambulance ride from Woodlands to the Westminster is thankfully brief – the emergency room is only ten minutes away – because we have another two hours of waiting ahead of us.

Mum's knee begins to swell until it is twice its normal size.

At around nine o'clock in the evening we are ushered in to 'see doctor', an attractive young man called Gabriel. With the arrival of Gabriel in our lives, it seems as if an armistice has suddenly been signed and our war is over. He glides around the room like a dancer, lifts Mum's hand to say hello, turns his twinkling eyes in my direction, and tenderly prods Mum's knee. Despite this beautiful truce, he drops another bomb on us.

I'm afraid it looks like your mum's kneecap is fractured, he says, as if he is whispering sweet nothings into our ears.

Oh my God, I gulp. My first thought is panic. Mum might be bedridden. *You mean she won't be able to walk?*

Don't worry, he says quickly, seeing my distress. *No need to panic yet . . . at least not before we get a full X-ray to make a proper diagnosis. Meanwhile I'll order a knee brace for your mum.*

That damn nurse, I growl.

One of the nurses here? he asks, suddenly worried himself.

I don't feel like going into it right now. I let my distress deflect his attention. *If she can't walk,* I whimper, *it'll be a disaster.*

Third world poverty is a disaster, he twinkles at me. *Global warming is potentially a disaster as well. A boat sinking at sea is also a disaster. Your mum not walking will be a problem, for sure, but certainly not a disaster.*

He's an angel, I think suddenly. An angel with a message for me. Keep things in perspective. Perspective's the first thing to go when you get tired, when you're overwhelmed. I shake my head, then nod quickly. I can't remember whether Gabriel needs a yes or no answer. I probably look like a madwoman standing there in emergency shaking and nodding my head like I don't know what's going on anymore. It's been a long day.

The knee brace arrives. It is light blue and makes us all laugh.

I took the liberty of ordering it in sky blue, Gabriel says to Mum. *You look to me like a sky blue kind of lady.*

Mum is giddy with all the attention. She hobbles bravely up the corridor in her knee brace, which looks like a wicketkeeper's leg pad and which also comes in a range of colours.

Gabriel muffles his mirth long enough to tell Mum not to walk too much, but not to stay completely bedridden either.

Got to get the balance right, he tells me as Mum limps around in a shaky semicircle then back towards us.

There's that word again, I think. Balance.

These things actually heal better when there's some movement to help the blood keep circulating, he tells me before turning to Mum, suddenly serious. *Now perhaps you can tell me exactly what happened to you, Joan?*

His sincere interest opens a torrent of breath and tears.

I've paid my taxes all my life. Or in this case my health insurance. Don't I have a right to proper care? she asks him, tearfully. *What do you think, Gabriel? I mean, sometimes I think they forget.*

Who do you mean by 'they', Joan? Gabriel asks.

It's a good question. We use the word a lot these days. They. We are 'us' and they are 'them'.

They should remember I'm somebody's mother. Mum's crying again. *I deserve to be well cared for.*

Gabriel looks at me and winks. His light-heartedness in the face of her distress is beginning to feel flighty rather than charming. Or maybe I'm just too hardened now to take things at face value.

I'll give Woodlands a call, if that's ok with you, he tells us. *Even if this nurse didn't actually cause your mum's injury, she certainly . . . ah . . .* he pauses diplomatically before continuing, *should have arranged for Mum to get here a lot sooner than she did.*

Mum feels validated and reassured, not just about her leg but about humanity in general. Me too. After Mum expresses fear at returning to her hospital, Gabriel arranges for her to stay in overnight.

I wait while she changes into a hospital gown. Curtains are drawn, routine tests are carried out. Later we're told that there is an irregularity in her heart, which Gabriel assumes has been caused by the trauma of the day's events. I wonder then whether a heart can be slowly weakened through lack of care and love. Whether a heart can break down from fatigue and loneliness.

I suddenly think of the asylum seekers at sea scanning the darkness for a sign of a distant shore. At least we had found our Gabriel. I wonder if there were any other angels out there calling them home through the night.

I remember some of Dad's favourite lines from *The Tempest*.

While storms wreck havoc with our vessels
And tempests whip up gales and frenzy
Remember dear heart my love is stronger than
Any man made craft and I will carry you
I will carry you to the edge of the world

Of course it isn't Shakespeare. It isn't really anything. It's just something a little like something Dad read to me once. It doesn't matter now, because I started making things up as I go along a long time ago.

Gabriel phones Mum's hospital with his report and a week later Nurse Nola is sacked.

Unlike Mum, who asks me to pray with her – *deliver us Lord from every evil* – I don't thank God. He or she doesn't seem to have much power in hospitals and I do not think that Nurse Nola, by any stretch of the imagination, could be considered a handmaiden of the Lord. Instead, I pray in gratitude to Mum's private health fund and thank the high-priced premiums she has so diligently paid during the last twenty-five years.

'Going through traumas of various kinds is par for the course in life,' my father wrote in a letter dated 1989. 'Come out of them wiser, more cautious, more tolerant, even happier. No hurry. No worry. No hassles. No sweat. Just remember to make every post a winner.'

The family come and go throughout Mum's difficulties. Paul visits us at home when he can and makes time to see Mum in hospital. I can tell her crises are a burden for him. Often he has to come in from work if things are serious enough for her doctors or nurses to call him, although he is always cheery and supportive. He is busy with his young sons, Finn and Kel, whom we see grow up from babies to children, and regrets sometimes, I think, that Mum is not a healthier presence in their lives. She feels this loss too, for him and for herself, and although Finn and Kel always arouse in her wide smiles and, she tells me, deep emotions, she seems unable to change the situation.

Stephen visits regularly, taking days off from his work to fly up from Melbourne, and when she can Janice flies in for short stays as well. Cathie is still a regular presence on the phone and in person.

Each visit is like a rebirth for Mum; the new energy feeds and revives her. With Stephen, who spends time deeply listening to her, Mum finds her inner calm and peace; Paul's breezy optimism gives Mum confidence in the future. When Cathie stays, Mum briefly regains her old determination and spark. Cathie also brings to the house the music and laughter that she and Mum shared so much of in earlier times, as well as visits from her wide circle of friends. Janice always arrives with a kind of buzzing light; Mum perks up whenever she comes to stay. Despite her obvious dismay at Mum's deteriorating health, Janice can still make Mum giggle and in the increasingly fragile space of Mum's home giggling is something I am not so good at anymore.

Each visit is like a renewal for me too. I try to be a good hostess now that Mum cannot easily play the role, although sometimes it still feels awkward to share things with the brothers and sisters from whom my life has separated me. These visits also bring to me a private sense of wonder, as if I am putting together some kind of biological puzzle, when I witness this woman, my mother, who has no favourite among her children, being the single body through which five such disparate life forces can interconnect and I marvel at the subtle ways Mum is able to balance us out even though illness is slowly weakening her own balance. Despite these times of welcome revival, though, the geographical distance that separates us all means that for a lot of the time it is just Mum and me getting through the days – or, as she describes it, 'the highs and lows, the ups and downs, the ins and outs' – as best we can.

I try to stay as open as possible with Mum when she returns from her regular stays in hospital. She comes home each time like a newborn. But now there is a different element to our experience at home. After settling back into these familiar spaces I begin to notice her looking past me, as if there is someone standing behind me.

Hello. Are you here again? she sometimes calls out now, even if I'm standing right next to her.

Mum, I'm right here, I say gently, careful not startle her.

She points towards the blank wall across the corridor. *No, not you,* she tells me. *Them.*

We both begin to refer to whatever she sees as 'them'. I am more adept now at going along with all the changes in Mum's perception. I know her drugs are making her hallucinate. At the same time, I secretly enjoy this evidence of her altered state and so I am not surprised – nor even, with a smile for my dead father, discombobulated – when she turns to me one day and whispers: *Ever since I've come home from hospital it seems like there's more than just the two of us here.*

Who do you think is here? I ask.

She is matter-of-fact as she explains: *In the hospital when I wanted to die,* she tells me, *every night I prayed to your father and your grandmother. I asked them to send me some help if they really wanted me to keep going. Do you think I'm crazy for thinking that sometimes it seems like they might be here with us?*

'What's crazy?' I could ask her. In these circumstances, exactly what is crazy and what isn't? I like the idea of spirits walking the corridors. Of angels watching over us. Sometimes I even envy Mum for seeing what I cannot see – the vague outlines of things from other worlds, messages from the dead and the dearly departed.

Sometimes she looks at me and I know she sees her mother. And behind me, perhaps, my father. Maybe we merge together in her visions, the three of us, a triumvirate of past and present making the future. The Buddhists would think it is all perfectly natural. They know we are just vessels for souls. Possibly I am sharing my vessel with my grandmother, sort of like an extended stay over, until Mum's better. And though I once told Dad I wished never to see him again, he's welcome too; in fact, anyone is who can make Mum feel more secure.

Joan: I was convinced that they were there with me, and you know that I've never gone in for all that ghostly hocus-pocus. If I can't see it or touch it, as far as I was concerned it doesn't exist. One of your sisters reckons it was probably the drugs making me hallucinate; perhaps I just needed them to be there. But they were there. I could feel their presence. Sometimes I could see outlines of things: shapes in the corridor and on the end of the couch – they were moving . . . hovering around me. I felt better, whatever was happening, knowing we weren't so alone.

AIN'T WE GOT FUN

Mum knew that for many people singing is a serious business. It brings out all sorts of insecurities and fears. Confident, articulate people can become bumbling messes in a music studio. Children also experience all kinds of terrors when they have to learn a classical song and not the pop songs they have practised in front of their bedroom mirror. There is no way to fake a voice in an empty room without resonance or microphone.

Many of her students heard for the first time their own voices recorded on Mum's old ghetto blaster; it was also often the first time they wanted to give up and never sing again. It was Mum's job to help her students through all these different stages, to encourage them through their difficulties and try to make their development as enjoyable as possible. She understood also that many teachers felt frustrated by the process as well: students who did not practise regularly, who had severe technical difficulties, or simply a terrible sense of pitch, could make the work of the singing teacher extremely demanding.

In an article for the Music Teachers' Association Mum advised teachers to maximise the things that made them laugh. In 1990 she wrote that 'a smile is the quickest way to combat the teaching blues and to connect with your students'. She even suggested getting up from the piano in the middle of a particularly challenging moment in the lesson and doing a tap dance with the students. 'Add a bit of nonsense to break the tension,' she wrote. 'And learn to laugh at yourself so that others will laugh with you, not at you.'

Dad would probably have found something to laugh at in everything that happened to us and he would have told this story a lot differently to me. He would have not just looked at the bright side, he would have found the dark comic textures underneath. He would certainly have told me not to be so personal, to be stoic as I did my duty and to keep my feelings to myself. Renowned for his word play and practical jokes, his sense of the absurd provided a strange counterpoint to his austerity. I sometimes wonder, too, whether his humour was his protest at the world of surfaces and respectability that might really have seemed laughable after the simplicity of his monastic life.

Everyone has a story about Dad changing into different clothes – hats, ties, sunglasses, even swimming goggles – for each course at the dinner table. It was a way, one relative observed, of asserting his identity during all the talk about music, a topic that usually dominated the conversation at dinner.

Cathie remembers simple things – like going round and round the roundabout nine or ten times in a row whenever new friends drove with us for the first time. Or screaming in the stairwells at his school as if someone had fallen into the quadrangle. Kym remembers how he used to love to sit back and watch us all. *You were his entertainment. He'd love just watching you all interact around the dinner table, all this banter and music. I remember going away and just buzzing. I thought it was wonderful all these things happening.*

Barbara Clarkson brought her two daughters to learn violin from me while I was still living at home. I taught them in Mum's music studio under the house. Barbara remembers a father who was very involved with his children. *Your father seemed to be really trying to inspire you all in a way that other fathers didn't,* she tells me. She speaks of the musical rope that surrounded the family and situates Dad on the outside of the chaos of sound and music, calling to us in the centre of the whirlpool with his poetry, his crosswords, his funny stories, his practical jokes, and his Latin declensions. Trying to bring order to the confusion around us, to balance up the music with language.

Dad wasn't interested in small talk and never went to the pub. According to Paul, social chitchat just passed him by. *Rather than do small talk he would just do something pretty weird,* he tells me. *He never told jokes. He expressed himself very well in words but also in ways other than language.*

Cathie remembers a man who was not judgmental, who had seen a lot of 'real life'. As headmaster of many schools throughout his religious tenure he had been subject to intimidation and violence as part of his job. He was threatened with guns and once even had his house set on fire. Dad never divulged by whom – disgruntled parents, families, former students? Cathie tells me:

> I can imagine in those days the Catholic schools would have had a lot of the socially disadvantaged, poverty, broken homes, all that sort of thing. So he was very slow to make judgments about people. He never once made a comment about the way I conducted my life. He just said quietly once or twice to let him know if I needed help. I think he was just beyond all that moral stuff. He was much too practical and subtle to think of things in black and white. I think our life at St Lucia would have seemed like plain sailing to him after what he'd been through.

Dad didn't have mainstream passions. He didn't socialise much or have expensive hobbies. After he retired he liked crosswords in the morning, swimming in the afternoon and walking in the evening. According to Paul, Dad had a complexity to his way of thinking about things that allowed him, in the end, to appreciate simplicity. He was religious in the sense that he preferred to examine his own actions rather than point the finger at others; devout in his attention to the simple things around him; and human in the failings he saw in himself that he sometimes projected onto his children. But he was also a man with a poet's heart and he knew the world was a difficult place. 'Look after your brothers and sisters,' he used to say to me. 'Look after each other.' *He had a frugality to his life that just enabled him to be happy with what he had,*

Paul concludes. *He came across as a father who didn't really have anything – like golf or business or the job he had – that dragged him away from the family.*

In 1985, Dad wrote in another letter to Cathie:

> Tomorrow the Spring Hill baths close up for the winter. So I'll have to find a warm spa somewhere, perhaps at Vichy. I've been swimming twice a day at Grammar where I'm constantly saluted by old friends who ask me to come back just to talk to them at morning teas. Paul and Stephen rarely come with me now. I recall a summer when they swam 100 lengths morning and evening for which they earned a cent per lap. They are playing their first rugby game of the season on Saturday – not so much enthusiasm for the game, I think, as in previous years. They are not beefy enough now. Though both are taller, especially Stephen, whose hand-me-down blazer from Paul is tight and inadequate now.

I read in Dad's writing a man who was an elderly father to teenage boys, who wanted – needed – to keep working. His enforced retirement hit him hard; he often spoke about being asked back to do relief teaching – offers that never materialised. But he was a man who was also well practised in the art of surrendering his ego. He was, after all, at an age when many men were playing golf and going on retirement cruises, while he was still putting five children through school on a modest teacher's salary. He didn't stint when things got hard; he drove us all to school and offered himself up on the weekends to ferry his sons to football and cricket games and his daughters to orchestra practice and music lessons. I shared more than daily drives with him, though; I also shared his embarrassment when, from the schoolyard, I watched him make the lonely walk up the hill to the principal's office to ask for an extension for the payment of our school fees, because he couldn't afford to pay them. Sometimes I ached, too, to be his daughter and to feel, when I visited the large, well-equipped houses of my school friends, our lack of status and material things.

I once saw Mum and Dad perform together in public. One afternoon in the auditorium of the private school where Dad taught English, history and Latin, he gave a lecture on *The Great Gatsby*. I was thirteen and hadn't yet read the Fitzgerald classic, but I listened for over an hour as Dad read a carefully prepared lecture which consisted of extracts from the book interspersed with stories from the twenties – strange tales of speakeasies, flappers, goodtime gals and their dreamy beaus. Mum was part of the show too: during breaks in Dad's commentary she played and sang songs from the Gatsby era, numbers with titles like 'Yes, We Have No Bananas', 'I'll Be Loving You Always' and 'Ain't We Got Fun'.

In the morning
In the evening
Ain't we got fun?

Not much money
Oh, but honey
Ain't we got fun?

Mum and Dad were a good team. Mum's showgirl qualities and beautiful voice gave just the right touch of entertainment to the serious tone of Dad's words. I should have been embarrassed. Most teenage girls – even bookish, daggy, violin-playing teenage girls like me – would have been mortified by their parents making a spectacle of themselves, not just in public, but in front of that cruellest, most sceptical and hard-to-please crowd: a hall full of teenage boys who, under most circumstances, would have been itching to get out of the air-conditioned auditorium and onto the nearby football field or cricket pitch. But, as Mum commented truthfully afterwards, that day you really could 'hardly hear a pin drop'.

There was another quality to their performance, though, that I definitely would have been too embarrassed to pinpoint at the time, but which I can attempt to define now. My parents were what people might describe these days as 'kind of sexy together'. This realisation only comes with hindsight and an adult understanding of what being 'kind of sexy together' might mean. Not the overt in-your-face kind of sexy, but the underneath-the-skin kind of sexy that comes from something that's been worked at, from doing something creative together – from really playing together.

Or does the sensuousness of my memory have something to do with my ripening body sitting in a room full of teenage boys? Perhaps it was the ache inside Fitzgerald's language that aroused me. Or it could have been the slides my father used to illustrate his narratives: black and white stills of men and women staring loosely into the camera, lounging easily into each other with what I would later recognise as the casual physicality that comes from money, alcohol, sex and drugs. Whatever it was, it was there and it was palpable and I can honestly say I never saw them in that light before or after. I wonder, though, whether Dad was turned on and moved by the sound of things just like I was, whether he was more than just proud of my pretty blonde mother as she sang her parts in his carefully structured performance. Inside his robust body, did he feel the ache as well, the call of song and poetry, that divine whisper that would eventually call me too?

GALOP INFERNAL

I did not die, and yet I lost life's breath.

Dante, *The Divine Comedy*

Although there were hundreds of poems in the bookshelves of our home in St Lucia, I can't remember ever seeing a copy of Rimbaud's *Season in Hell* or *The Inferno* by Dante. I would discover these poems later, during a period of voracious reading after I left my parents' house. In Dante's poem, hell is a place where you are stuck forever, frozen by fear, madness or the suffering in your own mind. Rimbaud's vision of hell is like a mad bark from a howling wolf, poison seeping out from its wounds. It is a place of torment and of unfettered desire, yet it can also be a purifying prelude to the heaven of the 'divine love' that could bestow the keys to all knowledge.

Though Dad was a churchgoing Catholic all his life, I don't really know if he thought that the keys to knowledge were to be found in divine love. He had contemplated divine love for over thirty years in the solitude of his monastic life and in the end made the choice to walk out of the monastery's door to search for the keys to knowledge in his love for a woman – my mother – and his children. Perhaps if he contemplated heaven – and hell – he might have thought that he had found heaven on earth with us, in the house at 34 Warren St, St Lucia, and that the keys to knowledge could only unlock the doors to a family home and all the tears, laughter, shadows and light that it enfolded within its four walls.

Dad's preferred version of hell was contained, I think, in the poems of Milton, where hell is a loss, an absence of the paradise that is rightfully ours 'until one Man . . . Restore us/ and regain the blissful seat'. The blissful seat, the heaven on which we sit, can always be regained through hard work – the tasks of purgatory. Dad knew the value of hard work and austerity. It was not in his nature to have to purify himself through a complete dissembling of the senses, as Rimbaud did in his season in hell. He preferred his pain to be private and to treat his wounds with humour. If he was alive today he might shake his head in embarrassment to know that his second daughter became that 'beggar girl, that monster child' who, driven by her own will, made the journey into the underworld. He might also have thought that my youth had been idle, as Rimbaud thought his had been, and that, also like Rimbaud, I had allowed my sensitivity to waste my life. But he might have been pleased as well that the will which had driven me away also eventually brought me back to the house he had shared with my mother, her mother, and my brothers and sisters, driven me back to my mother so that I could walk beside her for a while as she passed through hell.

I am not really surprised that Dad would not have favoured Rimbaud's version of hell. If Beauty had sat on my father's knee he would have honoured rather than reviled her and, unlike Rimbaud, I do not think Dad thought morality a weakness of the brain. He might have agreed with Rimbaud about the power of the mind and its perception of things. If he thought he was in hell then he probably was. If he believed he was in heaven then the blissful seat would be restored to him and Beauty – without bitterness – would perch again upon his knee. If we had ever had the chance to discuss such abstract things, I hope he might then have turned his smile towards me and relieved me a little of my shame – this shame I still carry of being the wilful, curious, passionate daughter of such an austere, complex and humble man.

Mum's favourite version of hell was probably also the most entertaining one. In Offenbach's operetta *Orpheus in the Underworld*, Eurydice is no passive beauty waiting to be rescued by Orpheus. At the end of Offenbach's frolic, Eurydice decides to stay on in the underworld to pursue a life of pleasure, dancing and the fulfilment of her desires, perhaps because, as Cyndi Lauper sang over a hundred years later, 'Girls Just Want to Have Fun'.

This 'opera bouffe', a particularly French version of operetta written and performed in a burlesque style, is full of comedy, satire and farce – not to mention dancing girls. Serious music critics condemned it as a 'profanation of holy and glorious antiquity' and public decency was especially outraged at the *galop infernal*, the 'infernal dance', or 'the can-can', which was performed at the show's climax by showgirls in skimpy costumes.

Mum performed in *Orpheus in the Underworld* in the old Brisbane Opera Society when she was a young woman working in the typing pool at Queensland Railways. I don't know if she played one of the shepherdesses in the rural idyll at the beginning of the operetta, one of Pluto's consorts who shares his revels in hell, or one of the dancing girls who lift their skirts and twirl their legs at the end of Orpheus's journey through the underworld. I doubt she would have consorted or danced; I think she was most suited to the part of the shepherdess tending to her little lambs in a field of flowers. Although Mum loved to sing she was never much of a dancer, and certainly would not have felt comfortable at all in skimpy costumes of any kind.

After she married she threw herself into family life and tended to her own little lambs with the same commitment that she devoted herself to her studies and her teaching. She was always at heart a good girl – and raised me to be one too – and she grew to be, as her mother was, but unlike her tempestuous second daughter, a good, respectable woman. She was never beholden to the gatekeepers of serious music, though, and she disliked snobs of any kind. So I think that in her secret self she might have preferred a world filled with light classics, with the bubble of the opera bouffe, with songs of wit and romance, of passion and heartbreak that always seemed to find, despite their apparent ease, the perfect and delicate balance between words and music, between structure and emotion, between torment and delight.

One night during a Brisbane thunderstorm, Mum's doctor tries her out on a new Alzheimer's medication even though she has not yet been diagnosed with the disease. The drug causes a psychotic episode during which Mum tries to escape from her hospital ward, thinking it is a hotel full of German soldiers. She asks a laundry van driver to take her to the police. Ninety minutes after taking the drug, she is found hiding under the van, screaming at imaginary assailants, begging for her life to be spared. I hear about these events the next day when I arrive for a visit.

Mum is sitting up in bed when I enter her room. Her hair is uncombed and her eyes are open wide like saucers. Despite her distressed state, I cannot hold back my sudden anger: *I told them they couldn't give you any more medication without asking our permission,* I say, my voice strangled with frustration. *Did you sign something? Did you give them your permission?*

She holds on to my hand, her eyes huge and dark in her stressed face.

Linda, please, she begs me. *Darling. Be gentle with me.*

I am furious at the hospital, at Mum's doctor, at Mum herself. When the day nurse comes in, Mum takes her hand and holds out her cheek for a kiss from her, from anyone, probably, who would show her some tenderness. Anyone who isn't me.

This is Jenny. Jenny's my friend. Unlike you, she could have added. Unlike you, my mean, angry daughter.

I cannot mask the coldness in my voice as I address Jenny. *Do you know what happened to Mum?*

It's best that you talk to the doctor, Jenny begins. *We've been trying to get hold of her all morning. Apparently she's down in Sydney somewhere for a family wedding.*

I follow her out towards the nurses' desk where two other nurses are noticeably scowling at me.

Can you at least tell me what new drugs she's been given? I ask.

That's all available on the chart, she tells me. *You have access to that information here.* She gestures towards the desk. *I can get the head nurse to talk to you if you like.*

She is doing her best. I know she is doing her best. I will keep on telling myself she is doing her best.

Back inside her room, Mum is gesticulating wildly for me to come back.

She's one of them too, you know, she tells me when I return to her room.

One of who? I ask, unkindly. *I thought she was your friend.*

She whispers, as if we are co-conspirators: *They pretend once in a while, but that's just so you drop your guard and then they get you.* She continues breathlessly, holding on to my arm like a child: *I heard one of the nurses say 'We've got to get Linda. Get Linda. Get Linda.' I thought they were going to get you. I mean really get you,* she repeats as she digs her nails into my arm. *And then I didn't know where I was. I couldn't recognise anybody and then I realised that everybody I knew had been replaced and that everyone – EVERYONE – was in on it.*

When Jenny comes in to say goodbye at the end of her shift, she tries to kiss Mum, but Mum shrinks back. Apologising on Mum's behalf, I walk with Jenny to the lift.

I wouldn't normally say this, she tells me, offering me her serene face, which makes me feel calm just by looking at it, *but I want to let you know that even if your mother's doctor prescribes that tablet again for her tonight, we wouldn't give it to her. She has never shown any symptoms of psychosis. You'll never get the doctor to admit any of this. One thing most of them are scared of more than anything is legal liability.*

I know she is going out on a limb to tell me this. Even in the middle of all the craziness I can appreciate her kindness to me at this moment.

That's why they get the patients to give written permission. It covers them legally, she continues. *As long as the doctors never admit their mistake, they're covered. At this point in time your doctor would be most worried about the fact that you might sue her for incompetence or something. Anyway . . .* she trails off, *I've said enough.*

When I leave Jenny at the lifts, I am balanced perfectly at that moment between gratitude towards Jenny and bodily rage. My fury has nowhere to go, though; I know my family – and especially Mum – would not have the stomach for a protracted battle with the hospital. I feel like an utter failure, knowing I cannot speak the language of this strange territory to where we have been transported, and where we seem to have arrived clutching one-way tickets.

I blame myself. I should have handled it better, should have seen what was coming. If it was up to me, I would walk out of the hospital and never come back. It is not so simple for Mum. The medical machine sometimes seems unstoppable, immune to any recourse from those whom it can injure the most – the old, the sick and the vulnerable. Battling her disease has drained all of her physical and emotional resources; now there seems to be nothing left for either fight or flight. Not even the psychosis driving like a whirlwind through her body can give her an exit strategy: there is simply nowhere for her to go.

There isn't anywhere for me to go either so I start to run – through the hospital corridors, past the laundry truck where Mum had taken refuge, and up the driveway where I see a police car idling. I suddenly want to scream at them to: *Go inside and arrest the real criminals. They're inside in uniforms too, and they make sick people crazy.* But I don't raise my voice. I'm like Mum now, and I don't want to make a scene. Instead, I jog past the car muttering to myself like a madwoman, reduced to insane imaginings and delusions. I feel so winded I slow down to a walk when I make it to the road outside the hospital, from where I let gravity propel me down the hill towards Coronation Drive. The lights are flashing *don't walk* but I cross anyway, seizing this meaningless opportunity to break the law. My rebellion brings me a few aggravated beeps from the cars whizzing past me, but I don't care. I have made my stand against the machine, even if the machine is only a traffic signal and not the hospital up the road.

When I finally turn around and make it back up the hill to Mum's room, I take her hand and tell her I am sorry. I say over and over that I am sorry. I mean it. I'm sorry that I cannot help her more. Sorry that I feel so guilty. Sorry for fighting her; sorry for not fighting her more. Just sorry. She's too out of it to really understand what's going on. Her glazed eyes find it hard to concentrate on anything I'm saying.

I pull her forward towards me. *Mum,* I tell her firmly. *I think we should walk around the corridor. We need to get the drug out of your system.*

That's all I ever do, she tells me, dragging down hard on my arm. *Walk and walk and walk around and around and around. I don't want to go out there now. They might see me.*

She starts crying. I lean in and hug her, whispering close into her ear, trying to convey through my body the urgency of what I am saying: *Mum, I need you to concentrate and listen.* I need to be strong, I think to myself. I need to be strong the way I've never been strong before. *The drug will take a while to get out of your system and what's happening is a chemical reaction that's affecting your brain.*

Well, something's affecting it, she says with a wry smile. *We all know that.*

I suddenly like her so much, like that she can make a little joke in the middle of her psychosis. I wrap my arm around her and hug her.

Whatever you think in the next few days probably won't be true, I tell her. *But if you keep telling me, or Paul, or any of the family who ring up, we'll all be able to help you understand that what you're scared of isn't going to happen, isn't real. Ok?*

I can feel the panic rising in her again, feel her heart pumping against my chest, the disorder of chemical upon chemical swirling through her brain.

I have to get out of here, Linda, she whispers. *You have to do something. I can't go on like this.*

We talk about changing the doctor who prescribed the drug. Mum refuses, afraid of offending her.

It takes over a week for Mum's psychosis – and the drugs that caused it – to pass through her system. All through that week she accuses me of being 'in on the conspiracy'. Mindful of how distraught her brain has become, only being able to imagine the chaos of her mind, I make my visits longer and more consistent, sit meekly beside her bed as she raves about the hospital, the nurses and us, her children.

You'll all burn in hell, she yells at me one evening as I leave for home. *All of you.*

I don't know about hell. I never have believed in it, not in a religious sense. But as I listen to my mother's tearful apologies after the psychosis has passed, I recognise it is a place with which she and I are now both familiar.

LIEBESTRAUM

From the look of old photographs, my great-grandmother on Mum's side was not a happy woman. She also arrived in Australia by boat and was seasick for most of the journey. She grew to hate the sea during that voyage and once she landed in Sydney she vowed she would never set foot in it again. Instead, she settled herself and her fourteen kids in Tenterfield and never went near the coast as long as she lived. In old photos her face looks hard and tired. Disappointment has settled in the flinty blueness of her eyes and the narrow line of her mouth. I imagine she used her breath to hold herself in; that she learned to breathe like a gate opening and shutting on the shed at the back of her house where she locked her supplies of sugar away from her great mob of children who came home hungry from school every day.

She stopped crying after her fourth child, stopped breathing after her eighth and tenth died. She thought breathing might kill her too. She needed her body for other things: to wield sacks of potatoes, to balance two children, one on each hip, while another dragged at her skirts. What breath she had left she saved, like her pennies, for a rainy day, for when her children were cold, or when one of them died.

Her husband, on the other hand, had grown up on ships and had been a deckhand at the age of thirteen. His ruddy skin and piercing blue eyes speak to me not just of his Scandinavian blood, but of a life lived in chilly ocean mists. He had breathed in the sea for so long the ocean spray settled in his lungs; but nothing cold or damp would kill this man, whose pink cheeks told of someone who knew how to breathe, but who did not know how to share these secrets.

I wonder sometimes if my forebears ever felt the trauma of what was happening around them in the hard, brown country where they arrived; whether they had any compassion to spare for the other, more long-standing inhabitants of their new country, who found themselves, through the very fact of my ancestors' arrival, hurtled from the familiar into a terrible unknown. I hardly ever heard them speak of these other traumas. Perhaps, like thousands of other dirt-poor Irish, they were too preoccupied with their own survival to worry about anything else – like my great-grandmother, whose heart might have slowly hardened to anything other than her own family's existence as she got through the births and deaths of her children alone while her husband, my great-grandfather, whom Grandma called 'Daddy', was away on the water. From her 'mummy', *that busy little woman* Grandma would recall fondly, she learned her frugality – both the material and emotional kind – and never forgot its lessons as long as she lived.

In a letter she wrote to me in 1985, Grandma says:

> A week ago, an 'alien object' from outer space came down at Gumdale [a suburb near Wynnum] and the occupants invited a housewife to go up for a drive. She rushed inside and locked her door. Do you believe that? I don't know what I believe, but I think it's always best to keep an open mind about these things. Now, from the ridiculous to the everyday, I am wondering if there is anything overseas that can be done for the ears, like a tube for the ears. It's being done, I know. Deaf children are hearing through a device the doctors have found. I am wondering if it's 'common' over there. I'm not complaining. I certainly have a lot to be thankful for. I have no pain, or not much anyway, and good 'I' sight, but if I had a little better hearing . . . But don't take too much notice of my writing. I'm getting madder all the time.

There are photos of Grandma as a young girl, the startlingly blue-eyed, Swedish-Irish Christina Augusta Jurgenburg wrapped in fake fur and hipper, jauntier versions of the hats we saw her in long after she stopped being just a Christian name or even a Mrs Somebody else's surname, when she had become a generic title, someone that we referred to as 'ours' or 'my': 'our' gran, 'my' grandmother. There is one particular photograph taken on the *Fairstar*, the ship which took her around the world when she was seventy-three. She is standing on a stage with her violin in front of a room full of her fellow passengers, with the ship's band behind her.

Tell us again what you played, Grandma, we would ask her every time she got out that photograph.

Well, I played 'Liebesliede', 'Liebesfreude', 'Liebesfreunde', 'Liebestraum', and 'It's a Long Way to Tipperary'. I love this story, the names of the music she played:

Love's Song
Love's Happiness
Love's Friend
Love's Dream

Of course she could never really play well at all. Not before, not since, not ever. The violin she carried with her around her world perhaps represented to her the impossible. Or the possible. The possibility of music. The possibility, despite all evidence to the contrary, of love.

When I was older and could finally appreciate how difficult it was for Gran to actually string three notes together on the fiddle, I used to wonder what those ship's musicians had actually thought about her getting up to play with them when in reality she could hardly play at all. *You do the action for long enough,* she used to say, *you eventually master the practice. The important thing is you never, never, never give up.*

She never did give up, even though she never did get any better. But she kept on practising anyway, day after day, in her bathroom, where the acoustics were so much kinder than in the rest of her flat, right up until she was bedridden with the cancer that eventually killed her at the age of ninety-two. I appreciate that she never did give up, not the violin, not her family, not herself – that she kept going with her love and her dream, no matter how impossible it was for a woman of her class and circumstance, that she did not let life knock it out of her, this love of hers.

Four days before Grandma died she was involved in a strange incident that involved Mum as well. Gran was bedridden with cancer and suffering from jaundice when at three am one morning she got out of bed, packed up all her costume jewellery in a small leather case, tucked her violin under one arm, painted her lips with her favourite coral red gloss, and walked noisily – and unaided – down the back stairs. She had already lost the use of her legs and could barely speak above a whisper, and so Mum never suspected that the racket that woke her up after midnight was coming from her own mother.

Mum found her downstairs sitting on the old wooden rocking chair that she had dragged on her own from one end of the garage to the other. She was sitting near the garage door, which she had opened so she could look out onto the road and see the light coming in. She was waiting for someone, she told my mother in a booming voice. Mum was surprised, but did not force her back upstairs to her room. She just sat down too and asked Grandma if she minded some company while she waited.

I'm waiting here for them to come for me. To take me home, Grandma told Mum, a bit put out.

Who's coming, Mum? Mum asked her. *Who's coming to take you?*

My mummy and daddy and Yehudi Menuhin, Gran replied.

Mum was incredulous. *You're waiting for Yehudi Menuhin?* she asked.

Grandma's voice was loud and strong as she answered: *Yes. He thinks I've got potential.*

When Grandma began to talk about things Mum had never heard before, her voice sounded like a young girl's. Mum remembers: *She was talking so loudly I was worried she might wake the neighbours. I didn't want her to be upset when no one came, so I was just waiting with her until she got tired. But she didn't stop. She told me stories about her mother and father. About her love affairs. Things I'd never dreamed of. It made me realise what a life she'd had. Just little things, but a lot of little things all strung together making a big life.*

Gran finally jerked her head up just as she seemed about to stop talking and drop off to sleep. *I want to play 'Meditation' now,* she told Mum. *When you hear Yehudi play 'Meditation' you believed in the angels.*

Grandma took out her violin then and played like she'd never been able to play when she was young and healthy. I don't know whether Mum added this detail just for the effect of it; I doubt it, as Mum has never really leant towards the poetic. Grandma took her fiddle out, rosined her bow and played the opening bars of 'Meditation' from *Thais,* as if she was channelling the great Yehudi himself. Mum remembers how simple, pure and effortless it was.

Joan: As if all the difficulties she'd always had with the instrument, the fact she'd had no lessons, no one to teach her any of the things she so wanted to learn, nothing but

> her love of the instrument to keep her playing over the years. Everything just melted away and she found a direct route from her spirit to the instrument. As if all the things in her life that had prevented her from her doing that, all the things she had to do to survive, to endure, to take care of her family, just fell away. She finally had the luxury to make a few moments of pure, beautiful music.

Grandma often told Mum that she didn't want to keep living if she was in extreme pain. It was an understanding, never openly articulated, that Mum would make suitable arrangements to make sure her death was relatively painless. I imagine their conversation about this topic to be as unsentimental as most of their other dialogue throughout their shared lives as mother and daughter: practical, efficient, and to the point.

A few weeks before Grandma died the doctor told Mum that the cancer would soon begin to cause her terrible pain. He presented Mum with two choices. Either Grandma could go to hospital and receive the best care available, or she could stay at home with Mum. If she preferred the second option he would visit every couple of days to make sure she was comfortable.

Mum still cries about it – not the sadness of her mother being gone, but what she calls 'the absolute rightness of how she ended up'. The doctor told Mum that when the time came he would make sure Gran went with no pain. Mum wanted Grandma to die in her own bed. It was a gift she had been preparing for her mother ever since she had moved up from the coast to live at the back of our house. Later she remembers:

> She was never alone. I loved looking after her. I *loved* it. Do you understand? It was a privilege going in with her food every day and giving her kisses. She was like your father. They get so affectionate when they're nearing the end. I couldn't have asked for anything more than to be able to help my mother have the right sort of death. And the doctor was true to his word. When she started to turn yellow and the jaundice was right through her blood and the cancer had begun to make her uncomfortable he came down and gave her something to help her go peacefully. And she did. She had exactly the sort of death she deserved. And if I'm proud of anything in my life it's that my boys, both my beautiful sons, were with her every day and Stephen was there holding her hand as she took her last breath.

Stephen played cricket in the back yard with Grandma up until she was ninety. So did Paul. I still remember her running between the metal wickets, her laughter, her strong active body, her delight to be there with her grandsons.

'Keep the children at home as long as you can,' she used to advise Mum. 'Don't give them a reason to leave before they have to.'

Two days before her death my grandmother turned yellow and asked for rosary beads to be brought to her. She died in her own bed with the blinds open, her family nearby and several crucifixes hanging around her neck.

MY MOTHER'S MAD OPHELIA

Joan: If you haven't had the experience, you just think about it and then you let it go. But when you've had the experience, the sadness, the joy of everything taken from you, it's quite different to people who don't experience it. So in that way, it's very valuable, as a human being, to be able to go into a hospital and talk to people. They talk about their sadness and what's been taken from them. And while you're speaking to them, you try to point out to them that it's not all loss at all.

Throughout her teaching life, Mum attended hundreds of vocal seminars, conferences, workshops and master classes. She also read a large volume of literature about singing. While she felt most of what she had read, heard and seen was beneficial, she also sometimes voiced her personal concern that dialogue and approaches to the pedagogy of singing were in danger of becoming too scientific. 'Are we as teachers,' she wondered in an article for the Music Teachers' Association of Queensland, 'in our healthy desire to understand how the vocal parts work and to familiarise ourselves with scientific terminology, forgetting the essential tenet of vocal teaching: to convey information to the student in the quickest, clearest and simplest way so as not to create confusion, which inevitably leads to doubt, worry and tension?'

'Is the art,' she asked in an article written in February 1997, barely two years before she became ill, 'becoming a little stifled by the science?'

During one of her last hospital visits in the summer of 2002 Mum teaches singing to a Mary, *a Mary Mary quite contrary* Mary, who is depressed, obese and suicidal. Mary gives Mum massages in the evening when she becomes anxious and, in return, my mother teaches her how to breathe. I'm on hand one evening when Mum begins to pass on her knowledge to Mary. Though Mum has become increasingly frail, she confidently reaches her hands around Mary's unwieldy body as she begins to show Mary how to access her breath, how to fill first her stomach then her lungs and chest with air, how to arrange her mouth and lips to form a sound from that air. The room changes tangibly as the two women begin to breathe. Their fatigue seems to subside as their energy grows. I notice how sound can protect, eradicate weakness, disarm resistance. How Mary lifts up her chest as the breath travels upwards and out of her mouth.

Mum is firm and kind – her old professional self – as she transmits her knowledge. A tiny light fills her eyes;

they become sharper, more focused, more intensely blue. I remember that light from when I was a child, startled and sorry that I hadn't understood then – hadn't really understood till this moment – what that light was. The loss of that light had been her catastrophe. No wonder that no one can really say exactly what came first, the illness or the loss of the voice – whether the loss of the voice had been the illness, the cause of the illness, or a symptom of the illness. These questions don't really matter now, because just like the preachers say, I've seen the light – well, *a* light anyway. It is in Mum's eyes and it is in Mary's eyes too – Mary, quite contrary Mary, who has a body the size of a refrigerator and a wish to obliterate herself. Mary, who can now learn to sing with my mother's small hands holding her gigantic sides. Contrary Mary lets out such a wail that three nurses come running in to shut her up, and Mum too, both of them, these women with their wailing voices that fill the room, their eyes charged with light.

Mary is moved the next day – no one says where – but we are told that this sort of thing cannot continue in a hospital where people come to rest.

There is a hush and a hum in a hospital, a mechanical rumble so low sometimes it gives the impression it is coming from deep within the earth. It is not coming from the earth, but from machinery, from life support machines and dialysis machines, and televisions, and fridges, and microwaves and lifts. Everything is turned down low so that sounds do not become specific, so that, in the end, all these low sounds amalgamate into one low rumble that sometimes whooshes but mostly hums.

There is no earth in a hospital and the air is conditioned. There is no rain or excessive sunlight. You cannot drown in a hospital, although you can fall and break your hip in the shower. You can pick up infections in hospital that are unheard of outside. There are bacteria so virulent that they can, literally, make your blood curdle. You can go in for a routine operation and end up dead. That's the way things are in a hospital.

After Mary's departure, Mum spends so many hours walking and singing around the corridors of the ward that complaints are received from the other patients and she is asked to stop. There is a kind of surrender after this stay, as if she – or we – do not have the power anymore to withstand the machinery of the institution which seems unable to see the potential in this gift of my mother to sing along its corridors; that thinks she is as mad as mad Ophelia, unravelling in sound bites in front of them; that sees illness and decline instead of life, wisdom and possibility.

She is eventually discharged and sent home. She is quieter now, more subdued. The effort of surviving these hospital stays depletes us both. I find myself speaking incessantly to whoever will listen about everything that has happened. I babble, I groan, I question, I cry. And when everyone is tired of listening I take myself away, to walk alone along the beach or down stony paths in the bush, and speak to no one. Or, more precisely, I speak to the wind, to the sea, to the trees, and to the air. It doesn't matter now whether there is any response, or even if anyone hears me. I just know I need to use my voice, to speak, to sigh, to whisper, and to sing. To use my voice in different ways and, in doing so, find a new voice, one that speaks of unspeakable things: my shame, my regret, my loss, my wounds, a woman's voice, the voice of a daughter finally learning to love – and lose – her mother.

LEARNING HOW TO BREATHE

Dad taught all his kids to swim at an early age. He thought being balanced in the water had a soothing effect on the brain. Just as classical music was supposed to produce in children a more harmonious frontal cortex, or so it later became fashionable to think, swimming served the same function – to bring about equilibrium in both mind and body.

For a while he took me to swimming training in the mornings. I can't remember exactly when during my primary school years he did this, but I know it was before I started menstruating. I know this because when I began to bleed Mum would only buy me pads, not tampons, because she and Grandma still believed that swimming during your period – impossible anyway while wearing your 'protection on the outside' – would 'ruin your womb'. I do remember that the training entailed getting up before six am, even in the cold winter months, and driving from St Lucia to Jindalee to do laps of the fifty-metre pool there.

Dad was thrilled when I won a swimming trophy in Grade Three for a twenty-five metre freestyle race at the school swimming carnival held every year at the Valley pool. I was good at freestyle, enjoyed breaststroke, was terrible at backstroke, and didn't have enough upper body strength to roll my arms over in the butterfly. But I did enjoy the thrill of winning that one race. For a while afterwards we persisted with our training, and with our early morning trips to Jindalee. Perhaps Dad thought he had a future winner on his hands, or perhaps he just didn't want me to think that I could go on winning trophies and blue ribbons without hard work and effort. I began to resist him for the right to stay in bed, for the right not to shiver and dive into the freezing water, for the right to swim for leisure and not for victories. Even though the Jindalee pool had as its most famous alumni the shy Olympian Shane Gould, I had no desire to emulate her or any of the sleek-bodied athletes who kicked and breathed their way up and down the pool every morning, guided by mostly professional coaches and not by their fathers.

I don't know exactly what Dad expected of me, whether he thought I might turn out to be a good competitive swimmer, or whether he just wanted to give me the chance to become the kind of dedicated daily swimmer he was, to become a member of that serene aquatic group of 'lappers' who found the business of swimming up and down a single lane of the pool soothing and elevating for the mind. He did, however, think that if any of his children had aptitude for something he would do his best to instil the work ethic and discipline necessary to see it develop.

I never really enjoyed those early morning training sessions. They are, on the other hand, recalled fondly by Cathie, who remembers Dad buying one ice-cream between the three of us, Janice, me and her, then taking a big bite out of it himself just for fun. I can't recollect wearing goggles and so I particularly hated the sting of chlorine in my eyes and nose. I also disliked being damp and cold and shivering on the wet cement. Years later a Chinese doctor whom I consult about hormonal problems confirms that getting this cold and wet on a regular basis as a prepubescent could cause a 'damp and cold womb'.

I am sure Dad would have had no clue that our early morning drives through the sometimes crisp light of a Brisbane morning could result years later in a damp and cold womb. I doubt he thought about any of those 'women's things' in relation to me or any of his daughters. He was good with the business of educating and training boys and when daughters were involved I imagine that, in his equitable way, he thought what was good for his sons might also be good for his daughters.

There was one thing, though, that I loved about swimming, which, probably not coincidentally, was also the problem that Dad was least equipped to help me with: breathing. Not just breathing on one side, the right side, the male side, the usual side one first learns to breathe on – the side my father taught me to breathe on. Not even just on the other side, the left side, the female side. No. My quest was to learn to breathe equally well on both sides, to develop in my left shoulder the same ease of movement I had developed in my right shoulder, which allowed me to turn my head up towards the sky and gulp in air as my right arm came over in the second half of the basic freestyle stroke. I wanted to develop symmetry in my physicality. I bugged Dad about it constantly and he did his best to teach me. But I don't think he ever mastered this skill himself – breathing on the left side – so he could never help me become what I referred to as an ambidextrous swimmer.

In order to find solutions to my desire to learn how to breathe this way, he took me to a swimming teacher at the Gold Coast, a man called Kevin Dean – pronounced, I later dramatically reminded myself, to rhyme with the word 'mean' which Kevvie most decidedly was. Although Dad initially intended to sign me up for a whole term of lessons with the well-credentialled Mr Dean, I only lasted one short lesson as his pupil. This lesson began with Mr Dean picking me up and throwing me into the centre of his swimming pool, after which he stood on the side of the pool and yelled at me: *So!!! You think you can swim, do you?*

After a few more moments of verbal taunting, he then lifted from the side of the pool what I heard later was his most infamous teaching tool – a long pole with a hook at the end of it with which he would theatrically fish his struggling charges out of the deeper water. That day at the Gold Coast, while Mum and Dad watched from the side of the pool, I was one of those flailing pupils about to be submerged in what I had always found to be the benign water of a professional swimming pool. As the hook came down and found the back of my swimming costume, I was pinned like a captured mermaid by the tripod of Poseidon, who was screaming at me now in what I do recall as a particularly broad, blokey Australian accent: *Swim to me! Come on. If you think you're so bloody smart, swim to me!*

Dad had taught me to swim when I was a baby. Later he had tried as hard as he could to teach me to breathe on both sides, but under the long metal pole and hook of Mr Dean I could not keep myself afloat. In fact I could hardly breathe at all. At the time I truly believed that it was only because there were witnesses that he didn't let me drown, there and then. It wasn't over, though. Not quite. After waiting a few moments during which I struggled for air, he then fished me up out of the water before submerging me again.

At the end of my first swimming lesson with Mr Dean, Mum and Dad scurried out of there, me huddled and numb between them, promising the coach – untruthfully – to return the following week. For the rest of our Gold Coast holiday that summer, though, neither Mum nor Dad mentioned him to me again. Occasionally, he was referred to by all of us in later years, in a laughing, embarrassed kind of way, as the reason why I gave up swimming.

I never did learn how to breathe on both sides. For a while after my encounter with Mr Dean I could hardly breathe on the right side and even now I struggle to turn my face up to the left when I swim up and down the university pool at St Lucia, just as my father did.

Although Mum couldn't swim at all, she did spend many years of her life studying the techniques of breathing. She always described herself as a simple woman who liked to break complicated things down to their clearest, most discrete elements. Despite the hundreds of books she had studied and the thousands of notes she had sung, she worked very hard to explain in simple everyday language the mechanics of breathing to those who did not understand about the body and what it went through to make enough breath for a song.

Mum also had a collection of inspirational quotes. Here is one she wrote in one of her last articles for the Queensland Music Teachers' Association newsletters: 'The fine singer amazes. As the voice soars up we ask how this technique, this artistry, is possible. But the great singer shows us only beauty. We accept it as a gift.'

Mum was never much interested in finery. She didn't like tricks, vocal or otherwise. Fine foods held little appeal for her. She ate simply and frugally. Riches did not attract her either – she often told me money wasn't everything – although I know she adored the richness of a beautiful thought or word. But she felt the beauty of a great singer deep in her heart where words do not spring from. She felt it in her body; she longed for it with her own breath, and dedicated her life to celebrating, understanding and dreaming of such a gift.

Gifts come in unexpected forms. They sometimes come as a surprise or a shock. Sorrow and loss can be both beautiful and a gift. Falling comes as a gift too, to move us from one place to another. I have to fall and break before things can change for Mum and me, just as my mother falling brought me home again, moving me from one place to another: from the underworld to the outside world, from the darkness to the light, from anger to love.

* * *

I fall at about five in the morning in the bathroom, probably around the exact spot where my father fell out of the shower and died. Despite the cocktail of drugs she has ingested during the past few years to control her anxiety and depression as well as her various physical ailments – medication that includes Rivotril, Madopar, Celebrex, Avanza, Diazepam, Mogadon and Xanax – Mum is now waking up in terror at around three or four in the morning, unable to breathe. Her habit now is to come into my room while I am sleeping – as she does this particular night – and tell me, gasping, that she thinks she is going to die.

I haul myself out of bed, lead her back into the kitchen of her house and offer to make her a cup of tea.

Mum trails me like a shadow, calling out to me repeatedly: *I need to go to the hospital.*

I don't look at her for the moment, busying myself instead with the business of waking up and making the tea; the clanging of the cups and kettle are a welcome distraction.

Mum, I can't keep taking you to the hospital, I tell her without looking at her. *I just end up bringing you straight home again.*

Her voice then is a yelp, a cry of pain. I think as I hold my hands around the warming kettle that it is, at this moment, unbearable to hear.

But I can't breathe, she whimpers. *Listen to me, I can't breathe.*

I listen closer and it is awful to hear the breath locked inside her body. I turn around to look at her ashen face while I wait for the kettle to boil, her wide, scared eyes, her rigid mouth. I hear the rasping, wheezing sound of the breath forcing itself into the closed throat.

I move towards her. *I know you're frightened, Mum,* I say, standing close enough to touch her if I need to, if she needs me to.

I never thought I'd end up like this, she answers, looking around as if there are ghosts standing with us. *Your grandmother would turn over in her grave if she saw the way we've ended up. Not to mention your father.*

I look closely at her face. I don't know exactly what I am looking for: signs of her future, perhaps? I don't know whether she will be able to adjust her mind, whether there is anything ahead except broken sleep and terrible dreams.

The world seems suddenly altered. I feel winded, as if I have been running for centuries to arrive at this moment. I remember then, as if I am dreaming, how she once tried to teach me to breathe, how she tried to put her hands on my waist, how I struggled with her, thinking I already knew how to breathe properly, thinking that there was nothing I could possibly learn from her about what I needed to know.

'Breathe from here,' she said, pointing at my stomach, 'not from up here,' she added, pointing at my throat.

I see myself pushing her away, not wanting her to teach me anything. 'Too stubborn for her own good,' I hear my grandma call after me as I turn and run from her. 'Too stubborn to learn anything. She just has to learn to get over herself.'

She was right. It took me a long time to stop resisting Mum teaching me anything. Until I realised, after starting to write and sing my own songs, that perhaps I was born her daughter so she could teach me how to use my voice.

I reach out and rub my hand across her back.

Think of all those students you taught how to breathe, I remind her, pressing myself into her, willing out my energy towards her. *You've got to remember that now, Mum.*

Oh, it's no use, Linda. My chest is so tight I can't get the breath up. Nothing I do makes any difference.

I rub in a circular motion, recalling the soothing hands, somewhere in my deepest memory, of a mother reassuring her child. *Think of your voice,* I almost coo in her ear. *Remember your singing.*

Her reply is abrupt, resistant. She is in no mood for nostalgia of any kind. *There's no time for singing now. I need to go to emergency.*

She collapses her weight and sags into a chair, her shoulders hunched over her chest. Her hands clutch at mine as I try to extricate myself from her panic. I run to the library shelves in the lounge room and pull out books at random. Even though I've cleaned out a lot of volumes from Dad's old library and sold the old editions of encyclopaedias, our house is still full of books. We have books on psychology, on French pronunciation; German phrasebooks, books of Japanese haiku, old detective stories, and Readers Digest condensed classics. Behind the rows of dusty books, I find what I am looking for: a thin old hardback, still in good condition. Inside the front cover the publication date says 1904 and the title engraved in gold on its blue cover reads *The Science of Breath.*

I lead Mum into the lounge room and settle her on the sofa. Nestled in, I stroke her hair and begin to read in a voice a mother would use to read a bedtime story.

Breath is life, I begin. *Life is absolutely dependent on the act of breathing. From the first faint breath of the infant to the last gasp of the dying woman, it is one long story of continued breathing.*

Sounds like your grandmother's book, Mum sighs. *She was no singer, but she understood about breathing.*

As I read on, I can feel Mum relax; our breath eases and expands outwards with each moment.

The yogi knows that by rhythmical breathing one may bring oneself into harmonious vibration with nature and aid in the unfoldment of his latent powers. I can feel myself sinking further into my own body, as Mum sinks down against mine. *He knows that by controlled breathing he may not only cure disease in himself and others but also do away with fear and worry and other negative emotions.*

Can I tell you something, Linda? Mum asks. Her voice is softer now. Breathing properly has taken the edge off her panic.

I lay the book beside us and move my ear close to her mouth so she does not have to expend much energy to speak. *Yes, Mum.*

Perhaps I've never been really mature, she continues, her voice so soft that every word is like an exhalation of breath. *I mean, just because you get to a certain age doesn't mean you really grow up. I always tried to do the right thing. Go to church, look after my children. But perhaps you don't really grow up until things go wrong.* The tone of her voice is unfamiliar to me; I have never heard Mum speak like this before.

I always thought it was possible to take control of things, she confesses. *But some things you can't control at all. Or, if you can, you just don't know how to.*

I hold her lightly, as if she is suddenly the most fragile thing in the world.

I know, Mum. It's ok.

I just have to learn to take it. I mean, that's what it's all about, isn't it? Trying somehow to find a way to take things when they come. Life is hard enough just the way it is, but when you get sick, you just have to find a way to take it. I know she doesn't really need an answer from me, so I say nothing as we both gather breath.

I know I'll probably never sing properly again, she says with finality.

That's ok, Mum, I reassure her. *Singing properly isn't everything.*

I cuddle into her. *As long as there's breath in our bodies we can make sounds,* I reassure her. *Any sound is ok – a bark, a meow, a bellow, a squawk. Who says we have to sing words?*

She's not in the mood for laughing, not even at my best efforts. *But singing makes things bearable,* she tells me. *It always has.*

She is right. Perhaps that's why I gave up so much to find my song. To make things bearable – when they got unbearable.

She is suddenly wistful. *But there's something else,* she continues slowly. *I can't see meaning in what's happened to me. I studied for years so I could teach the meaning of songs, but this is life, and I can't see any meaning in this suffering at all.*

It's ok, Mum, I tell her. *Maybe there is no meaning in suffering.*

I remember when you were a little girl, Mum tells me. *You were always laughing.*

I think as I hold her that sometimes a voice can just break your heart and that I have never been moved by my mother's singing voice the way I am at that moment by her vulnerable speaking voice.

You were so bright and cheerful, she continues. *But I can see you've suffered. The world has weighed down on you too, hasn't it?*

Sometimes . . . everyone suffers, Mum. It's unavoidable. A fact of life.

What can I say, I wonder, except a few tired clichés? There is no time, I think, for anything else. The night will be over soon.

I never really suffered, though, she continues. *Not till I got sick. Not like I think you have. I saw what your future would be. I saw the self-doubt, the lack of confidence. I didn't understand why, you were always so bright, everybody said so. I didn't know how to help you. I thought you'd just get over it, like people do. But I knew that would be your flaw.*

She's right. And also, of course, she's wrong. Right and wrong, just like she always was. I smooth back her hair, and cuddle her again. After she falls asleep, I lift her up and carry her into bed. Thank God I lifted weights, I think, and did all those push-ups, so now I can carry my mother. It takes a few minutes to settle her, then I stumble back up the corridor to run myself a bath. I listen out for the sound of her snoring as daylight drips through the window. Perhaps it is at this moment, as I lean down to turn off the hot tap, that I lose attention and fall. It's not that I feel dizzy or weak. It is more like a letting go, this falling. A surrendering to the fatigue that is now overwhelming my body.

I fall on my side and lie there unable to move or make a sound. Perhaps I fall so I can sleep. Because I am so tired I could sleep even like this, knowing finally that I am unable to change Mum's situation, to steer her boat in another direction to the one in which it is relentlessly heading.

I remember a picture, then, that I saw once when I was a little girl in one of the old *Pictorial Knowledge Encyclopaedias* that had stood in the bookshelves of our lounge room. The image in this picture emerges in my mind as I huddle on the bathroom floor clutching my shoulders and arranging my head so it can lie peacefully on the cold tiles, an old historical image of the world drawn by an artist who still believed the world was flat and that sailors in boats would fall over the edge of the horizon when they finally reached it. For a moment, I see Mum and myself in such a boat, heading towards the edge of the world over which we will eventually tip.

I take in a deep breath. I can feel my chest expanding with air as I breathe right through the pain that is now throbbing in my left hip. From up the corridor I can hear Mum's rasping breath echoing through the house, diminishing in volume until it is only a faint sigh.

Book Three

HOUSE OF LOVE

INTERMEZZO

Mum was a student of people as well as a teacher of singing. She understood the connection between the body's fears and tensions, and the ability to release the song she believed was in everyone. She notes in an article she wrote for the Music Teachers' Assocation of Queensland in September 1995 that 'tense, energetic, ambitious people are more likely to have tense glottal problems, whereas phlegmatic types are more likely to have a breathy problem'. For problems of tension she encourages an 'inner smile', which helps 'deconstruct vocal chords'. She also suggests laughing exercises *down* the scale, 'not up'.

She became philosophical during her illness. Although she had hardly ever lived anywhere but her mother's house, she had observed life through the prism of music and seen many types of people pass though the door of our house and later her music room. They had stood before her and confronted with her guidance their fears, their inhibitions, and their tight larynxes. 'Leave your ego at the door,' she would admonish some students, mostly important men in their other lives, who became like quivering children when faced with the seemingly impossible task of singing in tune. 'Remember you are a star!' she would encourage the shy girl who practised and practised but who could never look up from the ground as she sang.

Sometimes she directed me to a vocal exercise that improved my resonance or released my larynx. She encouraged my inner smile. She told me not to close my eyes when I sang, but to open them up so that the audience could see what was in my soul as well as hear it. 'You have beautiful eyes,' she told me. 'And a beautiful smile. Don't look so serious. Remember, smile and the world smiles with you.'

So I try to smile, even when I feel like crying. And to leave my ego at the door.

Not long after I fall in the bathroom, Paul decides Mum should leave the St Lucia house. He doesn't decide this just for Mum's sake but for mine as well. It isn't something I'm proud of, the way I yell at her sometimes, the way my own physical helplessness erupts into frustration and anger at someone who is more vulnerable than I am. As usual, I am too stubborn and embarrassed to ask for help or admit I can't cope anymore.

My stubbornness is stupid and dangerous for Mum. I'm not helping things anymore by clinging to my role as her 'carer'. I am not even sure I am capable of 'caring' for anyone – not even myself – at this time. I am probably just making things worse. I am ashamed I can't initiate the move myself, and that my sunny-natured brother has to step in to change things.

Mum never comes back to the house, not even to say goodbye. Paul finds an old institution called Blue Hills, which is close to the sea and to where he lives in Sandgate, where Mum will stay for the next nine months. Later, we will discover it has many deep-rooted systemic problems. But for the moment, Paul tells me, we should be happy just to get anything.

When Mum moves into the Blue Hills hostel, I am too ashamed of how we parted to call her. It is foolish and neglectful of me, but I leave it up to her to contact me. Though I tell myself she's better off away from me at the moment, I am anguished and bereft at our sudden parting. I try to communicate this by sending flowers to the hostel, but it is nearly two weeks before Mum and I speak to each other again. Because Paul is close to Blue Hills, he helps her move and visits her daily. He tells me to take a well-earned rest, but when I don't hear from Mum, I wonder whether she is punishing me because I fell when she needed me. I call several times, but am only able to leave messages. She has no private phone yet and the public phone is a long walk from her room. I also discover later that the hostel's policy is to discourage a lot of contact between new residents and their families until a suitable settling-in period has passed.

When she eventually calls we speak as estranged lovers might, polite, considerate and tactful, as if we know that much work will have to be done to find a new intimacy now that the old connections have been broken. Mum tells me that she has begun a new routine of daily walks from the hostel to the beach and back again. When I finally dare to visit she shares with me the details of these journeys by foot to the water. She tells me she dresses in floral blouses, her favourite tweed skirts and sensible walking shoes for these sorties beyond the gate. Close to the edge of the beach she stops to breathe in the sea air; then she sits on a bench near the children's playground, swinging her legs as she often does, quite unselfconsciously, if her feet do not reach the ground. At the milk bar opposite she buys herself a lime spider – lemonade and ice-cream mixed together in a long frosted glass – or, on the way back to the hostel, a cappuccino with one sugar and plenty of froth from the little coffee shop on the corner.

I'm happy to hear that Mum has new territories to explore, no matter how insignificant they might seem. In her rapidly diminishing world, even a slow walk five hundred metres down a street to a concrete path close to the water's edge constitutes a grand adventure.

There are other unexpected bonuses as well: she begins to make new friends. One of these new friends is Marta, whom I first meet walking arm-in-arm with Mum along the musty corridor of the hostel's fourth floor. Marta is speaking, or wailing some might say, to Mum, while Mum nods in agreement with her. Mum tells me later she can't understand a word of what Marta is saying. *But I have seen the numbers on her arm,* she explains, *and I can hear in her voice that she is traumatised by something.*

The numbers on Marta's arm are from the two concentration camps, Dachau and Auschwitz, where she spent much of the Second World War. I recall Mum's psychosis in hospital when she envisioned herself in such a place, unable even to visualise the horror of the reality. Marta and Mum make a strange pair. Neither understands a word the other says, but each listens patiently as the other rambles on, knowing not to interrupt the flow of words. Mum is, as she puts it, 'the new girl in town'; Marta, on the other hand, has been a resident of the hostel since the early 1960s and is still unable to speak much intelligible English even after half a century away from her birthplace. Despite being isolated by her trauma and her broken speech, she lives in her tiny room with its stained carpet and peeling walls as if it is paradise.

Then there is Bert, the namesake of Mum's father, who takes a shine to her after their paths cross several times during their respective morning walks. Though Bert's progress is hindered by the large metal frame he pushes along in front to steady himself, his incapacity only makes Mum seem more like an ingenue when, with a bow and a smile, he greets her and calls her 'the lovely girl'.

He lost his own wife, she tells me. *She was a lovely girl just like me. So of course when I see him I smile. Nothing wrong with that. It's simple, really, after everything's said and done. I know he slows down and waits for me sometimes. He settles himself on the seat until he sees me coming back up the road from my walk, then he stands up and pretends he has only just started walking towards me. I know he likes me and he likes to see me smile.*

I would have kissed Bert myself just for making Mum smile. We are even more thrilled to discover that Bert is actually the father-in-law of an old friend of mine. I imagine happy endings: Mum finding love again with an older man, skipping like a girl beside him, or dressed like a bride as they walk slowly around the driveway of the hostel. For one wild moment I even imagine a union blessed by their gods, their families, and by whatever angels that have brought the two of them together.

But her infatuation goes the way of a lot of things in her life: she begins to distrust him and wonders if he is, after all, just after her money. Eventually she shuns his smiles and avoids the driveway on her morning walks. I don't know whether this mistrust is a cruel side-effect of her disease, a symptom of dementia, a response to feeling neglected at the hostel, or just a lifelong habit. Whatever it is, after a few weeks I don't hear much more about Bert. Or about Marta.

When Mum begins to deteriorate again, I listen to her renewed fears, her bad dreams and her fluctuating moods. Although I meet and befriend helpful and efficient nurses and carers while Mum lives at Blue Hills, it is obvious that they can do little to alter the sometimes degrading circumstances of the residence. A few years later the hostel will figure prominently in exposés on the care of the elderly on several current affairs shows, and Mum's stay culminates in a physical altercation with one of the nurses' aides who, for a period of several days, brought the right medication at the wrong time, or the wrong medication at the right time to Mum's room and ordered her to take it. I finally grab it out of his hands and demand to see his superior, after which he demands to see either my husband or my brother, refusing point blank to deal further with any more 'uppity and irrational women'.

LOVE LETTERS TO LORD BYRON

Dad never cared much for the work of the poet Lord Byron. Perhaps Byron's work was too excessive for an austere man like Dad, who preferred the verses of Wordsworth, *whose sound was like the sea,* and his visions for a more egalitarian world. Dad was especially fond of Yeats' love poetry, though. I know he loved my mother's girlish beauty and still yearned for her to turn her charms upon him long after the first stage of their love had ended, but I know he really meant it when he offered these words of Yeats to my mother: *one man loved the pilgrim soul in you/and loved the sorrows of your changing face.* I sometimes wish he was still around so he could call out to Mum as her body stiffens and her face begins to freeze. I don't really know how Dad would have felt about my Byron. He would probably have warned me, as he had many times while he was alive, about my choice of friends and associates. Perhaps he also warned Mum to be careful or feared that she might have been distracted by someone like Lord Byron. Or even that she might have answered his call of love, if the call ever came. Whatever my father's fears for her, by the time I met my Byron, not a poet or a Lord, at a party in October 2002, Mum's soul had well and truly become acquainted with the dark night and so she might well have answered the poet's call when she was living in the hostel at Sandgate, where she grew increasingly disorientated and anxious during the final months of 2002. She might even have called back to the poet Byron, in her growing dislocation:

bid the strain be wild and deep,
I tell thee, minstrel, I must weep,
Or else this heavy heart will burst;
And break at once – or yield to song.

I am ready to yield to more than just song when I meet my Byron. Even though I have gone out with a few people during the past few years, I usually told prospective partners that I wasn't available for any kind of serious relationship, that I was 'committed elsewhere'. It probably helps that Byron is a practising Buddhist and has gone through his own painful reconstructions – from the wreckage of a broken marriage, a troubled son and, in the past, his own mother slowly dying in a nursing home. Despite being humbled by life, Byron is still a vital, optimistic man who is used to being in charge. I wonder at first if his vitality will be too much for us, but things change when his heart melts, as he tells me later, after hearing me sing my songs in Mum's lounge room. A melting heart, rather than a broken one, is something both Mum and

I can appreciate and so we both welcome Byron into our lives although we are at first as tentative as we might be as travellers journeying for the first time to a country whose language and ways are strange and unfamiliar.

On Christmas Day 2002, an overcast, humid day, Byron and I drive down to Blue Hills laden with brightly wrapped presents, cards, balloons and streamers. I have booked us all dinner in the hostel dining hall, but Mum is too distressed to leave her room and is only interested in getting her Parkinson's medication. Sometimes watching her wait for her medication is like watching a junkie wait for a hit: all the energy drains out of her body until the drug miraculously revives her, about twenty minutes after she swallows it, as if she is a dead person coming back to life.

During this visit, I am not alone for the first time since I left Raphael in Bellingen. It feels strange to have company, but Mum likes Byron. She thinks his shaved head and Eurasian face make him look like Yul Brynner from *The King and I*. This Christmas, after finally taking her medication, she even tries to 'Whistle a Happy Tune' with him. She also likes his flattering, cajoling way with her, but I wonder if he is too eager to please and suspect his sudden involvement in our lives. But I overcome my natural reticence by remembering my grandmother's words: *Never look a gift horse in the mouth*. So I let myself be wooed by his attentiveness to my mother and imagine I see in him, just as I think my mother can, the same kind of man she imagined my father was: gallant, attractive, paternal.

The day after Christmas we all drive down to Byron's house outside Brisbane. When we arrive Mum lies down and tells us that she is ready to die. She holds out her hands to us and whispers G*od bless you all* in the faintest voice, as if her body has already gone, lids flickering over slits of blue that journey glassily across the ceiling where all the seraphs and angels are apparently waiting for her. It's hard to tell whether it's the real thing or whether she's just rehearsing like she used to rehearse for her other performances. I start to wonder, why is heaven always up there? Hasn't anyone ever thought it might be down there, across there, or over there?

I remember what your grandmother said about dying, she whispers as I hold her hand. *It wasn't the actual dying. It was how long it took.*

I lean in and whisper back: *I don't think you are dying yet, Mum. And if you are, we're here with you.*

But she is dying in a way. Every day the old certainties, the old routines, the old ways of thinking are falling away. Her home will soon be sold. She doesn't even have any familiar furniture left. Her room is hardly big enough to contain a single bed and a small television, let alone her photographs or music. She is a refugee now, one who would perhaps prefer to die than start all over again in a strange, lonely country.

With her eyes closed and her cheeks sucked in above her thin dry lips, she looks like her own mother as she was about to die. Perhaps it is an omen for the future that I look more like Mum every day. The day before Christmas, as Mum and I walked along one of the hostel's corridors, a perky nurse had smiled at us and said how alike we looked. I had wanted to tell her that, though I'd always looked more like my father, I had grown prettier and more open since I'd cared for my mother, grown kinder, too, and more patient.

We stay at the house for two days. On Boxing Day night, when Mum is on a high after her drugs kick in, she goes around cleaning the house with Cole Porter booming from the CD player. In a festive mood, I take out my violin and play some of her favourite tunes – 'Night and Day', 'You're the Top', and 'Begin the Beguine' – while she and Byron take a turn around the lounge room floor. We have fun together for the first time in months. It is like a party. A real celebration. But Mum gets too worked up and begins to rave: *Everyone thinks I'm mad, but I'm not mad at all,* she yells as she dances around the room. *You don't know how miserable you get in those places. You ring for the nurses and they tell everyone that you just want attention and it's so simple, so obvious that, yes, you do want attention! You're old, sick and alone and you want attention. What's so crazy about that?* She drops to a chair, exhausted. I suggest we breathe together to calm down. She still remembers how to do this. I hold my hand against her stomach and encourage her to fill it with air.

When she speaks again her voice is softer. *Don't you think it would be crazier if you thought that's how it was supposed to be?* she asks me. *Someone paid to look after you, but not paid well enough for them to be kind to you, not quite well enough for them to not treat you like you're shit!*

We're both shocked by her language. In my whole life, I have never heard Mum swear. It reinforces just how miserable she is; how the possibility of a smile from Bert or a walk around the dark corridors with Marta has done nothing to ease her sadness.

That night it is hard to get her settled. Outside the hostel she is like a child set free on holidays and her moods constantly fluctuate. *I'm like your little baby,* she calls out to me as I tuck her into bed, settle her down with a kiss and tell her that the dark shadow in the corner is not a dangerous stranger. She tells me then, as she has told me a hundred times, how I used to keep her and Dad up all night, bouncing up and down between them in their bed with all my wild energy, and that if and when I finally get myself a husband and have kids, I might understand how tired you get and how important it is to take control of the children or they will take control of you, how you have to become less like a mother and more like a general with a small army of kids to feed and organise, day in, day out.

My father loved my mother, I imagine, from the time he first saw her on the banks of the Brisbane River to the last day of his life. It couldn't have been easy when they first married, a middle-aged man recently out of religious life with a blue suit and little money. What could he offer her but his beautiful thoughts and words? According to a relative who met them on their honeymoon, she had never met two such lovely, innocent people as my mother and father holding hands and smiling like angels while they discussed their future together.

'Can we have an affair of the heart?' Dad would write to Mum. 'Can we have an affair?' Perhaps Mum was too busy for such things. Most people were. And so when Dad thought to call words of love to my mother, she was too preoccupied with children, study and her burgeoning teaching career to hear him. So he would have called, if he had tried – I don't know if he did – into an empty space, or, rather, a space filled with utilitarian words, with everyday things and the business of surviving. And my mother, if she had heard the poet's sigh brush her ears before he descended into his lonely world – is there a word or place in the underworld for a spurned poet? – might have yelled across at him as if he was just another annoying distraction to her business and said, as I heard her say a hundred times: *Not now, Ben, I'm busy.*

Later, after their difficult years, a period which perhaps only ended with the first of my father's three strokes, Dad became like a romantic boy towards Mum all over again so it was like first love for him, a man in his seventies bringing his girl a rose. He used her second name then – Elizabeth – to herald this rebirth in their relationship. He hardly called her Joan again during the last years of his life. Joan: it always sounded a practical, industrious name to me. In Hebrew it means 'a gift from God'. Perhaps she was that to him when he came out of the monastery: an innocent, smiling gift from God. It took many years for her to become, in his eyes anyway, someone else, another name. After their difficult years she became Elizabeth, 'the abundance of God'.

Cathie remembers this vividly: *I don't think I ever heard him call her Joan in the last six months of his life. He would often say to her: 'Elizabeth, can we have an affair?' Mum simply responded to Elizabeth like it had always been her name.*

Dad used to impress Mum's students then, the way he would wait outside her music room door with her morning tea on a silver tray, a single red rose in a pewter vase positioned beside the china plate on which he had carefully laid her toast and marmalade. And sometimes there would be a special note, a secret love note, just between the two of them, which made Mum blush like a schoolgirl and bluster at her students, in an attempt to salvage her professional dignity: *Oh, typical Ben!*

The night after Christmas, with Mum in the next room, I open up to love for the first time in years. I'm too tired for raging passion though. Byron and I lie beside each other softly like survivors of a war, with an understanding about the ephemeral nature of things. I am afraid of being touched, ashamed of the fatigue which weighs down my body. I mistrust my senses; I don't feel beautiful anymore. But when Byron reaches out to me, I do not turn away.

Knowing Mum is in the next room doesn't inhibit our intimacy; it only makes it sweeter, more private. I receive Byron's touch with tiny sighs and sudden intakes of breath. I don't dare laugh or moan, though, or make a sound that might disturb Mum. Our encounter is a mime, a silent movie. A humble exchange.

Thank you, I whisper as daylight falls through our window. Byron thinks I am thanking him, but I am really thanking the passing of time and the fact that I seem to have finally grown wise enough to be grateful for love, to not take it for granted. That I have been humbled enough by my failures to appreciate love, in whatever form it takes, when it comes along, and to say thank you when gratitude breaks through me, and even when it doesn't.

INTERLUDE

After months of offers and counter-offers we finally sign a contract to sell Mum's house in January 2003, but I delay the settlement for another six months. The rest of the family regards my procrastination with a mixture of understanding and anger. One sibling advises me to 'go easy' and learn to communicate more clearly about what steps I am taking to facilitate the sale of the house and the subsequent access of Mum to the profits from the sale. Another tells me my stubbornness is 'not helpful. Never has been'. It seems that what at first was considered care and protection is now considered to be less benign, even a little sinister perhaps. In some ways they are all right. I have also grown weak and tired over the four years I had been with her, and it is hard for me to leave the home I now consider, for the first time, to be one.

The house is not officially handed over until June the sixteenth of that year after a frantic week of packing, cleaning, throwing out rubbish and organising furniture removalists.

Cathie comes with colleagues to sort through Mum's music and arranges the moving of the pianos. Some of Mum's large collection of music and pedagogical material is donated to the university; some is distributed to interested family members and old students, while the pianos go to the care of friends. Paul offers to pay for the removalists and cleaners, but is too busy with work and family to do much more.

Byron sees my need, though, and like a hero arranges help for me. He is there for me too, although his presence sometimes makes me tense. I am used to managing on my own and our arguments concerning my not wanting – or needing – him around while I deal with the business of leaving home for the last time are fraught and unsettling.

I don't follow Paul's advice to give everything to St Vincent de Paul. I'm not yet ready to consign everything left of my mother's life to the dusty oblivion of a charity store. After a lifetime of disconnected indifference, I find myself unable to discard the past entirely, not because now it is 'my past' but because, in the sharing of my life with my mother's, it has now become 'our past'. I discover surprising evidence of Mum's gifts – gifts she had always denied. She often told me that she didn't have an artistic bone in her body, but as I pack her things in cardboard boxes – her china, her old crystal – I see the few beautiful things she loved and created herself: the jumpers she knitted for us as children, beautiful woollen one-piece, two-piece and three-piece ensembles, decorated with patterns of fir trees, roses and edelweiss. I discover other things as well, such as the tablecloths she had carefully embroidered with bluebirds and roses and neat crocheted edges. Yellowing with age they look like tribal artefacts from an old, lost female culture.

The day after settlement, I crash into bed at a friend's house and don't get up for a week. The same day the family home is sold Mum is offered a freshly painted self-contained unit in the Garden of Eden Hostel on the north side, a beautifully maintained complex with both an independent living section as a well as a nursing home, mass every Sunday and a regular program of activities for the residents. Because of the large amount of money that has just been deposited into her account from the buyers of her old home, she is able to accept immediately. I will later wonder how easily she is able to leave Blue Hills, how she goes without even saying goodbye to Marta or to Bert, neither of whom is ever mentioned again.

Joan: Self-pity can only last so long and then it must go out the window with a lot of other things. I also learnt in the dark years about my daughter. Actually that's probably the most important thing of the whole experience. I learnt her character. Not that we weren't friends before, but we became really close. It was a very valuable experience. And I got to listen to her violin again. I loved hearing her play all the old favourites. Sometimes I even played them with her, though my piano playing was nothing to write home about. But her violin was so strong and confident that I could rely on her to pull me through.

When I was a young girl playing in eisteddfods I couldn't always rely on Mum as my accompanist. I didn't always feel confident that she would start at the right time or keep going when I faltered. Once during an eisteddfod when I was eleven, she got confused and our whole performance fell apart. I was playing 'Czardas', a piece of gypsy music considered an unsuitable choice by the more conservative entrants, who favoured Mozart and Beethoven. As the piece became faster towards the end, Mum's rhythm slipped and stumbled. She began to miss notes and then entire phrases. In response to her obvious difficulty, I panicked and began to race. My bow slid across the strings and the crisp attack necessary to play the final *bravura* section became impossible; we ground to a halt before the final flourish, which, in an ideal world, would have been followed by thunderous applause and a first prize medal in front of all the much more highly fancied entrants.

But, in the real world, I was humiliated. I staggered from the stage in tears, clutching my violin and music as if they were the only support I would ever really have. *It's ok to fail,* Mum said later. *Don't be ashamed of failing.*

But at that moment I didn't want her wisdom or her philosophy. I wanted only for her to say sorry and to assure me that next time she would not let me down, that I was the eleven-year-old and she was the mother and I had the right to her support.

Mum felt there was no need to apologise. She expected me to roll with the punches. To pick myself up, dust myself off and have another go: to forget about what had happened and move on to the next challenge. I was too young to realise that while I was learning, she was learning too, that I was sharing her dreams in a way that eventually would help me realise mine. *It's character building,* she told Dad. *And life's all about the character,* she would repeat for my benefit as I huddled on my bed, alone and ashamed, mortified by the memory of my latest public humiliation in the cause and service of music.

Friends all around me were giving up music but I wasn't allowed to.

Don't get ahead of yourself, Mum would admonish me. *You just have to keep working and the rewards will eventually come.*

She was right, of course. But she was also wrong. The joy of music was always there inside me, but it was locked in a skeletal system made rigid and hard through fear and endless repetition. These were things Mum did not foresee for me perhaps. Much later I chose to see it benignly as a difference in tastes – what suited her did not necessarily suit me. And later too, just as my own body unfurled, the physical freedom of making my own music transformed this old pain into pleasure.

But until then I was good in a crisis and I got through. Like all the women in the long line of my female ancestors I got through. Sometimes I imagined them behind me, all those women, aunts and cousins and grandmothers and great-great-grandmothers, heads bowed in prayer, shoulder to shoulder, never unfurling or breathing deeply, patiently hauling along with them all their simple pain and pleasure – these good and practical women – and their ability, above all, to get through.

PANIS ANGELICUS

Cathie: I was very lucky to spend the last six months of Dad's life at home with him and Mum while I was studying at QUT [Queensland University of Technology]. What I really noticed in that time was that Dad was such a great patient. I think he loved the fact that Mum was looking after him. I often thought how awful it would be to be invalid and dependent on someone who didn't love you, or who was cruel physically, mentally or emotionally. Mum was always patient with Dad and treated him with dignity.

I remember a week before he died he was sitting on the veranda in the winter sun and he turned to me and said that we should use a certain funeral house for his funeral as it had a special deal on at the moment. It would have appealed to his frugal ways: the idea of a cut-price funeral. I do recall feeling like he was not really with us that Sunday. He seemed far away, as if he'd already left. But he seemed incredibly peaceful, which was very comforting.

Barbara Clarkson was passing our house the day Dad died in 1993. Although she hadn't seen Mum and Dad for years, that day she experienced a strong impulse to drop in for a visit. My father was falling over in the shower just as she knocked on the front door through which her two children had passed so many times for music lessons. He was dead before she got inside. She remembers:

> I held his head in my arms and tried to resuscitate him while Joan was ringing the family. And then, the strangest thing. Suddenly I was aware of this incredibly cheeky presence in the bathroom. It was like a little quirky leprechaun up by the ceiling. There was this bright feeling. It wasn't light; it was just a very bright, sparkly feeling and his voice, which I hadn't heard for quite a while, said: 'It's ok, Barb. I've gone.' And then so strongly I heard him say: 'I just want you to tell Joan that I'm happy. I'm really happy.' And then it disappeared and I had this amazing feeling of relief and joy with this message to impart to a very distressed wife who was on the phone. So I just went up to her and said: 'Joan, he really is dead. But I've just had the strangest experience. I heard his voice. I felt his presence and he was really very eager for me to tell you that although he was gone he was really very happy.' And I could feel her lighten under my arm and she looked at me as if I had just told her something utterly normal and said: 'Did he really? Did he really say that?'

We flew in for my father's funeral from all corners of the country. When Paul gave the eulogy, he spoke about how my father had taught us all to swim in the ocean, how to tread water when the waves got rough, and find our balance as we bodysurfed back to shore. My sisters and I provided the music for the service. Cathie played the organ, I played the violin and Janice sang. We played duets, solos and trios through tears and sniffles. I played 'Ave Maria' and 'Air on the G String' by Bach and my sisters sang 'Panis Angelicus'. At times my sister Janice found it hard to sing, but took deep breaths and continued to fill the chapel with her pure soprano voice. At the end of the funeral, relatives we hadn't seen for years congratulated us on the music, rather than commiserated with us over losing our father.

I've always said that Ben would have loved his funeral, Mum tells me later. *He would've loved that great talk Paul gave. And the music! Oh, the music! He would have been so proud. He would have sat back and thought to himself what a great show they put on just for me. At times during the service I thought I could hear him say it himself. 'Thanks for putting on such a great show, Joan!' Oh, he would have loved it!*

After Mum moves to the Garden of Eden at the end of 2003, we find ourselves speaking in hushed tones about 'mysterious universal forces' and 'miracles'. It isn't that inexplicable, though, as Cathie called on many of her contacts in the Catholic community to ask for help in finding Mum better accommodation. But despite these logical explanations, after the trauma of the last few months, I feel we are entitled to grasp onto this sudden turn of events as a serendipitous change in fortune. Any progress is good progress, although Mum's brother expresses his dislike of her new residence for being 'too clean, too ordered, and too isolated'.

Mum's bad dreams begin all over again soon after she moves to the Garden of Eden, just as I make the difficult decision to move – temporarily, I tell him and myself – into Byron's house across the other side of town from St Lucia. I don't know whether her dreams recur because of the change in environment or because of the change in medication. When I visit her now I find notes she has written to herself on scraps of paper secreted in hiding places all over her room:

'I feel as if everything that has happened is my fault and that something I did in my past has ruined my life.'

'Oh Lord, I fear I am not long for this world. Please watch over me and deliver me safely into your kingdom.'

'Is it something I did? It must have been something I did. It must have been something I did. Something I did . . . something I did . . . I did something?'

'Bad dreams. Always bad dreams. I do not sleep. Always bad dreams.'

She spends her days investigating her past for clues as to why her life has taken the turn it has. She develops what her psychiatrist refers to as a 'morbid preoccupation with self-blame'. I don't find this state either aberrant or difficult to understand.

Unable to even contemplate a live-in relationship, I disengage from Byron and his offer of love and support soon after I move into his house. Unsure where to live and whom to love, I revert to familiar habits. I begin to swim in the mornings and walk in the evenings, just like Dad had done years before, to handle my exhausted emotions and the self-blame that now begins to overwhelm me too.

* * *

Sometime before he died, Dad wrote what turned out to be his last letter to Mum. It was typical of Dad's style that he didn't leave this letter out for her to find and hadn't even written her name on the envelope. He had left it in a drawer, thinking probably it would be found by accident, as it was by Cathie weeks after his funeral.

Cathie: I found it among some writing material in one of the drawers of the old dressing table in the back bedroom. It was a love letter a couple of pages long, written in Dad's beautiful, lyrical handwriting, and it was asking the same things he always asked: for Mum to have an affair of the heart with him. I gave it to Mum straight away. I never asked her for it back to read or grilled her about details. I guess I felt it was between the two of them and left it at that.

I can't say if Dad intended Mum to find it or not, whether it was a work-in-progress, or if he had intended to give it to her personally, but the letter created, at the same time, great joy and grief. I hope Mum kept it with her to read over again when she felt alone during the years after he was gone.

'I'm lost without my swim,' my father wrote to Cathie in 1982, eleven years before he died. 'I'll migrate I guess, one day, to Mediterranean lands for warm waters, or take, as I did one day recently, to long walks, a little lunch in my pouch, no money in my pocket, under the warm winter sun. Take care always. Love Ben.'

A MAVERICK IN THE LOUNGE ROOM

> Sunday, 23rd May, 1.30 pm, Joan Neil's residence, 34 Warren St, St Lucia. Topic: *My Principles of Teaching Singing to Beginners up to Two Years trained: The first lesson Appraisal and Where do we go from here?* Discussion will include Posture, Breathing, Basic Psychology; Demonstrated Exercises for the Vocal Parts (jaw, tongue, lips, and soft palate), Common Vocal Faults, Focus and English Diction. Please bring a plate of 'interesting food' for celebratory 6th Anniversary High Tea.
>
> Joan Neil,
> Music Teachers' Association of Queensland Newsletter

At the end of 2000, Mum's old friend and teaching colleague, Lyndsey Parker, contacted me about nominating Mum for a special award from the national board of the Music Teachers' Association. Many in Mum's old teaching network lost touch with her after her illness took hold. Mum contracting

Parkinson's disease shocked them enough, but only the staunchest of her friends could cope with witnessing the psychotic side-effects of her medication. There was discomfort, dismay and fear. Perhaps her friends sensed that someone they had known and admired had passed on and that someone unfamiliar had taken her place. If Mum felt their absence she rarely mentioned it. Along with the disappointment she might have felt, she was also embarrassed and withdrawn, content to suffer her degeneration in private.

Joan: In some ways I think it was harder for my teaching colleagues and my students. They saw the progress in big leaps. When you live with it daily you just see the changes from moment to moment. Take my face, for instance. For me or for anyone around me every day it wasn't that my face suddenly grew rigid overnight. It happened slowly. You got to notice all the little changes and you gradually got used to it. But when someone didn't see me for weeks or months, when they visited they suddenly had to confront me with my face all seized up with that blank expression. I could see the shock in their eyes. Their pity. And sometimes fear. And then . . . often . . . I would never see them again.

Lyndsey asked me to write up a special report that listed all Mum's achievements as a teacher, board member and lobbyist for the teaching of all types of music. 'You'd be able to put it together much better than I could,' she told me, encouragingly. 'And of course, as her daughter, you'd know about all the things she did.'

I didn't really know much at all and was forced to ask her friends and my sisters for information. Marjorie Anderson was one of Mum's most loyal friends, who stayed in regular contact with us while Mum's health worsened. At the beginning of 2001 she agreed to meet me to share her memories. We got together in a sunny corridor of the Westminster. Marjorie told me that Mum started the Queensland branch of the Singing Teachers subgroup of the Music Teachers' Association. Peering at me over the top of glasses similar to those my mother first wore when, after years of sight-reading and playing thousands of accompaniments for student recitals and exams, her eyesight began to fail, Marjorie remembered those early days:

> The national group didn't exist when Joan first arranged an informal meeting of singing teachers in her house at Warren Street. Your mother's idea was that we get together on a regular basis to share ideas and offer support to each other as teachers of singing. Your mother was very generous and, if you don't mind me saying, ahead of her time. Nowadays everything is well organised but in those days we were all on our own scattered across the city, beavering away in our little music rooms, if that. Your mother heard about an organisation in America dedicated to just this sort of thing. Of course, there was nothing like that here so Joan got the idea to start one up months before the national group convened.

Marjorie was insecure about committing her memories to tape so spoke from notes she had prepared earlier. Just like Mum would have done, I thought, or hundreds of other diligent, hard-working women like her trying to do their best. Afraid, though, that their best might not be good enough. The story unfolded gradually over several cups of tea from the hospital café and as Marjorie spoke to me, I slowly began to realise that the story of the evolution of the Music Teachers' Association from its early days in Mum's lounge room was as much a part of her history as it was my mother's, and that these women created that bit of history around our old family piano.

Finally, as Marjorie took off her glasses and carefully put down her notes she began to reminisce more freely:

> I took the minutes of the first meeting actually, which took place on 23 March 1978 in her lounge room. In her address to the group your mother set out her agenda of wanting to create an inclusive and supportive network which did not just include classical music teachers, but which embraced all styles of music, from musical comedy, jazz to pop and rock'n'roll. And your mother offered your place anytime we needed to meet. When the national group formed the next year we didn't want to give the impression that we were in any way opposed to it so we amalgamated fairly quickly into the national organisation. But before that for a few months it was just us and your mother in her lounge room at Warren Street. She really started the ball rolling.

Lyndsey Parker contacts me again in October 2003. I have forgotten her wish to have Mum recognised for her work in the Music Teachers' Association. Despite the slow progress – the national board only meets once or twice a year – there are a couple of sympathetic members now who know first-hand how much Mum did for music teaching in Queensland. Lyndsey tells me:

> Your mother was a real dynamo. As far as I'm concerned one of the reasons why the universities and conservatoriums opened up their programs to include studies in jazz and popular music is because of the work people like her did at the ground level for all those years. Others may not agree, but we know what went on at the grass roots. She always believed that music should be for everybody, not just the privileged few. For a while she was our representative on the board of the university music department. They, of course, wanted to keep things exclusive. The old guard didn't want to let the so called riff-raff in. Your mother wasn't an aggressive lady. She was very pleasant about the whole thing. But she just kept plugging away until changes were made.

Mum tells me herself how much of an ordeal those early meetings at the university were for her:

> I'd be so nervous my cheeks would turn bright red. I'd have this conversation with myself in my head: 'Now, Joan, you've got to say something now or you'll never be game to.' I mean, there I was, this suburban music teacher, this mother from down the road, and there they were: Doctor This and Doctor That, and all these concert pianists and opera singers. It took me years to get over my sense of inferiority. Some of those university types were just *snobs* when it came to any music other than classical

> and opera. And they did vote me down the first time I brought it up. And the second. And I think the third time as well. But eventually, you know, if you keep plugging away, changes will happen. Still, I think they used to shudder when they saw me coming. Not her again, they were probably thinking, her and her wild ideas.

As well as the official things she accomplished, there are things I personally remember: that she failed twice in her attempt to gain her Licentiate and Fellowship in singing, prestigious awards from the Trinity College of Music in London; that she shared the news of these failures while cooking us our very favourite things – jam drops made with butter and strawberry conserve – as a special treat; that we never thought to comfort her, and that she did not cry; that she absorbed the disappointments of these setbacks and resat both exams until she passed.

When she finally received her Fellowship in the mail, she caught the bus into the city especially to see me where I was working at the Elizabeth Arden counter in Myer during the Christmas holidays. 'I knew you'd be happy for me, Linda,' she told me as I danced around her in the middle of the store's cosmetics' section to celebrate. 'I had to tell someone.'

Lyndsey is disappointed when she rings me a month before Christmas to tell me that the citation has been delayed again. Even with the support of board members who knew Mum personally, other members feel she has not achieved enough at 'an official level' to warrant special attention. She has never taught in a conservatorium or a university, shepherded any nationally or internationally well-known students, or networked with overseas teachers or professors. She has done all her work in our lounge room, or, when it was finally built, in the music room under the house. Working without the support of any accredited organisation, a maverick in our lounge room, Mum's grassroots endeavours are still not deemed worthy of any special note or commendation.

EXULTATE JUBILATE

During the second half of 2003, Mum's intense nightly dreams continue; her disorientation worsens and the nurses at the hostel now openly refer to her 'dementia'. A month before Christmas, Mum's nurse, Heavenly, rings me to tell me Mum has now become incontinent. There has been an altercation about her wearing incontinence pads in her underwear.

I put them in her pants and she takes them straight out, Heavenly complains. *Then she tells me not to treat her like a baby.*

I wonder if Heavenly is, or will be, true to her name. *Did you discuss it with her beforehand?* I ask wearily.

No. But it makes sense, doesn't it, that she wears the pads?

She sounds as tired as I am. We are two tired women discussing underpants and pads over the phone.

You'll have to get her at least a dozen pairs of new underpants, she tells me, *because she's ruined most of her old ones.*

I'm too worn out to ask her to speak more respectfully about the state of my mother's underpants. *Please don't force Mum to wear the pads if she doesn't want to,* I say. *I'll have a chat with her about it. But you've got to understand this is a big thing, this loss of control. It might take her some time to get used to it.*

I don't know why, but suddenly I recall that I studied *Othello* in my last year at school. I remember also how I found a book called *Shakespeare and his Critics* in Dad's library under the house. How amazed I was to read, as I pored over the fading pages of the book, that Shakespeare had been the subject of so much disdain and critical abuse. I remember in particular one critic from the eighteenth century, referring to the 'Laws of Tragedy', and, I suppose, to the Greeks and to Aristotle, had dismissed the entire play because Othello's final jealous murderous act was prompted by such a seemingly trivial accessory as Desdemona's handkerchief.

'How could a tragedy of such grand proportion', the critic wrote, 'rest on this womanly accruement; this trivial piece of linen and lace? Perhaps we should rename it "The Tragedy of the Handkerchief"?' To an eighteenth-century thinker, I suppose women's things seemed too insignificant for tragedy. Now the issue of Mum's underpants and her growing incontinence seems a kind of turning point as well, one that also rests on these trivial womanly 'accruements', these cotton undergarments that surely in the grand scheme of things could not be considered tragic.

After speaking to Heavenly, I drive down to Mum's retirement home to see for myself the state of her underpants. On my way to Mum's room, Desley, the hostel's occupational therapist, calls me into her office. She looks harried as she shows me a pile of screwed-up music on her desk: *Your mother has accused me of stealing this,* Desley tells me defensively. *But I've just rescued it from the rubbish bin, where I believe your mother has thrown it. Fortunately, I found it in time. But I thought I'd let you know the situation in case she tells you I've taken it.*

She is a large, eager-to-please woman who works up a slight sweat as she tries to smooth out the crumpled sheets. The rest of the yellowing music is lying in shreds in an old cardboard box. She is matter-of-fact as she continues: *Her playing has deteriorated a lot during the last weeks,* she tells me, and I don't like myself for noticing – or thinking that I notice – a slight tone of triumph in her voice, as if the loss of Mum's competence on the piano means she is now less likely to make any 'ruckus in the common room' and upset the other residents who would have to witness Mum's disintegration on a daily basis. *Sometimes she tears up the music in disgust,* she continues more kindly. *You can take it with you if you like. Keep it safe for her.*

I look through the music. There is an old copy of Mozart's *Exultate Jubilate,* Bach's *Ave Maria* and 'Your Tiny Hand Is Frozen' from *La Boheme*. There are the old light opera tunes which she used to sing as a girl: 'We'll Gather Lilacs in the Spring One Day', 'Be My Love' and 'One Day When We Were Young'. There is a whole Schirmer album of Schubert Lieder as well as abridged albums of music from *Paint Your Wagon* and *The King and I*. There are also excerpts from *The Well Tempered Clavier* and *The Art of the Fugue,* as well as sheet music of 'Jalousie', 'Autumn Leaves' and 'Purple Moon'.

I don't care that Desley sees me cry as I carefully smooth out and reorder what's left of Mum's favourite music. I know this was no random selection, but a conscious effort to destroy the remains of her once splendid collection of song. And because Shakespeare is already on my mind I think of one of Dad's favourite lines from *The Tempest*, delivered by the magician Prospero when he is about to give up his practice of magic.

I'll break my staff,
Bury it certain fathoms in the earth,
And, deeper than did ever plummet sound,
I'll drown my book.

Perhaps no one would think an old woman screwing up her music and consigning it to the rubbish because she couldn't play anymore was comparable to a grand Magi on a fabulous island. Perhaps if I try to connect these two seemingly disparate beings, another critic, like the eighteenth-century writer who blasted Shakespeare for his vulgarity, might blast me too. But Prospero is only a figure in a play after all. Mum might never be called a great artist like Shakespeare – she was only a singing mother of five kids teaching music in the suburbs – but just like him, I imagine, she does understand what he was talking about as she prepares to leave her life's work, abjure her own *rough magic*, and tear up all her favourite words and music.

PARKINSON'S SUCKS!

Mum was chopping carrots for our evening meal when she found out that she'd become a Singing Associate of the Trinity College of Music in London. We *oohed* and *aahed* at the splendid news, but none of us offered to take over cutting the carrots for her. Mum never made a big deal of her achievements; she was always thinking of the next challenge, which at that moment was cooking a meal of meat and three vegies for her husband and kids. I like to think now that she celebrated her success by the way she started singing while she chopped the carrots. She didn't suddenly burst into song though, not as she sometimes did for our amusement, or just for the fun of it, chasing us around the kitchen with a broom, or singing operettas while she stirred the mince on the stove. That night she sang discreetly, as if her satisfaction was private and deep.

It had stormed during the day – one of those Queensland electrical storms that make the sky look ill. It had recovered, but from where I was sitting at the table I could see through the kitchen window the still greenish sky framing Mum in the kind of deeply textured landscape that I'd seen in the old movies that she loved. It was a lot to take in, what was going on inside and outside the kitchen – the backdrop, the cast of children wriggling around her, the domestic soundtrack swelling gently beneath her. She looked like the star of her own musical and I felt like one of those Hollywood kids hanging around the set of a film that I wouldn't realise till much later was one of those timeless classics that your own kids might be able to watch with you over and over on Saturday afternoon reruns.

Mum probably was too busy chopping to notice that the sound of her knife slicing through the vegetables onto the board below created a kind of rhythmic counterpoint to the melody of the classic song she was singing under her breath. Like the chop chop chop of the carrots . . .

Day and night
You're always the one.

Five days before Christmas 2003 Mum is admitted to St Agatha's Hospital near the Brisbane CBD. The hospital has been suggested by Mum's new neurologist, Dr Goldman, who comes highly recommended as one of the country's leading experts in Parkinson's treatment and whose rooms are just down the road, making it easier for him to 'keep an eye' on her. Dr Goldman also happens to be 'a friend of a friend' and his affable way of communicating encourages a new sense of ease.

Mum always gets a new lease of life when she has a new doctor and especially approves of Dr Goldman because, like Dr Silver, he is 'so handsome', although as I joke with her, she seems to have a habit of finding all her male doctors good-looking. Dr Goldman also apparently works at the cutting edge of recent developments in Parkinson's disease, and we are thrilled that Mum has once again the possibility of a fresh start.

After examining her, Dr Goldman is upbeat, but proposes another overhaul of her medication. We are told her stay at St Agatha's may last for a couple of days or a couple of weeks. I don't ask for any more specific information. I am better at understanding the euphemistic language of the doctors and can now easily interpret the phrase 'it's best for her to go in for further observation' as 'we need to fix up her medication again'. I have realised that often no one really knows what is happening and that, just like any other human being, health professionals are often stumbling around in the dark, grasping at solutions to impossible situations.

I'm having a break at the New South Wales' north coast when Paul rings to tell me that this hospitalisation is to be extended. He is about to leave for holidays with his family and is worried Mum will be alone in hospital with no relatives around to visit. He asks me, just as he did five years earlier, if I can drive north and stay in Brisbane with Mum 'for a few days' while her medication is sorted out.

Mum always advised her singing students to keep a practice diary. A diary helps you keep track of your progress, encourages you when your spirits flag; it also reminds you that all major developments occur one tiny step at a time. I was never organised enough, though, when I was younger to do anything as incremental as this. I also had terrible handwriting. But there are times when a practice diary would be really useful. When perspective is gone. When the changes are so overwhelming that days go by in a blur of fatigue. When life speeds up and the balance between outward activity and inner reflection seems completely out-of-whack.

During the final days of 2003 and early 2004 my face begins to resemble the same blank haunted face my mother had when she first experienced fear and anxiety at the beginning of her illness. I don't know how to rest, though, to unfurl my unwieldy body and mind and heal. Worst of all, I stop singing too.

I begin my own practice diary to record things as they happen. Perhaps not recording things as they happen will make time disappear, along with Mum – and me. Perhaps the diary will help me see – not now, but one day – the bigger picture created by all the tiny moments that now seem to be occurring randomly and often without meaning. Later I will fill out the entries in order to make more sense of this randomness as Mum's illness progresses. But the diary I make at the time lists dates, times, and transcribes conversations. Exactly what I am practising during these weeks is unclear. The entries are sketchy, patchy and thin. They reflect the halting twilight state of our lives at this time of transition.

19 December 2003: I go up to the fourth floor, full of dread. As a concession to Christmas there are a few bits of gold tinsel decorating the corridor railings. I pass open doors and see people lying immobile on their beds. Everything is grey.

I hear opera when I enter Mum's room. There is a nurse giving her tablets and Mum is hunched over on the bed. For some reason I notice her feet don't touch the floor and that she is wearing a nightie I haven't seen before. She looks tiny and old, like a sad Yoda. The nurse is brusque. I can tell that Mum has been 'uncooperative'. Tablets I have not seen before are lying on the tray. The atmosphere in the room seems full of tension. I wonder what has gone on before my arrival.

Are these new tablets? I ask.

No, they're ones she's always taken, she tells me.

I notice the nurse is defensive. I'm good at that now, making nurses defensive.

According to the chart she's taken it for a good while before she came here, she concludes.

She goes back to fussing over Mum and ignores me. I don't blame her. Not really. I'm sick of myself too.

Mum is in the middle of a Parkinson's freeze and can't move. She asks me to take her shoes off and put them back on numerous times. Nothing makes her comfortable. She tells me she feels as if a thousand little insects are crawling up and down inside her legs.

21 December: Mum's hallucinations begin suddenly on the morning of the 20th. The nurses whisper to me that they are symptoms of 'aggressive dementia'. I notice, though, that they only began with her new medication. The new drugs make her babble like a crazy woman and I feel again, as I have many times during the past few years, that illness has become like a thief in our lives, robbing Mum over and over – of her dignity, security, self-respect and even, sometimes, her sanity.

When Mum tells me she has been sexually attacked by some people who came into her room I tell her it was all a bad dream. Her paranoia is to do with sex and with people trying to control her. She talks about an old man touching her when she was a young girl and says that God is punishing her for being touched 'down there' and that her psychiatrist interrogated her on behalf of the Masons, 'in order to get information'.

It is all crazy stuff, but I converse with her as if what she is saying is all perfectly normal. It seems the best approach. When we return to her room I find there has been a medication change. She is now on a drug for schizophrenia, prescribed to reduce her dreams and 'psychotic behaviour'. When I research the drug on the Internet I discover that its side-effects are increased hostility, paranoia and feelings of persecution. I don't feel vindicated. I just feel tired.

Sometimes, Mum talks less like a madwoman and more like a wise woman. *Your father was a very thoughtful, tender man who loved me,* she suddenly blurts out to me as I am about to leave one night. *The church should never have insisted on no contraceptives. That's what broke your father's heart. Losing our intimacy like that. Probably gave him the stroke, the bastards!*

Her mood shifts as she walks me to the lifts. *But the way I looked after your father is the story of our love,* she tells me. *It was a tender spiritual love. Affectionate, respectful, caring. That's what's life all about . . . reaching that level of love.*

She begins to sing as we wait together for the lift.

Love that hovers
over lovers
speaks in song.

I know the song and join in. Other people waiting for the lift turn away, embarrassed.

She stops and says: *I sang this song to your father.*

I know, Mum, I tell her. *I remember.*

Sing with me, she says, her eyes glistening. *I love it when you sing with me.*

And the music answers . . . she continues, *swaying to and fro.*

I hum along for a bit, until I remember more words.

Mum stops singing and waits for me to sing the next line. *Telling you, it's true, it's true,* I warble.

Someone giggles. Another voice joins with Mum as she responds, singing . . . *I love you so.*

She stops and bows before going on, announcing to the lift which has arrived at our floor holding what might be her final audience: *This is my daughter. We're just singing together.*

I get into the lift, turn back and face her as I hold the button down to keep the door open a little longer. The couple next to me join in with Mum and me to sing the final line of the song: *I love you so.*

There should be an orchestra in the lift. There should be technicolour. A choir of angels. A curtain closing. Rapturous applause. But as the lift doors close, no one claps, not even the couple beside me who sang with us. I imagine Mum walking back to her room, humming as she goes, at the same time forgetting and remembering all the melody of her life, her mind a confusion of love and music.

When Mum's psychiatrist rings later, I ask him whether it is true that the brain can degenerate over time by taking so many drugs. He avoids directly answering my question and instead philosophises over the phone: *You cannot change the past so there's no point, really, is there, in thinking about it?* I wonder if he believes I am the one with the problem.

22 December: Mum is so rigid she has to be lifted out of the bed. Her hands are like claws. For the first time I pray for her to be taken quickly. I don't want her to suffer any longer than she has to. I hold her hand and stroke her leg. Her limbs are twisted and so stiff that when I lift her onto the bed I have to force her legs downwards.

Talk to me, will you, Linda? I just want you to talk to me. I want to hear your voice. Tell me what is happening to me. Tell me what has happened. I just want to understand.

I don't know what to say. I'm tired of talking. There seems no point at the moment. Talking seems to have got us nowhere. So, instead of talking, I do what I did when I first returned home five years earlier – I get out my guitar and sing one of my songs. When I sing I am revived. I hope Mum is too. A couple of nurses pop their heads into the room, smile, and walk away.

After a few verses Mum turns slowly towards me and asks: *Who taught you that song? Did I teach you that song?*

She's forgotten a lot of things. I don't mind. I don't mind at all. *No, Mum,* I tell her. *I made it up myself.*

She is crying when she says to me: *I'm so proud of you.*

I know that with those few words she is acknowledging to me that I have finally found the thing I have searched for; found the thing I never thought I would find by returning to her. I have found my song and I am singing it for her in the hospital surrounded by machines and steel and grey, empty corridors. I understand, too, in ways that probably could never be conveyed verbally between us, that she had drummed her music into me for so many years when I was a child in the hope, perhaps, that I would find in it, as she probably had, a means to discover myself and my own emotional expression. It wasn't a matter of being famous or some kind of star. Even a practical woman like my mother knew that finding my song had little to do with finding an audience for my song.

She doesn't want to hear any more after that. She has heard enough, I imagine, to last her a lifetime. Now she just wants silence. She tells me it's not that she doesn't like to hear me sing, it's only that she can't bear it. I'm not insulted. Some things *are* unbearable.

She wants to pray, but it's so long since I've said a prayer; I say only half a Hail Mary and let her finish the rest.

'Don't keep secrets on stage', Mum once advised her readers. 'Let it all hang out.' Anyone who knew her personally or was taught by her can hear the emphatic way she might have delivered these lines. I sometimes hear my father's thoughts in my mother's words. Not that I think she didn't believe in everything she wrote and thought about singing. Rather, I can see what he passed on to her; what luck it was to have found a man with his love of poetry and words to settle down with her in a Brisbane suburb. I can also read in her words the determination that would have made her find a way to get where she needed to go, even without him. And for him, my mother would have been the singer, not just the song, the physical embodiment of all the dreams that poetry had put into his heart. In return for manifesting his dream, he gave her his strength, his passion, his enthusiasm and, despite his resistance sometimes to her earning money and singing in public, his adoration.

Mum hinted once that Dad didn't always like her singing on the stage. I try to understand his misgivings, to put myself in his shoes. In those days the stage might have seemed a rough business. To him, perhaps it would have seemed safer for her to sing at home. But Mum was down-to-earth and practical enough to know that you had to do the hard yards, to do the rough menial jobs to make any thought become a reality. That was her gift to him, the knowledge that sometimes you had to step up to the spotlight, open your mouth and sing out, louder and bigger than if you were just whispering softly next to your beloved. She knew how important the body was to her art. She knew that the stage was larger than life. Knew that song, like an act of love, was physical poetry.

'Draw your audience into yourself', she wrote. 'When you are uninhibited and really concentrate on your lyrics and words, your voice will blossom.'

25 December: On Christmas Eve I received an offer of a writer's residency in New Delhi beginning in November of 2004. It is an opportune Christmas present, the offer of Christmas next year in another country. I can feel our story drawing to a close and wonder whether, unable to finish it myself, forces outside are conspiring to end it for me.

Cathie's in town for Christmas. Paul, Kym and the boys share lunch at the hospital with Mum, Cathie and me. Friends with gifts and greetings drop in all day to visit, but by the afternoon Mum is tired of Christmas and wants to rest.

As Paul and his family are leaving, Kel sees a picture of Mum taken by Paul in London in 1997. In the photograph she is smiling like a girl while she strolls through a leaf-strewn park.

Do you know who that is? someone asks Kel, who is a gregarious and lively child.

Yes, he answers, his face turning up to us like the sun. *That's Grandma Joan when she was still alive.*

28 December: Mum rings and tells me she's become disfigured in the night. When I arrive she is on the phone. Mum's relationship with the phone is always a good barometer of how she is feeling. When she is depressed she hardly speaks at all; when she is anxious and wound up she can't stop talking. I play her a couple of songs to calm her down; she tells me to stop because my voice is too shrill.

She tells me later that she did not want me to sing because it made her so sad. *I crossed my hands on my chest with my rosary beads,* she whispers to me, *and I was just lying there ready to die.*

I couldn't see any other way and you singing made me realise what I was leaving. And I wanted you to stop. It hurt me.

Why did it hurt you to hear me singing? I ask, although I already understand why.

She sighs, as she often does these days. *Because it reminded me of everything I've lost.*

In the afternoon of the 29th I travel down to the Gold Coast for a swim and dinner with friends. As I unfurl near the sea, I am suddenly in love with everything, the water, the sky, the air, everything that is not to do with sickness and hospitals. The next day, as I travel back from the Gold Coast for another attempt to see Mum's doctor, I see a large black and white sign on the side of the freeway that says PARKINSON'S SUCKS!!

Yes, I scream as I pass the sign. *It sucks. It bloody well sucks.*

I appreciate the rawness of the sign's language, its simplicity. As I bang my hand down on the steering wheel, my eyes stream with tears. I am determined now to write the story of what has happened to Mum. To us. To find another voice. A musical writer's voice. And I will call my book simply this: *Parkinson's Sucks.* Along with a myriad of other things. Forget metaphor. Forget poetry. Sometimes two words screamed out on a concrete highway say all there is to say.

But it is not just Parkinson's that sucks. Dr Goldman has promised her an early appointment on the 30th. When I arrive at the hospital Mum has been up for hours, excited by the prospect of a visit from her neurologist, who now calls her 'my girl'. I notice she has powdered her face and put on her special dark lipstick, as well as the diamante earring and necklace set that Dad bought her just before he died. She lies on her bed in her red and white Christmas frock, hands clasped demurely, and when I tell her she looks beautiful, she acts coy, like a Tennessee Williams heroine waiting for her gentleman caller.

At eleven o'clock, after three hours of waiting for her gentleman to call, Mum's makeup begins to cake as her body grows rigid. At eleven-thirty, she has a session with a physio called Audrey, who teaches her how to sit up and down correctly, how to stay calm when anxiety takes hold before her tablets are due, how to navigate herself physically through the rigidity that gradually takes over her body during the course of the day.

After Audrey leaves I go home, have lunch and take a short rest. I feel uneasy at the thought of Mum waiting much longer. I am just being paranoid, I tell myself, I am 'tired and emotional', suspicious, like Mum, of everyone and everything now. Still, unable to sleep, I ring the hospital to see whether the doctor has turned up.

The only news is that Mum has spilled some of her lunch onto her freshly washed dress and that her lipstick has bled into her makeup and is now staining her teeth. She pretends she doesn't mind waiting, but I recognise Mum's passive acceptance as a precursor to a deeper anger that she will only articulate later to me.

At seven-thirty in the evening when I go back up to the hospital there is still no sign of the doctor. Mum and I do not speak about our disappointment; instead we numb ourselves with television, sweets and meaningless chat. At nine-thirty, the time I discover that Mum's doctor has just phoned the nurses to say he is not coming in at all, Mum is curled up like a baby on her bed.

I refuse to curl up, though. I am a silent storm in the corridor, pacing up and down beside the nurses' desk until I work up the breath to speak.

Did he ever actually intend to come? Or was he just trying to mess with my mother's mind? I ask petulantly.

My sarcasm is ugly; my disdain is ugly as well. The whole scenario, as far as I am concerned, is, as my grandmother might have put it, as 'ugly as sin'.

She depends on him, I say through a gritted smile, trying to calm myself down through long, slow, deliberate yogic breathing. *And if she depends on him, we all depend on him.*

The nurse, trained to remain neutral in the face of irate patients and their families, watches me impassively as I rant at her. She asks me politely if I would like to fill out an official complaint form. I feel futile, useless, hopeless, helpless. I shrug my shoulders and walk away, the fight, like hope, gone from me entirely.

31 December: On New Year's Eve I visit Mum on my way to a party. She is in her room wearing a dress as blue as her eyes, flat tan shoes, and socks that make her look like a girl about to head off to school for the first time.

Her mood, for the moment, has brought her up out of bed. She greets me with a smile, links her arm in mine and walks with me down the corridor.

I'm much better today, she tells me.

I hate myself for not trusting what she says. Hate that the whole cycle of mood changes and drugs has made it harder to trust her, wondering always when the next crash will come.

She can tell how tired I am and this time it is she who leads me along, swinging my arm high up in the air as we walk towards a seat in front of a window that overlooks the city. It is a balmy evening, one of those Brisbane nights that catch you by surprise during summer, when things cool down and bodies unfurl from the effort of coping with the heat.

Mum puts her head on my shoulder and tries to rouse me out of my dark mood. *Come on, Linda. Smile. Remember it's the face you show the world that's important.*

It sounds so absurd hearing her say it that I have to laugh. Absurd to still believe in showing a face to the world after everything she's been through. I admire her, though, for still trying. And I love her for still believing in what her mother told her, despite all evidence to the contrary.

For a few moments I enjoy our shared happiness as we watch the Brisbane skyline in the distance. I suggest then that we exchange our New Year's resolutions. Mum resolves to not be so negative – about life, about the future.

Perhaps the negativity is just chemical, I tell her. *The moods could just be chemical.*

Everything's chemical, Mum replies, *even music. It's all about arranging and rearranging chemicals. Now how about you? What's your resolution?*

> I tell her my resolution is to do with her: I would like her to trust herself more and speak to the doctors as if they are her equals and not her superiors.
>
> *But that's the way we were brought up,* she tells me. *To trust in those people.*
>
> *It's not like I think they're always wrong, Mum. But they're not infallible either. You stood your ground with music. You made a stand there. Why can't you do that with your own body and mind?*
>
> *Now I'm a sick old woman,* she tells me, burrowing closer into me.
>
> I am prepared, of course, to excuse her, forgive her anything, for the pleasure of this burrowing, for this moment, and for all the moments we have shared since I came home, to finally know her and to be known by her.

As we sit together on New Year's Eve, I am in no hurry to leave. I am in no hurry to go anywhere. I am even too serene at this moment to fret much about what might have been if, at the beginning of this whole saga, we had known what we know now.

Mum senses my disquiet and rubs my arm. *You can go mad with regrets, you know.*

I know. Mum herself never believed in them. She rests her hand on mine: *All that matters is that we're here now. And just think, you never would have come home if I hadn't got sick.*

Oh, so that's why you became ill, is it – I laugh, pinching her – *just to get me to come back?*

She is suddenly serious: *Mothers will do almost anything to take care of their children. You know that.* I wonder if I do. *You do,* she continues, as if she is reading my mind. *You've been like my mother. I can call you Mum if you like.*

Look where you've ended up with me trying to look after you, I say, suddenly stricken by the thought of all the things I haven't done – and still don't do – well.

In the loony bin, you mean, Mum? she laughs.

Now that was *crazy,* I tell her, not exactly laughing with her. *Except I don't think you were the one who was mad.*

We are quiet for a little while longer. I take in a deep breath. I think of how many more such conversations are left for us to have and also of how many conversations I didn't have with my father before he died. *Sometimes I feel I should apologise to you,* I tell her. *To you and Dad – for not living a more normal life. I know it wasn't always easy for you both.*

She squeezes my arm as she says quietly: *Maybe we weren't always easy for you either. Just because we're your parents doesn't mean we know what you need to do. I could see you didn't belong to me, you belonged to the world.*

I am still surprised when she speaks like this, as if there has always been a secret self in her – among the hundreds of other selves – that only hinted of its existence while she went about the business of her life.

What's normal anyway? she continues, echoing the question that I have put many times on her behalf to doctors, nurses and carers.

I don't know, I laugh again. *You tell me.* I turn to look at her; her face is bright pink in the neon light reflected from outside onto her pale skin.

Can I share a secret with you? she whispers, leaning in closer to me. *I've seen a lot of things during the last few years. Things I would never have dreamed of in my whole life. And all these things have taught me one simple thing: nobody knows.*

Nobody knows? I ask, looking back out at the skyline.

Nobody knows at all. She squeezes my arm as my face falls again.

So don't worry. You've got nothing to be sorry for. You didn't waste a second. You just had different things to do. And look what you've got to show for it now.

And what have I got to show for it? I play along with her, smiling once more.

Smiling and falling, I think. Up and down. That's our life now.

She sighs. I can tell she is growing tired.

Mum . . . I ask, tapping her on the arm.

Mmm, she mumbles, drifting off with her head on my shoulder.

Tell me . . . Mum? I prod her.

She doesn't say anything else, but I don't mind. I am growing more used to fragmentary things, snippets of dialogue that begin and end before they are finished. I even enjoy the lack of conclusions in our lives. I am just happy to be sitting there with her, thankful that we can share any kind of conversation with each other as one year turns towards another.

31 December 2003: At midnight I am playing my songs at a small gathering beside a swimming pool at a block of units in

St Lucia. The party takes place close to our old home, which has recently been bulldozed to make way for high-priced rental apartments. I don't drive up Warren Street anymore. I always take the long way around so I have never seen the construction site. I hear, though, that the hoop pine trees my grandmother planted at the edge of the property over fifty years ago are still standing after it was decided that they were too tall and strong to safely cut down.

There is a clairvoyant at the party who tells me I was a troubadour in a past life and that I will not be fulfilled until I find my voice again in this life. She tells me my songs are like poetry and that they could make a stone cry.

HOUSE OF LOVE

Mum felt that a singer should be an actor and a poet. A singer should be facially alive, physically calm, and musically confident. Interpretation can be, in some respect, spiritual. It should come from the heart and soul of the singer. She was also very sensitive to the position of the singer in any kind of competition. Although she adjudicated at dozens of eisteddfods all over the state and was actually writing comments for some nervous competitor when she first experienced rigidity in her shoulder, she never forgot her own humble beginnings as a frightened young singer hoping for the best as she stepped tentatively into the spotlight for the first time. She even wrote a special note for examiners and adjudicators at the end of one of her last articles for the Music Teachers' Association newsletter: 'Remember to always try to put performers at their ease with encouragement and kind words as singing is such a lonely and vulnerable art.'

* * *

In June 2004 I travel to Scotland to attend a conference. The last time I had been to Scotland was with the Youth Orchestra tour when we stayed in Aberdeen and played Brahms, Dvorak, Tchaikovsky and Shostakovich. This time I will stay in Stirling and perform my own words and music. Byron is still in my life and is excited to see me travel for the first time. Even though I have never fully committed to our relationship, we are still in contact intermittently throughout 2004.

Two weeks before I am due to leave for Europe, Mum falls and breaks her hip. She is given a hip replacement operation and sent back to the Garden of Eden within days of surgery, with no rehabilitation or physio program in place. Her hostel has assured us they will attend to her rehab, but when she arrives there has been no notice of her coming; her bed is unmade and her room unprepared. Mum waits alone in a corridor for hours while a staff member is found to attend to her needs. Three weeks later little has been done towards her rehabilitation. I make terrified phone calls. I threaten the occupational therapist in charge of Mum's rehab with legal action, accuse her of moral negligence. I dream I am mad, demonic, hateful. I dream that my own mother – and everyone around her – hates me and what I have become.

As usual, Paul steps in to soothe the troubled water. *It is time for you to have a break,* he tells me firmly. I do not, as I usually do, disagree.

The conference goes well. I spend three weeks in Paris and am dazzled by the city of lights and by an artist who lives there. There is no romance, though: he is married, and I am still too worn out to love. Towards the end of my stay a friend introduces me to a French sculptor who looks into my eyes and tells me knowingly that I must not let my family's sadness penetrate me one moment longer. I tell him I understand the French like the sensual life too much to be connected to suffering for very long, but that I come from stoical Anglo-Saxon stock. We endure; we persevere, I tell him. It is not sexy, but it is our nature. We suffer because we know how to. He agrees with my cultural stereotyping, but disagrees with my decision to go home. He tells me my liberation is in my own hands, but I miss my mother too much and feel her pull on my heart still. He hand-feeds me morsels from his kitchen and invites me to model for one of his sculptures, but I am still too connected to things back in Australia to be tempted by his offer. Before I fly home from Europe, I promise to return soon, to pick things up, he assumes, from where we left off. My immediate plans, though, are to get back home in time to attend a meeting with Paul about Mum's upcoming transition from the independent living section of the Garden of Eden to its nursing home.

Paul carries a foolscap pad as we sit together across a table from a nurse who tells us that, due to Mum's worsening condition, this will probably be Mum's last move. He talks briefly about our brother Stephen, who has phoned the previous evening with an offer to care for Mum full-time if we need him to. I wish I was more like Steve, who is like our father, or Paul, who is round faced and friendly like my mother's side of the family; wish I hadn't been pierced so deeply by Mum's suffering; wish I had learnt to become detached and smooth like a proper, functional person. I remember a time when I was smoother, less ruffled, before I became so attached to Mum and her illness. I try to suppress the feelings of shame and regret that arise in me when I feel like the devil in the family, marked by the dark shadow of instinct and uncontrollable emotions.

Cheryl, the kind, efficient woman in charge of nursing, takes us for a tour of the nursing home. The rooms are smaller than the rooms in Mum's independent unit and in greater disrepair. Paint is scrappy on the doors and walls and the toilets are noticeably smelly.

Later, outside, Paul says he cannot even notice the upcoming scents of spring: *I have no sense of smell at all,* he admits to Cheryl, laughing. He is such a cheery man, I think, just as Mum always said he was: happy-go-lucky, seemingly unmarked by sorrow, still believing the best of everyone and everything. Compared to him, I feel wrung out, joyless and – just as Mum sometimes said about me – guilty of taking everything way too seriously.

Before we part, we sip tea and water at the coffee shop. He tells me that my approach to things is not always productive. *It's not like I don't care about Mum, Linda,* he says, smiling. *But I don't like conflict and don't think it's necessary.*

Afterwards we walk together down to visit Mum. She's been moved to a facility with security locks after developing a habit of 'wandering' and falling in the grounds of the hostel, away from the watchful eyes of the nurses. Her face is bruised from a recent fall; she is sitting in a crooked line of women silently watching television. I resist the temptation to run to her and hold her. Stifle the impulse to call out: *This is wrong. This is wrong. This is all wrong.*

I smile quietly as Paul embraces Mum; when it is my turn to say hello I stroke her cheeks. She is happy to see me; she looks like a bruised and battered child smiling up at me with her sad blue eyes. When Paul leaves, we kiss goodbye for the first time in months. Afterwards, Mum and I walk outside on a path around a caged bird in the middle of the hostel's concrete patio. We talk about Paris and Toronto, Mum's other favourite city. She has not healed properly from the hip replacement operation; her head is now noticeably bent at an angle and she walks – or shuffles – with a distinct limp. I hold her close to me. I hold her up. She is restless, hardly able to talk. I feel the life force less and less in her body.

That night I pray that she doesn't linger. I pray that she doesn't fall again.

She does fall again. Two days later. She falls in private and calls out for help. I am unable to find out the exact time between her fall and the arrival of help so I don't know how long she lies on the cold concrete with her eyes closed and her forehead swelling. According to her neurologist, she will fall again and again until she stops walking, stops moving. We are advised to buy her a wheelchair and teach her how to use it.

She is lolling in this new wheelchair when she receives her commendation from the Music Teachers' Association of Australia. Miss Betty Del Fuego, a nationally prominent singing teacher, attends this ceremony, which takes place in a little alcove off from Mum's room in the Garden of Eden nursing home. Lyndsey Parker is also there, as well as Marjorie Anderson, Paul, Finn and Kel, and some family friends. Betty and Lyndsey haven't seen Mum for years and are visibly distressed by the large discoloured lump on her head as well as her inability to open her eyes or speak.

We only find out later that her system has shut down from the shock of the fall. At the time, though, all we can really do is reassure her old friends that she is worse than normal. They go through the ceremony with tears in their eyes, and after cakes and tea they leave hurriedly so they can cry and grieve out of Mum's sight.

It's an absolute tragedy what's happened to Joan, Lyndsey and Betty whisper through their sobs after they place the framed certificate in Mum's hands. *After all the work she did for so many in her life. It just doesn't seem right.*

What seems right or wrong isn't really that relevant to me anymore.

Byron is at the ceremony too, to support me and to honour Mum. We still see each other, although we are more off than on. He is still fond of Mum as she had been of him. I think she hoped – as he did – that we would marry. She said once it would be good for me to at least try it. Byron tells me he is planning to go to Vietnam to work with orphans, to help develop business plans for the locals. He doesn't quite know what he is going for, I suspect.

He and I walk together outside for a while, around the neat circles of carefully groomed flowers, up and down the long slabs of concrete and across the green clipped lawn. He stops suddenly and takes my hands. *You could come too, you know. They need people to help them too.*

Byron's shaved head and angular, Eurasian face makes him look like some exotic animal. I remember a childhood photograph he once showed me, of a boy with dark brown glowing skin, standing beside a pale, fair-haired woman. *It wasn't easy in those days being dark skinned with a white mother,* he told me, shrugging off my wonder. But it wasn't the contrast of his Indian looks with the Celtic beauty of his mother that had startled me. It was how he was now as white as his mother had been in his boyhood pictures. I did not understand how that could happen, how dark skin could become white skin; how one dominant strain could be replaced by another. Could you will yourself to change colour? I wondered. Had he? Or had it happened incrementally, over time? A slow evolution from one shade to another, caused not by will or attrition, or even by desire, but by some mysterious internal process. When I asked him about it Byron put it down, in his cosmic new-age way, to meditation, and to becoming, over the years, more like his mother than his father.

Outside the entrance to the nursing home, Byron is suddenly serious. *Why don't you come with me to Asia? We can have an adventure. Your mum doesn't need you so much anymore.*

I don't reply as I look at how the sun shines off his smooth round skull, how at certain angles he looks like Gandhi looked in his later life.

We can go as friends, as lovers, as husband and wife, he continues. *It doesn't matter. We could go to Vietnam. There are mountains there that can apparently take your breath away.*

He puts on his sunglasses then; they make him look like some kind of celebrity guru, waiting for the light in the light, I joke to myself, while he waits for an answer from me, as he seems to have been waiting ever since we met.

What if something happens while I'm up a mountain somewhere? I ask then, noticing, as I speak, the helplessness in my voice. *And no one can contact me. What if she falls again?* I continue, scuffing my right foot lightly across the ground, not wanting to speak much more and draw attention to how obsessed I sound, how obsessed I am. *And I cannot see her because I am enjoying the beautiful view?*

They can call you on my mobile, he laughs. *They can email. They can find you. There is always a way to get in touch. But you're worn out. You need to have a break.*

He huddles around me then, not pressing in too hard, almost as if he senses my fragility at that moment. It feels old-fashioned somehow, the way he places his arm around my shoulder, one of those gestures from men I used to hate so much, as if by receiving such concern I might become too vulnerable and less able to survive on my own. These days I am better at receiving, but still I know, just as Byron knows, that I am not ready for what he is offering me.

I know you can't answer me now, he continues, letting me off the hook. *But think about it . . . and let me know sometime . . . when you're ready, what you're feeling.*

I nod, unable to say anything. Unable to give him back what he wants – or needs – from me. He doesn't press me anymore; he just smiles, bows, turns and heads off to the car park. I watch him walk away and I hold close to the thought that it will not be for the last time. That life can come and go too, that there will be something – or someone – up ahead for me, waiting, when my time with Mum is over.

A week later Mum is lying motionless on a bed in St Agatha's Hospital. The sign above her bed says NIL BY MOUTH. Her neurologist had considered the lump on her forehead sustained through her fall serious enough to warrant urgent scans. These reveal no bleeding in the brain, but several cracked ribs. At the time she is admitted I come down with a virulent flu and take to my bed as well. Like Mum, I do not open my eyes or speak. Two days later, on my birthday, I take flowers to Mum's ward. I sit beside her bed and talk to her, say sorry to her, cry for her. It doesn't matter that she doesn't answer. If she did she might just tell me, as she so often did during my life, to 'pull your head in and stop taking everything so seriously'. It turns out she has not opened her eyes or orally taken in food or medicine for over seventy-two hours and that this time, perhaps, she may have given up. Decided to stop breathing, once and for all. I ask her nurse if this is what usually happens when people are about to die.

Sometimes, she answers, adjusting Mum's pillows. *Often they just stop like your mum has. Usually they wait for permission from the family.*

She peers at me closely while she speaks, watching for my reaction. She seems sensitive, used to dealing with death. I imagine her delivering these facts to other families waiting for a parent to die. She speaks softly, yet her words are firm. You can't argue with death, I think. Or with people who have decided to die. Best to just let them go.

But then again if we can rehydrate her, she continues, *the muscles might start working again and she can take in food. Otherwise we might have to get the family's permission to put a tube in her stomach and get food to her that way.*

What if she really doesn't want to? I ask, more out of curiosity than anything else.

She bends down to find a lever and skilfully adjusts the height of the bed until Mum is lying all the way back down. *That's a decision for the whole family,* she says.

Cathie: I can vividly recall the Sunday in late 2004 when Paul called me and told me that St Agatha's wanted us to make a decision about life support if the need arose. That afternoon I had to go and accompany a number of my senior students in their final recital. One of the boys was singing 'Going Home' by Copeland and Britten. I don't think I have ever played with such intense feelings about the text and music of a song. I had to fly down to Brisbane the next day so you can imagine what I felt a lot that day about this song called 'Going Home'. Going Home. You understand sometimes exactly what those words mean.

The available family – Cathie, Paul and I – gathers in a conference room at the hospital, along with Mum's psychiatrist, occupational therapist, physiotherapist, and a nurse called Jenny. We discuss Mum's declining health and the possibility of Stephen coming up from Melbourne to care for her full-time. Both Paul and Cathie refer to him as a 'special person' and by the end of the meeting, the occupational therapist does as well.

We are presented with statistics: at night now, Mum must be turned every two hours. Two nurses are required to move her from bed to chair to shower and back again. The physiotherapist tells us Mum's toes have curled inwards and are now rigid. She is hardly able to pivot on her feet, can only stand on 'her tippy toes' and is not ever expected to regain mobility, a euphemistic phrase for never being able to walk again. She will eat mashed and vitamised food for the rest of her life; water will never again pass between her lips, to protect her lungs from flooding and developing a pneumonia that might kill her. We are informed that her delirium is being caused by the severe dementia associated with the 'aggressive' Parkinson's she suffers from, as well as the urinary tract infection which she has contracted from the catheter that has been removing waste from her body for the last month.

Everyone sounds reasonable. I feel lulled by their smooth tone, nod my head in tandem with my brother and sister. The doctor, whom Mum also once called the 'handsome one', has a baby face and a peaceful demeanour. I notice my sister likes the doctor and that she wants to be liked by him. My brother exercises that easy banter which men of professional standing exchange with each other. I can't imagine either risking an altercation with each other or asking a question which might be considered offensive.

Sometimes there is such a thing as a tonal imperative: if the resonance in the room was musical, it would come, perhaps, from a septet by Haydn, or if it was a song, perhaps it would be a perfectly arranged pop song. Everyone's part is ordered, note perfect, even mine; despite my head being filled with atonal lines of my own devising, out loud I don't make a false note.

I ask only one question. It is a question I suspect no one wants to ask, but one that everyone would like answered: *How long do you think it will be before Mum dies?*

My voice is not like my mother's. It is more unschooled than hers. I will never earn a fellowship or a doctorate with my voice. Not like Mum did. Her voice developed in a cultural context; unlike my voice it knew the rules. It sang in a home, in the kitchen, practised in the lounge room, it performed with babies at its feet. It learnt from other well-qualified singers, it existed inside a framework. It scored As, Bs and Cs in exams. There are pieces of paper hanging in frames that attest to the sophistication of my mother's voice. It practised its scales, learnt to project, developed a resonance. My mother's voice was all body, was all her body, it filled every empty space; such a voice can stop another voice, like a pretty mother can stop a plain daughter from unveiling her unique beauty and showing it to the world.

You must sing your songs, an African woman once told me in a shop called Saraswati on Campbell Parade opposite Bondi Beach where I played a gig so I could earn enough money to eat for the next twenty-four hours. *You have been put onto this earth to sing about the sadness of women.*

Now, in the hospital, no one wants to answer my question. As my sister sobs quietly, the baby-faced doctor thinks for a while before answering that he cannot answer my question.

My brother closes his notebook decisively at the end of the meeting and says *Mmm.* I rub my sister's back. We walk together down the corridor to say goodbye to Mum. I feel briefly comforted, glad to be walking with my family, wishing for a moment that I could happily walk with them again, wishing for a smaller moment that I could forget all that I knew so I could be fully and peacefully included in the circle that is gathering and forming itself as my sisters and brothers return from other parts of the world in order to keep vigil over our mother. I wish that I hadn't been such a rebel, such a fighter, wish I had not questioned and probed so much; wish I had been able to be sweet and amenable, as my mother might have wanted me to be. Because I understand now that, for Mum, recovering from her illness, or being right, or having to know, or understanding herself or the life that has brought her to this point, was not as important to her – and never would be – as her kids getting along.

We gather around Mum's bed. Cathie is smiling again as she strokes Mum's hand and tells her she has sent a bottle of scotch down to Melbourne for Stephen's birthday. Paul looks distracted and tired. I think about what it has been like for him: devoted, as my father had been, to his young family, while pulled back always to the needs of Mum and his other family. On call to both of them. And, despite his sorrow and his stress, still smiling. But he is edgy and anxious to leave; he wants to miss the peak-hour traffic and he has errands to do before he can go home.

That night I dream I see Mum at the end of a white corridor like the one I walked down at the hospital. She's wearing a long white dress and is lifting off the ground. As she levitates in the air I hold on to her ankles. I watch myself holding on to her. I know, despite all the words I have said about letting go, that I am not letting go of her. That I am pulling on her as perhaps I always have done, dragging her down from her ascent with my need of her. I've never believed in angels, not actual ones, and I don't hear a heavenly choir as I dream. But I see what perhaps my mother sees as she reaches down to pry my fingers from her ankles: that holding on is useless. That letting go would be like a giant sigh, a final exhalation of pain and suffering, like throwing ballast off a hot air balloon so that it can float heavenwards.

You don't need to fight anymore, Mum tells me. *You only need to love.*

THE VIEW FROM HERE

Some people didn't really like the way Mum spoke in a radio documentary I made about her in 2003 in which I used the interviews I recorded while she was still able to speak coherently.

I wish you could have been a bit more positive, they told her. I understood what they meant. To the outsider, still living in the mainstream of life, a tragic voice is an affront. People on the go, people who work and toil, need uplifting and Mum could offer nothing of that anymore. On the other hand, I had lived with her illness and her voice for so long that I was used to its faltering pace and sense of fragile wonder and loss.

After the documentary was broadcast I received letters from people thanking Joan for telling her story. It was hard for her to listen when she herself first heard it. She did not like to hear her voice so weak and uncertain.

Will anyone really be interested in listening to this? she asked me. *This sad old woman?* Then she cried and said: *This is a beautiful thing that you have done for me.*

I called the documentary 'The Asylum Seekers', because I often feel that illness makes us like refugees looking for shelter as we travel long distances away from our home. When it won a gold medal at the New York Radio Festival I told her that it seemed there were people who were interested after all.

'What would happen if all the members of my family disappeared?' the writer Maurice Halbwachs asks. 'I would maintain for some time the habit of attributing a meaning to their first names.'

Today my mother is one of the disappeared. As a way of finding her again – or finding her for the first time – I have attributed meaning to more than just her first or last name, although for a while I became interested in finding out the meaning of both these things. I have tried, at various times, to find meaning in her illness, in her life and the collective life of my family. Mum herself never felt there was any meaning to her illness. She did not transcend it; she did not manage to find hope in the middle of her suffering. In the middle of her suffering was just more suffering. Sometimes I feel that all I have left is her voice, the memory of it, the hours of recordings, the traces of it in my voice. In all these ways, I have tried to hear her voice again – not just the voice she sang with, but the voice she used later when she could not sing anymore.

Trauma, psychoanalysts say, has a timeless quality to it. Which is to say, I suppose, that it does not pass away with time. It remains as fresh as when it was first felt. But Mum, thankfully, doesn't feel her trauma anymore. Nor, I imagine, does she grieve. Her life is simple these days. She lives with Stephen in a house that Cathie and Paul own at Brighton, the suburb next to Sandgate where Paul and his family live. Stephen, who left behind his life in Melbourne in November 2004 to move up to Brisbane, cares for her full-time. He goes about his days with a quiet dignity that has enabled my mother's life and her dying to also be both quiet and dignified. Her body never recovered from its last shutdown and progressively over the past four years it has stiffened to the point where each day there are only tiny windows of movement and life when she is roused from her vegetative state. During these gaps in her rigidity Stephen lifts her from her bed and wheels her out to the toilet. After she is finished in the toilet she is then wheeled to the lounge room, or, if it is fine weather, outside onto the veranda, or down the ramp to the back yard, where he hand-feeds her mashed-up food. The rest of the time she lies rigid yet peaceful in her air-conditioned room – cool in summer, warm in winter – in which the radio is always turned on low to ABC Classic FM.

And so it is left, as it usually is, to the survivors to do the grieving. To feel and feel again the trauma of the disappearing. To write the names of the disappeared over and over.

Cathie: When Stephen made the decision to leave his life in Melbourne to take on full-time care of Mum, there was some resistance from the medicos involved to us taking her out of hospital where she was dying. After a number of meetings, finally they agreed. The point that was made to

> us by the doctors and nurses was that no one would be able to look after someone in Mum's condition at home, virtually on their own. But Paul made a salient point that I feel surprised had not been considered before: 'This is what always used to happen only a few decades ago,' he told the doctors. 'Most of the elderly and infirm were cared for at home. Why do you think it's such an impossible thing to do?' I think the crux of the discussion was that today people would have to give up income and this was not a common experience. I thought this was very sad. Perhaps materialism and the pursuit of personal happiness through wealth and power have made us mean.

When Stephen arrives from Melbourne to look after Mum I can tell everyone in the family is relieved. He has been involved in Mum's declining health over the past few years from a distance – through phone calls and letters – and up close through his regular visits. By coming north now he brings fresh energy, as well as his strong, healthy body, to soothe the family – and Mum – from their distress. I feel sorry that I am too tired to be as gracious as he is, or to hear the praise he receives for coming to Mum's – and the family's – rescue.

Sensing my bruised emotions, my friends rally around me, but I know I should only feel happy for Mum, for all of us, that we don't have to worry about our mother being properly cared for anymore. I feel spent, though, as if I have outlived my usefulness, just as it often seemed to me during the past few years that Mum had outlived hers too.

I feel tired in my bones as I prepare to journey across to

India where I plan to live for the first four months of 2005 as part of a writer's residency in New Delhi. My good fortune has not come out of the blue. While I have been in Brisbane I have developed as a writer as well as a songwriter and now I am rewarded with opportunities such as these.

Byron is sorry to see me go and feels aggrieved that I can leave the country with so much unresolved between us, but my desire for change and relief is ruthless and I depart in the middle of November 2004. This month also marks the beginning of the period during which Stephen looks after Mum full-time and, in effect, keeps her alive when all of us, after the NIL by MOUTH episode in hospital, expect her to die.

The purpose of my residency in New Delhi is to write about India, but everywhere in this wild and vibrant and overwhelming city I see, hear and read images of the mother: 'Mother India', 'Mother's Milk', the 'Mother Ganges'. Overwhelmed and exhausted, I cry nearly every day for the first two months. My tears are welcome: they drain me of my fatigue and restore in me the ability to feel. It doesn't take long, though, for my body to weary of the pollution and stress in Delhi. I move north to the pilgrim town of Rishikesh, where, close to the source of the 'Mother Ganges', I think about how to write about my mother and the things through which we have passed.

Stephen sends regular updates via email as well as photographs of Mum. I follow her progress anecdotally and through peering at the images on the computer screen. I notice incrementally how her physical state improves during the first few weeks and months of Stephen's watch. I am happy to see Mum improving and guilty for not being there to help, for not being able to care for her the way Stephen can now.

She puts on weight and looks better nourished, but she is permanently incapacitated now and spends her time in bed or in a wheelchair. She is still capable of listening to Steve read out the emails I send about my travels. In his brief emails back to me Stephen tells me she listens with interest to them and occasionally says *Oh* or *Mmm*.

The rest of his communications are filled only with details of her medication or the state of her urine. Though I miss Mum, in my secret life I am glad to be where I am, so I can rid myself in private from my guilt and remorse. My body also changes, unwinding every day from the stress of the past five years, unfurling like a newborn in this mad, fecund country.

I took my violin to India, although I don't really expect to write songs. I don't dare to think that any music could come from my tired spirit. But then, a miracle: after the first few weeks of sleep and discovery I begin to write songs again, this time strumming the violin instead of the guitar to accompany myself. In a foreign country my lyrics are different. My voice changes too. Released from service, I feel music coming from somewhere deeper in me.

I extend my stay in India long beyond the four months I have planned. At the end of six months, I travel to Nepal for a new visa and write songs while looking out from my balcony roof toward Mt Everest. I travel east to Darjeeling then west again to Dharamsala where I do a ten-day Buddhist retreat. The Dalai Lama is in town and holding talks just down the road. Every day, while I am silent, he speaks about compassion and forgiveness to the thousands of pilgrims who have gathered from all over the world to listen to him.

When I emerge from the retreat I write letters of apology to my sisters. To Paul and Kym. 'I am sorry for disturbing your lives. With my anguish. My guilt.' I receive no replies. I suppose, logically, that everyone is getting on with their lives.

'What have you got to be sorry for?' my friends ask me in emails. I can't really answer their question. I don't know where my sorrow comes from, why I feel the need to be forgiven, whether I am mourning for my mother or for other things I have lost. I spend my days walking up hills and back down again. I sip tea, play my songs with other travellers in small cafés, laugh, love, cry and breathe in the Himalayan air. I email back to my friends: 'It will take some time to understand exactly what has happened, but for the moment I feel that I have suddenly opened my eyes and the view from here is beautiful.'

Still, I do not return home. Instead, I travel to Paris for the summer where I play violin with Arabs, sing for Jews and entertain the French in cafés and on the street. Influenced by the music halls, street musicians, accordion players and the gypsy fiddlers who frequent the Metro, I unfurl my heart and write more songs.

'I am happy again', I write to a friend. 'Happy during this glorious summer in Paris.'

I hope Mum is happier too. She was a never a woman who begrudged any of her children their adventures She would be pleased, I think, if she could comprehend my letters home, that I am singing and making music again, that I am walking the streets and smiling, that I am once again a woman who loves, a woman who is loved.

Stephen writes to me during that time that he 'read your letter out to Mum who occasionally interjected with "Oh, Paris . . ." or "Oh, violin eh?", but mostly "More apple pie", I'm afraid.'

It takes me a whole year to return home. When I finally see Mum again in December 2005, I am not shocked by her rigid body or her twisted face. I don't feel sad at all; I am just happy to be with her and to imagine perhaps that inside her bent frame she is serene. And I know I have been right to stay away for so long because there is no fight or sorrow left in me in regard to her. I wonder if she is where she always needed to be – in a quiet, restful place. I think of the home she left in St Lucia and all the places through which she travelled to finally arrive here, with her grandchildren, her sons and all her people around her.

It is hard to adjust to being back, but I still prefer to be close to where Mum lives so I can visit her regularly. At the beginning of 2006 I settle back into a flat at West End just up the road from the banks of the Brisbane River where my father first saw my mother, and begin to write a book that will share with others the story of that fortuitous meeting – what came before and what came after: a book about breath, about love and learning how to live.

A SHORT HISTORY OF MUSIC

The Larousse Dictionary of Music, which is also useful as a short history of music, defines the vibrato as 'an effect [. . .] whereby a singer or instrumentalist imparts a throbbing quality to a note by oscillating between it and a pitch slightly below. [The louder the note the singer sings], the more pronounced, usually, the vibrato – and the oscillation can become so wide that the hearer may be left in doubt as to just which note is being aimed for. If the technique is applied to a fairly rapid passage the result can be quite unnerving and totally unmusical (except apparently in the opera house).'

I have always had a love-hate relationship with vibrato, just as I sometimes did with Mum. When I was a little girl the vibrato of a violin used to fill me with deep, mysterious emotion. I later discovered that my grandmother's old recordings of violinists such as Michael Rabin were the result of recording equipment of the day that sped up the live sound. Contemporary digital remixings of these early recordings have tried to slow down the tempo of these original recordings, thereby making the pitch and vibrato sound more authentic. In old recordings, though, the vibrato seems to oscillate so fast that it sounds like a shaking, or a tremor, or someone crying; listening to it often made me want to cry. I only understood later that it was an unnatural, unrealistic sound so that the emotion it produced in me might have been unnatural or unrealistic as well. Later, I also discovered that the whole area of vibration was a contentious one and that it only came into common use in the third decade of the twentieth century.

In his autobiography *Unfinished Journey*, Yehudi Menuhin, my grandmother's favourite violinist, wrote: 'To teach vibrato, [my teacher] would shout, "Vibrate! Vibrate!" with never a clue given as to how to do it. I longed to achieve vibrato, for what use was a violin to a little boy of Russian-Jewish background who could not bring a note to throbbing life?' In a later documentary about his life he is pictured sitting cross-legged on a yoga mat, recalling his childhood as a young prodigy: 'When will I be able to vibrate, I used to wonder. I couldn't sing without a lovely sound.'

A violin without some vibration can sound raw and flat. Sometimes when I listen to certain country and western fiddle players, the vibrato is so wide that I think an old man with no energy must be playing. Yet excessive and excessively quick vibrato can rob a musical line of all its meaning. I used to love the sound of a vibrating high note on the violin. It still moves me, and others, too, comment on how they are affected by the sound of a violin, viola or cello vibrating. But I do not find singers who produce vibrato so appealing. In fact, except for Maria Callas's voice, especially in recordings after her heart was broken when the wide, shaking vibrato seemed to suggest someone hanging on with all their power not just to their career but to life itself, I have always found it unattractive. I do not like vocalists warbling or swooping either. Yet I love it when a violin swoops and wavers and vibrates; such sounds sometimes seem unearthly to me.

Mum told me once that the reason she loved the violin was that it produced the sound closest to the human voice. Yet I have never found the sound similar at all; the violin sound has always seemed more abstract, more free, and at the same time, considerably more intense and moving. This may be because I prefer a simple folk song sung in a natural, unproduced voice to the drama and penetration achieved by a fully trained vocalist. On the other hand, I love the violin playing all kinds of dramatic and intense music. When I sing my simple songs, I aim for a totally pure sound, devoid of any oscillation at all. But though my mother and I may have differed widely in our taste in music, art, spirituality, medicine and lifestyle, in one singer we found what we both loved: a singer without a fussy, penetrating vibrato who could sing art songs and folk songs with the same ease and dignity; who was equally loved by the critics and the 'ordinary people'; whose gifts were, for the most part, untrained, yet who achieved in her short life an artistry and resonance that belied her simple and unschooled beginnings.

Like my mother, the British contralto Kathleen Ferrier left school before she turned sixteen; unlike Mum, though, who went to work in the typing pool of Queensland Railways, Kathleen began her working life as a telephone operator in Blackburn, England. She married early, to a man called Bert Wilson, and managed to win a local music competition in both the vocal and piano sections; this encouraged her to try for a professional singing career. Though she took music lessons, as my mother did, she never attended any music academy, university or conservatorium; she had natural gifts – most notably an unusually large throat – that enabled her to develop into one of the world's finest and best-loved singers. During the Second World War, Kathleen gave many concerts for an organisation called the Council for the Encouragement of Music and the Arts. Her greatest artistic and professional achievements, though, came after the war when she became renowned for her exquisite and moving performances of Mahler, Bach and Handel, her work with contemporary composers and conductors such as Benjamin Britten, Arthur Bliss and Malcolm Sargent, as well as her performances and recordings of British folk songs, in particular 'Blow the Wind Southerly'. She died of breast cancer at the age of forty-one and was famously carried off from her last public performance on a stretcher.

These days Mum sometimes goes to sleep with a recording of Kathleen Ferrier singing 'Blow the Wind Southerly', among other folk songs, playing on the CD player next to her bed, in a voice in which the vibrato is subtle, appropriate, beautiful and moving. Steve says it soothes her. The vibrato in these recordings seems much more than just an effect or merely a technical oscillation. Sometimes when I listen, it seems to sweep across the sonic space like a paintbrush creating a landscape in sound. And as I listen I sometimes think I can hear – and see – in the music and lyrics of this and other British folk songs, the melancholy topography of my father's birth country and the brooding, bleak life he left behind to travel all the way to the other side of the world where the sun, as well as the bright, sunny beauty of my mother – and her high, vibrating voice – awaited him. Sometimes I imagine I hear him call to her. And though in many people's eyes Mum would now be considered a 'vegetable', I imagine she might like to sing back to him, as she still sometimes does, in her distorted, broken, and vegetable-like voice.

Blow the wind southerly, southerly, southerly
Blow the wind south the bonnie blue sea
Blow the wind southerly southerly, southerly
Blow bonnie breeze and bring him to me

Is it not sweet to hear the breeze singing
As lightly it comes from the deep rolling sea
But sweeter and dearer, my heart is wandering
The welcome of my true love in safety to me

Cathie: Today I love visiting Mum and Stephen. The house has a feeling of joy, serenity and generosity that is tangible. I have learned not to try and help Steve too much, but to work out what I can do for him – bring scotch, good red wine, and the occasional meal. He has a routine that needs to be respected. But when I see how much care Mum is living with, I realise this is what real love is – it is this giving of

> yourself. I think Steve lives a life full of value and so do all those carers in this world who are doing a similar job.

Four times a day Stephen crouches beside my mother as she lolls in her commode wheelchair in the bathroom at Brighton and gracefully wipes the shit from her bottom. The bathroom has been especially renovated so Mum can be moved easily to the toilet from the bedroom and back again. The shower curtain in the bathroom features giant yellow sunflowers and the cupboard above the sink is made from brown wood. The walls and ceiling are white as are the soap holders and shampoo bottles, although some, presents from Marjorie Anderson, who still never forgets Mum at birthdays or Christmas, are decorated with pink and red roses.

The work of love, muses philosopher Gillian Rose, teaches the heart what the mind knows, and the mind what the heart can understand. The house of love, I might add, is where this work lives and breathes. It is not easy to be graceful when wiping someone's bottom. I know parents do it all the time, but babies are on the whole soft, tiny and beautiful creatures; they are not old, bruised and broken as my mother is these days. Stephen still looks like a movie star and so sometimes if I catch sight of him in a certain light as I walk past the bathroom, I think that someone famous and beautiful is in there with Mum, waiting with a wad of toilet paper for when her bowels finally move, as he has done every day now for the more than four years he has been caring for Mum.

Bowel movements are a favoured topic of conversation between Steve and me these days. Bowel movements and desserts, which, despite Mum's advanced stage of decay, are still her very favourite things.

Steve used to like a scotch in the evening, but he doesn't drink spirits much now, although Cathie always brings him a bottle of Johnnie Walker Black, bought duty free, whenever she returns from one of her many overseas trips. He keeps these deluxe bottles for special occasions: birthdays and Christmases. He prefers a glass of good red wine, half a glass usually, at around eight to eight-thirty pm as he eats his dinner in front of the television. He goes to bed early, around nine-fifteen pm most nights, so he can be up at five to begin again, the next day, the work, the duty, the effort of love.

In the bookshelves in his bedroom Steve has collections of essays by eighteenth-century philosophers, works by Russian and French writers, and modernists such as Joyce and Beckett; next to his computer in the lounge room he keeps the complete series in hardback of Proust's *Remembrance of Things Past*, which he bought from Sean, his best friend from school who is still his best friend twenty years on, and who now runs an online bookstore. On the plain laminated coffee table in front of the sofa he keeps the television guide from the local *Bayside News*, the free newspaper that lands on his lawn every Wednesday. He watches a bit of television every day in between feeding Mum, washing her, cooking for her, wheeling her to the toilet, turning her over, attending to her broken skin, as well as the wound that still regularly weeps on her hip. He sees a bit of the morning shows, the midday ABC news, some British drama, as well as the SBS nightly news. Sometimes he downloads old movies from the Internet and the last time I visited him and Mum there was a copy of a Johnny Depp movie, *The Libertine*, on his computer desk. *What was it like?* I asked him, always eager to hear his opinion on anything. *So-so*, he replied, determined to remain neutral, just like Dad was, and not offer an opinion on anything.

The plant that I gave him for Christmas when he first came up to Brisbane is doing beautifully, as are the two red Christmas plants I have given him in successive years. He swims every day at the local pool in summer, travels to the heated pool in the next suburb during winter, and worries that falling customer numbers will eventually force the closure of both pools. He regularly peruses the newspaper inserts from the local supermarkets for specials on food items that Mum might particularly like – Tim Tams are a regular favourite, as are banana, carrot and orange cakes – and he is on first name terms with his neighbour Mavis, who still, maddeningly, sometimes calls him Jeff or Peter. Janice regularly sends him copies of the *Times Literary Review of Books* and the *Times Literary Supplement* as well as the *Threepenny Review* from America, and when I visit they are sometimes folded over on the kitchen table, available for me to take if I want to. He is renowned for his spectacularly thoughtful gift-giving at Christmas and on birthdays and for the cryptic messages he pastes onto the newspaper in which he always wraps the presents he now usually buys on eBay.

Before he came up to Brisbane to look after Mum he worked as a petrol station attendant, during which time he was on several occasions the victim of armed hold-ups. His philosophy was always to let the thieves take what they wanted, because nothing in retail, or perhaps in the oil business itself, he concluded, was worth dying for. He has a freakish gift that he flatly refuses to share with visitors or even, no matter how much I beg, with me: he can whistle all the minor parts of Mozart symphonies, beautifully, perfectly, complete with full dynamic and tonal range. I think – though he has not confirmed this – that he can also whistle Beethoven's late string quartets, including the elegiac Opus 132, which I imagine must sound perfectly balanced between the light and the dark, between sorrow and comedy, when whistled and not played by cello, viola and violins. As a child he could also tell you the name, make and model number of most Japanese cars made during the past thirty years and he has told me never to buy a kombi van or Volkswagen of any description. He is also the only person I know whom I could ring, as I did recently, to identify a nagging tune in my head: 'Is this Brahms' Lullaby?' I asked down the mobile after humming the melody. 'No, that's Schubert's Serenade,' he replied gently but firmly before getting back to the cricket.

He loves cricket, playing it and watching it, and just the other day we sat together, with Mum between us, watching some of the one-day games of the controversial Tri Series between India, Australia and Sri Lanka. He still enjoys footie on the television and playing cricket in the back yard with Finn and Kel when they pop in to visit with Paul and Kym, who help Stephen in any way they can. Every month, for instance, Paul gives Steve a buzz cut with his old hand-held clippers. Other times he will drop off a pair of new sandshoes or sandals to replace Steve's old ones. Paul lives the most so-called 'regular' life of all of us and now handles all of Mum's finances, but he is able to describe Stephen's life with understanding and admiration. To Paul, Stephen has always had his 'priorities worked out' and they get on as well as they did as kids. For Finn and Kel, having their 'Uncle Stevie' living with their 'Grandma Joan' in the next suburb means he is always available for a game of footie or cricket with them in the front yard, the same way Paul and Stephen played as boys with Dad.

Stephen is especially close to Janice, with whom he shares a gift for laughter and mordant humour. When Janice visited recently, she and Stephen induced in Mum sudden, surprising fits of laughter. I am jealous when I think of them laughing along with her. I do not think I make my mother laugh, not like they can. I wish I had their gift, as my father had too, of inducing hilarity in this woman who loved them – especially, I imagine – for how they could make her smile.

'Life goes on,' one of Mum's friends said recently, in a particular tone that made me think she might need some reassurance that it actually does. And, of course, it does. But some things change too. Steve is not a trained nurse, for instance, but is now somewhat of an expert regarding the different ways that Mum could suddenly die.

'The wound on her left hip has never properly healed,' he told me during a rain break in the cricket telecast. 'So if an infection gets into her bloodstream that'd be it pretty quickly.'

'A couple of times,' he continued, muting the sound on the television while I swung my legs back and forth over the edge of Mum's empty wheelchair in which I was, for that moment, sitting, 'I have caught her choking on some food. Once on a banana. In a second she went blue in the face. It was horrible. I started bashing her on her back. I bashed her so hard I could have broken her spine, but at that point I wasn't worried about that. All I could think was what a horrible, violent way to die, asphyxiating to death on an undigested banana stuck in your throat. Another way she could go is if some liquid goes down the wrong way and finds its way into her lungs. That would also be the end very, very quickly. And, of course, if she goes into hospital for any time at all she'll be dead pretty much in a matter of days. So really it's best for all of us to be prepared for those things.'

Cathie: I guess my response to the inadequacies of institutions in caring for people has mellowed with time. But while it was happening all of us were angry, outraged, frustrated and shocked at the quality of Mum's care and at the ignorance of some of the people doing the caring. If I had a warning it's that it's probably best to accept that no doctor, nurse, therapist or professional carer is going to be as interested in your loved one's life and health as you are. And take as much responsibility as you can to ensure the best of care. I do realise how lucky we are that we have had family members looking after Mum. You don't spend all your time worrying about what might or might not be happening while you're busy with all the other things you have to do in your own life.

There is a ritual that Stephen and Mum perform together each time he lifts her in and out of bed. I call it their dance and they are now well practised in its choreography. There are only brief respites in the day from the full-blown rigidity which afflicts her body; these usually occur forty minutes or so after my brother has crushed up her medication and mixed it in the thickened drink which he then spoon-feeds her. Sometimes this is a painstaking process which itself can take up to half an hour. Often I have watched him say a word over and over for her to repeat so that her mouth will form the exact shape for him to be able to push the spoon containing the crushed-up medicine through the gap between her lips and teeth and down into her throat for her to swallow.

Mum, he says, holding the spoon close to her lips and his lips close to her ear. *Can you say Rumbarala?*

Or *Mum, can you say tee tippee ta ta?*

Can you say far and away ha ha?

Sometimes it might take a minute or two of Stephen repeating the phrase *tee tippee ta ta* or *rumbarala* before Mum, with head lolling and eyes still closed, replies in a faint slurring voice *tee tippee ta ta.* Stephen then slips the spoon between her crumbling teeth and deposits the sugary mixture into her mouth. Another waiting game then begins: sometimes it might take twenty minutes or so for Mum to swallow the medicine. During this time Stephen will stay bent over my mother, tickling her throat gently to loosen up the rigid muscles in the hope of stimulating them enough to become aroused and creak into action.

After the medicine is down, it is time for Mum to be taken to the toilet on her special commode wheelchair. To begin this ritual, Stephen draws the sheets gently away from her body and says: *Ok, Mum. Toilet time.* He stands at the left of her bed. On the right of the bed hang pictures of Mum's two grandchildren, Finn and Kel. Next to these is a small print of an angel by a Renaissance artist and a calendar made by Nepalese village women which I sent to Mum during my writer's residency in 2005.

Slipping his left hand under her neck he pivots her body towards him. He then puts both hands around her waist and hoists her up towards him so that she is standing chest to chest with him: chest to chest with her son, who looks just like my father did as a young man, when Mum was still a child. She is standing on tiptoes then as Stephen takes her right hand and puts it around the left side of his neck, leaving his right arm folded around her waist like a dancer ready to lead his partner to the centre of the dance floor. Mum's legs are purple and rigid as he taps her right arm with his left arm and says: *Come on, Mum. Left arm up.* And as she has practised and performed a thousand times already since she moved with my brother to the house at Brighton she lets him lift her left arm up to place it around the right side of his neck. Sometimes her lips and neck strain with the effort of holding on to him but the muscles that are still strong in the right upper arm of her wasted body testify to how many times she has held on to her son's neck and not let go. And sometimes my brother's neck shows the strain too, underneath his passive face, as he puts his right arm up her nightie and slips off her underpants without looking down, and in one quick graceful movement spins her around on her tiptoes and pivots her gently towards the wheelchair.

It is not a dance you would ever see in a public place; it is private and full of intimate, familiar effort. Because they have executed it so many times it might even seem, to the causal observer, completely mechanical. But there are moments in this dance when I see my father's face in the face of my brother as he holds my mother; only this time it is my mother who is older than my father. While he is fathering her, I know Stephen is also mothering her, as she mothered him. Others might find it grotesque or macabre, but often as I watch them I am struck by the thought that not only is it one of the most beautiful dances I have ever seen, it is also one of the most beautiful things I have ever seen. And though I have become an avid chronicler of family events, I don't dare photograph this great unfolding piece of art that is my brother's service to our mother.

Cathie: You can see the influence of our father in everything that's happening now. That and the good humour and the ability to cope with solitude – to not need a lot of external stimulation for a happy life. And the older I get the more I appreciate Dad's quietness. If there is any one thing, though, that stands out for me about Dad it was his love for his family. That and his Mona Lisa smile, his dry sense of humour, which both the boys have inherited, and his ability to keep a straight face when the rest of us were doubled up with laughter. Do you remember playing tennis after mass on a Sunday morning when he would lob

> Mum from side to side – she had no backhand so she just kept changing hands? Then Mum would start giggling and this encouraged Dad in his mission. All the time while he was doing this he would look very serious, which of course made Mum giggle even more.

Ten days before my father died in 1993, I hitched up to Brisbane to see him. I didn't know he was dying then; he had been sick for several years since his strokes. To him, I looked terrible in those days: a blowsy bohemian from a respectable family playing electric violin in bands around the Sydney underground. The thing about having an older father is that you're still a young woman when he is an invalid. He's not meant to be dead when you're still wild at heart; there's no opportunity for wise conversations or reconciliations. No comforting apologies or forgiveness. So all I have now is one last tiny memory to place like a fine jewel at the end of this string of gems that I have laid out side by side so that they might catch, reflect and refract the light.

My father is lying in my mother's bed. It is late afternoon and he is, as usual, listening to the ABC on the radio. It is still hot and he is only wearing his pyjama bottoms. They are faded yellow with a pattern of tiny white horses on them. Dad never cared about what he wore so I don't think he would have picked out those horses especially. What I mean, I suppose, is that the symbolism of those horses – the freedom, the wildness – did not mean anything in particular. Probably someone gave them to him or bought them for him from St Vincent de Paul's.

He is lying on his stomach with his head to one side when I walk into the room to say hello. He looks thin and exhausted. His greying hair is combed down across his forehead and tufts of white hair push out from his underarms and chest. In his weakness he looks even more like a vagrant than when he especially tried to look like one, in the days when he would taunt my mother, and amuse his children, with his unkempt appearance and shuffling walk.

His eyes are half open when I enter the room. He peers at me and then whispers something. But I can't hear it because of the radio. Dad loves playing games, so I know that he is play-acting a little. I go along with his game and make a big deal out of bending over him to hear what he says, but I still can't make out his mumble. I hop up onto the bed, crawl around and lie beside him. I curl up around his body as if we are two spoons, him and me, my father and his daughter, as if we have been spooning each other our whole lives and not just at this moment for the first time. He growls a little as I hold him and says: *Mmm, that's nice.*

We lie together like this, hardly moving, for over half an hour. We don't speak; instead, we listen. Or rather, my father listens to the radio and I listen to him listening to the radio. Alistair Cook, I think it is, reading one of his *Letters from America,* Dad's favourite radio program. I notice as I listen that my father is a soft breather. I also notice as I breathe in time with his soft breath that he doesn't sweat. Or rather, that he does not smell when he sweats. It is the first time I have realised that he doesn't smell and that in my whole life I have never smelt his body odour. I remember

Mum telling me once: 'Your father was a prince. And his name means "blessed".'

A blessed man, I suddenly think, who leaves no smell.

My father.

After the program is over he reaches up a limp hand and switches off the radio. Outside, my brothers, who are also visiting, have just finished a game of cricket and downstairs Mum is taking one of her students through last minute vocal preparations for an upcoming examination. It is late afternoon, almost early evening, and the light is an ache of deep yellow and lilac. I am still curled around my father as he turns his head towards me, opens his other eye and says, as if he is passing on to me all the secrets he has learned in his long and sometimes difficult life: *Always remember, Linda,* he tells me. *You can never have too much affection.*

There are no more words after that. Just another theatrical sigh as we are called to dinner and the warm Brisbane evening turns into night.

During the months after my father died the right side of my body was stricken with sciatica that became so severe I once had to be taken to Emergency in a wheelchair. It was, friends later told me, as if my father's old affliction had moved into my body because the suffering he had left behind him was not yet ready to leave the earth. Eventually the pain was so bad that I was considering drastic measures such as cortisone injections or hospitalisation. My thoughts turned very intently then to my father. I had not thought about him much during the period before his death. And if I had I was always more concerned with myself in relation to him than with him in relation to me.

One night the pain in my side was so intense I couldn't move from bed just as he couldn't for nearly a whole year after he retired from teaching. I didn't struggle with the pain. There was no point. I just lay in my bed and tried not to move. Keeping absolutely still was, I had discovered, one of the best ways to minimise the trauma. I then thought of my father in a way that made me feel as if I was inhabiting his body as he lay immobile on his bed. Or even that he was inhabiting my body at the moment of his own death. I could sense, for a few seconds, his whole life stretching back from that moment of passing to when he was born; from the old man to the young child. I saw the distance he had travelled across continents and over oceans and through towns and cities. I saw the young man in his clerical collar, the mature, still-virginal man in his wedding suit, the older man in his swimming goggles and togs, gliding along lane six of the university pool. I saw, through his eyes, his wife, my mother, and his children, me among them, a vague curly outline in a crowd of curly children, holding out my violin for him to tune, not because I knew he could but because I wanted *him* to tune it, not my mother who usually did it. But he would not take my violin because music was my mother's area, the woman's domain, not his.

It was a particular experience to have then my father's memories in my consciousness, to feel him as he was at the moment of dying. And then I felt my breath pull hard at my body as if something was sucking me down inside myself. My throat tightened. I heard a rasping sound as I sucked the breath back in. My right side was in spasm; I could feel my back arching involuntarily, fighting the trauma in my muscles, as if my body could not support its own pain anymore. And then, as if my father was there – not just standing beside me but somewhere inside me, inside me and the pain – I felt him give me something. I let my breath out slowly and sucked it in again, more gently this time, then exhaled once more. I felt him do this too, at the same time, him and me together in the same body. A few more times we breathed in the darkness. I felt like crying. I felt as if he might feel like crying as he gave me this gift of dying; this gift of knowing his dying and, subsequently, mine as well. Of knowing through his dying how to live. Of understanding that it is that simple – to just breathe and let go. To breathe until you stopped breathing.

At the beginning of 2007, I sing my songs as part of a small concert in Brisbane. It has taken me a long time to get back into my music. During my year abroad in 2005 I rediscovered, through travelling, the wonder of the art my mother had lost forever, the art of singing. And I did climb another mountain, the hills of Anapurna around Kathmandu, the roof of the world where I lived for two months at the end of 2005 and where I recorded a whole album of love songs in a tiny acoustic studio beside a Buddhist temple.

The concert is held in West End at an old Cypriot club. I've been nervous about re-entering the marketplace with my songs, uncertain how my fragile tunes will be received in what I have always perceived to be a hard-edged and demanding environment. I am different now to how I was before, when it was my passion and my instincts that made my life and my music possible. I worry that I have become too serious and fragile rather than clever, wild and amusing as I'd once been with so little apparent effort, when I was just, as Mum used to say, doing my 'own thing'.

As I walk into the hall I see in a far corner Michael Franklin wrapped around his guitar, as sometimes men wrap themselves around their lovers, as he once might have wrapped himself around me. Or vice versa. I feel awkward in this once familiar environment.

Hey, Michael calls out. *I saw you were playing. It's good to see you here.*

I don't even think before my next words to Michael tumble casually from my lips: *You can sit in on my set if you like.*

He smiles at me. *Sure,* he says, squinting at me through his thick wire-rimmed glasses, like a wise old owl. *That'd be fun.*

Later, Michael joins me on stage. During my set I hardly even notice he is there, he fits in so smoothly with the meanderings of my melodies, with the movement of my words, and the breathy fragility of my voice. At the end the audience whoops it up and I am relieved that all the little songs I have nurtured in Mum's lounge room have been so warmly accepted.

They liked it, I whisper across to him as we take our bows. *They really liked it.*

Sure, Michael replies. *It was a good set.*

Thanks. And thanks, I tell him, smiling. *Double thanks.* I clip my words just like he does. Just as I always have done. I remember now, as if by surprise, that I once loved this man. That I am a woman who has loved, who has been loved.

I also remember something else Mum once told me. 'Some things never die. They just change. And then they change again.' I had never taken much notice of her when she said these kinds of things. They always sounded like 'old wives' tales' to me. I never really thought, as many daughters do, that Mum understood anything I needed to know about life or about love. I remember also how in New Delhi, two years earlier, I had dined with a billionaire philanthropist who admired the way I played the violin. After dinner he turned my hands over as he said to me softly: 'We always say you can trust a musician because where there is music there can be no violence.' I was surprised. I had always been too aware of my passionate, tumultuous emotional nature to think I could ever be seen in such a light.

But now I realise that perhaps both Mum and the billionaire were right. I had spent a lot of time trying to get over love, get through love, or forget about love. To wait for love, and the fierceness in my heart, to die so I could move on. It is useless to think that love dies. I understand at this moment, though, that it can change and that music can help to bring about that change. After all, here I am with the man for whom I had written my very first shaky, out-of-tune love song, and all these years later we can still play love songs together. Not as lovers, not as partners, not even as friends. Just as two musicians who can forget about everything that has passed through the fleeting miracle of a song.

SWEET MYSTERY OF LIFE

Cathie: I remember when Mum first became ill I had recently moved to Townsville with a broken heart. I was a very sad girl, prone to moments of great sorrow, grief and self-pity. When Mum was diagnosed, it gave me the opportunity to focus on someone close to me in a worse situation. I am sure this helped me, even though it took me a long time not to be unhappy again.

The first time I felt that my heart was broken, I heard my mother singing. I can't exactly remember why I'd gone to visit my parents that day. It was after Michael Franklin and I had broken up and I had been walking around in pain for weeks and so my reasons for doing anything were not very clear. I came late in the afternoon. Dad was out the back of the house in the garden when I walked around the side of the house and sat on the green vinyl couch outside the music room. Mum was inside giving a singing lesson to an elderly man called Harry, who had come to learn to sing after his wife died.

'Gives him something to do, poor thing,' Mum commented about Harry when he first arrived at her music studio hunched over from grief. He had been broken, hardly able to breathe. Mum coaxed him slowly, assuming he needed to talk more than to sing. She would allow him to come for lessons just for company, if that was what he needed, she told us. The absence of his wife, though, brought forth a miraculous gift. At the age of seventy-five, with an already forgetful mind and arthritis in both hands, Harry discovered, with Mum's help, a tenor voice so sweet and sonorous that it could have come from a young man in the prime of his life. 'And he had never even sung in the shower,' Mum remarked, amazed that after a lifetime of not singing, a fully alive voice could still unfurl, like a child from a womb. She never stopped being amazed at things. Music was her way, as it was for all her family, to this amazement.

Grief is unfamiliar when you first feel it. It can hurt you physically, like a fist pressing into your stomach. In my parents' house, it felt unseemly, as if I had brought a wild animal home with me. I was numb as I sat outside Mum's music room that day. I couldn't even cry. I only felt alive from the neck up.

Inside Mum's music room, Harry was singing one of Mum's favourite songs, 'Ah, Sweet Mystery of Life'.

Ah, sweet mystery of life at last I've found you
Ah, at last I know the secret of it all.

I couldn't see Harry; I was facing away from the music room. But I could hear him. I had to stop myself from screaming at him to shut up. I couldn't stand to hear his sweet voice, couldn't bear the sentimental lyrics, the rising and falling of the melody, the swooning and the swooshing of the voice. They do it deliberately, I thought, these songwriters. They know how to wring the tears out of you. I won't cry, I promised myself, pulling tight on my breath. I'll decide when – and if – I ever cry again.

I heard Dad, who was down the back of the house somewhere, singing as well. 'All the longing seeking striving waiting yearning,' he warbled from behind the bushes in the back yard.

Then Mum began to sing as well: 'My heart has heard the answer to its calling . . .'

Harry joined in as they all finished the song together: 'For it is love that rules for evermore.'

I stood up to go. I'll sneak out without anyone seeing me, I thought. Without having to face anyone. Or listen to this music for one second longer. But I couldn't move. I clenched and unclenched my feet to get some energy into my body, but I was still completely rigid. My chest felt like rock under my skin. Something was dead inside me.

Mum came out then. Her face was bright pink from the effort of singing as she called back to Harry: 'Oh, look who's here, Harry. Have you met my daughter?'

'Don't,' I gasped at her. 'Don't . . . don't . . .' I couldn't get any other words out.

She looked at me more closely. 'You're as white as a ghost.'

I shook my head, aghast at her seeing me like this.

'What's happened to you?' she asked, her bright voice pealing in the gloom of the shadows around me. 'What's wrong?'

'Don't,' I kept repeating. 'Don't.'

I heard Harry call out discreetly from the music room: 'Anything wrong, Mrs Neil?'

His speaking voice was another anomaly after hearing him sing – it was an old man's voice, cracked and broken.

'Everything's fine, Harry,' she called back to him. 'She just needs some air.'

I needed more than air. I needed something I couldn't identify. Something it would take me years to find.

'You're not breathing,' Mum told me. 'It hurts more when you stop breathing.'

'I can't.' I shook my head as I buckled over on my side on the couch. 'I can't.'

'You can. And you will.'

She didn't approach me. She didn't lean down and touch me. She just let me lie there.

'You're not like me, Linda,' she said as she hovered over me. 'I can see that your emotions go up and they go down.'

She swept her hand up high before dropping it down low.

'Mine are more like this.' She moved her hand in a straight line above my face. 'I always wanted a placid life. It gives me time and space to sing.'

I resented her so much at that moment, for her placid life, the certainty of her stability. The stability I thought, then, that I would never find.

'But if you are going to live your . . . um . . . passionate life . . . then you'll need to know how to keep breathing. Especially when life hurts you so much that you think your heart will stop.'

Dad called out from the back yard then, as Harry started to sing again. Mum didn't react. She just kept looking at me while I lay there. She was silent for a long time. It was unusual for her to be silent for such a long time, but I guessed she had nothing to say to me. I felt her there though, in her silence, felt her presence more than I ever had through her words or her song.

'We're not as different as you think we are,' she finally said, before turning back into her music room where Harry was waiting for her to teach him how to breathe.

I was twenty-two when I travelled to India for the first time on my own, old enough to risk the adventure alone, but still young and inexperienced enough for Mum to lose sleepless nights over the thought of me going. Still, she tolerated my 'mad vision' to travel to India and follow the path of Mahatma Gandhi. She was even sanguine when I became obsessed with the principles of nonviolence and turned vegetarian when, to prepare myself for my trip, I embarked on a serious study of Gandhi and, in particular, his theory of nonviolent resistance called *satyagraha*.

Grandma and Mum travelled down with me from Brisbane to Sydney to see me off on this, my first big solo adventure around the world. It was a glorious Sydney day at Circular Quay when the three of us ate what would be our last lunch together for at least six months. Grandma was as excited as a girl at the thought of my grand adventure. The previous evening when we bunked together in a room at Mum's cousin's place in Eastwood, Grandma tried on my backpack and said giddily: 'Oh, I wish I was going with you. I wish I was going too.'

Mum was less excited. She was never as restless as her mother, never yearned for travel the way Grandma and I did. I think she thought, more than either of us, that everything she needed was just exactly where she was.

It was magnificent on the harbour that day as the three of us looked together at the Sydney Opera House. I wasn't that interested in the building though. I was thinking about my own death for the first time in my life and wondering if I might disappear somewhere in the wilds of India and never see Mum again. Or I might fall off a mountain somewhere into a snow-filled valley as I had read climbers of high mountains sometimes do. I thought also about how the Tibetans practise the art of living as if they are about to die: that is, they live each day as if it might be their last and therefore leave nothing they need to do undone and nothing that they need to say unsaid. I thought then of all the hundred things I would leave unsaid if I did die, all the whispered words, all the sounds and sighs that I had kept locked inside.

I was sure that I wouldn't miss Mum. That she wouldn't miss me. I wish I can say now that I turned to Mum and told her I loved her. But of course I didn't. I was 'too wild at heart', too intent on my own needs and my own drive out into the world to realise her significance in my life. There was still a long way to go, many years to travel to find what I needed out in the world, where I would be mothered and fathered by many different people, so that I could return home to meet my mother as if for the first time.

But in case I did die, I turned to her and said: 'You know I always wanted you to say "I love you". I needed you to say it to me so I knew that you did. Not in an off-hand dutiful kind of way. Sometimes it seemed like you were always so busy singing and teaching and doing things. You never had the time.'

She seemed exasperated as she often was with me these days. But she was polite enough to wait until Grandma was out of earshot before looking me straight in the eye and saying: 'Grandma and I have both come down with you to see you off on a journey from which you might never return. We have bought the tickets, packed our bags. We're here with you. Right now. That means something too, you know. That's also love. That is the action love takes.'

I felt sad standing there next to her as the sails of the Opera House shimmered in the afternoon light. Despite being made of solid stone and steel, they looked as if they could just lift off there and then and sail off down the harbour into the sea, light and easy in the breeze. I felt sad because I understood that I had hurt her by saying what I said. I wondered if my journey abroad might give me some perspective to help ease the ache in my heart to feel such a stranger standing next to the woman who gave birth to me. Or if something one day might be revealed to solve the puzzle of our differences.

'It is not always found in words, no matter how beautiful they might sound,' she continued as her eyes were also drawn to the beauty around us. And I wondered if she felt it too, that ache in her heart, the same way she felt it when she sang a song, or listened to my father read a poem to her during a quiet evening. But she was a practical woman, above all, and I knew what she was saying was right and that one day I would understand perfectly what she was trying to tell me. I just couldn't at that moment. It was, as my mother was always fond of saying, just not our time.

It would take an illness and a homecoming for me to know my mother; and even further on, it would take the writing of a book, and the gathering of a hundred stories and memories, for me to know my father. But it would take years of music and it would take a hundred songs to find the language and the vibration that would make me less fierce and more peaceful – with her, with myself and with the world around me.

'It is also in the actions we take to be with you when you might need us,' my mother continued. 'It is all very well hearing a beautiful poem, or a piece of music, or even to sing a glorious song, but it's what we do for each other that counts.'

EPILOGUE: JOY TO THE WORLD

Cathie: I think that living with someone with Parkinson's or dementia makes you more tolerant of illness, particularly mental illness. Now I always include hospitals and retirement and nursing homes in the concert schedules of my school and community music ensembles. I always tell my students that the very young, the ill and infirm, and the old deserve the very best music we can give them.

When I see Mum these days I always sing to her the songs that she knew years back. I take her hands and conduct the music with her as I sing and this sometimes makes her start to sing too, and then for a brief moment I can see a tiny sparkle in her blue eyes, which these days are mostly vacant.

Like any good Shakespearian tragedy, there is also comedy at its heart. I couldn't help smiling one day recently as Steve and I were talking on Skype, when from the quasi-coma she appears to be in most of the time, Mum suddenly called out, 'Do you two ever stop talking?'

> As for the family, in many ways the difficulties we all experienced, even the disagreements which we inevitably had, seem to have passed away with time. Time is all we have, really . . . and when you lose someone you look back on all the times you didn't understand that simple thing: time is all we really have. And we don't ever get it back.

There is a picture of Mum as a young girl at the beach. She is wearing a one-piece bathing suit and her curly blonde hair is woven into plaits. She is kneeling on the sand, a bucket and spade beside her and a sandcastle newly built in front of her. The photograph is slightly blurred, as if either the hand holding the camera was shaking as the shot was taken or else Mum could not stay still for the few seconds the photographer needed to focus the camera and capture her on film. There is a feeling of movement in the photograph, as if Mum cannot be pinned down or captured by anyone; her mouth is open in a luminous smile and her eyes are fixed on someone or something to the left of the camera. Just visible in the corner of the shot is my grandmother looking across and smiling at the person taking the photograph of her daughter, who is apparently unaware of either her loveliness or the fact that her loveliness is being appreciated. She seems at one with her surroundings, completely comfortable in her graceful physicality. I have looked at this photo many times wondering what it is that my mother is looking at while everyone is looking at her. Who is she with beside her mother? What is she thinking as she moves about like a sunray on the sand? Who is she smiling at?

Once when I was perusing the picture I suddenly thought how little you can ever know about anyone else or what is inside of them and that sometimes you have to live with that not knowing as you would a mystery. And then I noticed that what I had thought for years was Mum's radiant smile was actually something else. At this moment, all the different elements of the photograph – the cameraperson, the sun, the sand, the castle, the shaking hand, the mother and the daughter – finally coalesced into a whole. I stopped seeing only the separate details and instead saw what my grandmother would have called 'the big picture'. I could almost feel my perspective physically shift as I realised that what I had always thought was a picture of Mum smiling on a beach was actually a photograph of people – my grandmother, the photographer and who knows how many more around them – listening to a young girl, my mother, looking brightly into the distance as she sang to herself in the sunlight.

Christmas Day, 2007: Cathie is home from Hong Kong for Christmas and I am sitting in the lounge room holding my violin on my lap next to Mum, who is in her wheelchair. Steve's in the kitchen preparing her lunch and Cathie is sitting on Mum's other side, a book of Christmas carols open on her lap.

It's been a good day so far. Mum was alert in the morning, although she doesn't really know it is Christmas. The weather is not as hot as usual, it's quite balmy in fact, and the trip down to Brighton from Brisbane has been surprisingly pleasant for this time of year. We have been singing Christmas carols today and during our collective song Mum opened her mouth and began to sing along.

This year Paul is driving around Australia in a motor home with Kym and the boys. Janice is still in Tasmania, but will pass through Brisbane early next year on her way back to England. Family members come and go from each other, I think, orbiting like planets. Colliding sometimes, damaging each other from the impact of our accidental intersections, before being hurled back again to continue our voyages in the darkness of space. I wonder then whether some of us will always need to return over and over, as I have, drawn back to the centre by something inexplicable and magnetic in our drive to love those whom we know and to know those whom we love.

After lunch Mum is wheeled back into her room and settled into bed. I hang around for a bit and watch television with Cathie and Steve before nodding off, as I usually do on Christmas Day, for a five-minute nap. When I wake up I go into Mum's room with my violin to say goodbye. Even though her eyes are shut and her head is lying stiffly to one side, I play again some of her favourite Christmas carols, the ones we'd sung before in the lounge room: 'Hark the Herald Angels Sing', 'Silent Night', 'O Come All Ye Faithful' and, to finish things off, 'Joy to the World'.

Just as she did when I played them in the lounge room with Cathie and Stephen singing along, Mum starts to make some noises underneath the melody of the violin. It is not exactly singing, and it is not exactly a song, but in the circumstances it is something just as wonderful.

When we finish, I put my violin down gently on the end of her bed and lean in close to her face so if she opens her eyes I will be right there where she can see me. It is miracle enough that she has sung with us, but to be recognised on the same day would really make it seem like Christmas.

Did you like the music, Mum? I whisper into her ear.

Of course. She speaks, as she often does now, as if she is hearing voices and passing on their messages to us. *But I really have to practise some more . . . before I sing in public.*

But you were so good, Mum, I tell her softly. We have all had to learn to speak more quietly as Mum has grown so fragile, to become gentler, with her and with each other, just as our father so often urged us to do.

Her inarticulate murmuring now reminds me of someone returning from far away, with many strange tales to tell, settling in for a long stay.

I lean in close, my voice wavering. *Do you know who this is, Mum?* I ask her.

Her eyes are closed. Her face has lost all of its fat and the flesh that remains stretches out across her bones like the skin of a drum. But Stephen has rubbed Olay moisturiser into her skin morning and night so that, despite the blood clots and bruises that mark her face, her skin is smooth and glowing.

I smile as I stroke the loose folds of skin on her upper arm. *What's my name, Mum?* I ask, remembering how she would tell me how annoying I was as a child, always asking questions.

Don't be silly, she rasps at me. I remember her as a mother to that child, always trying to quieten me down, to stop playing around, and to take things more seriously. And then later when I grew up how she would tell me to stop taking things so seriously. You can never win, I joke to myself, and then I can't help myself from laughing out loud, from enjoying this moment with her, from trying to spin it out for as long as I can.

Who am I then? I ask her. *Tell me who I am and I'll stop bothering you.*

I can hear the neighbour's festivities of song and laughter and from the house on the corner a sudden brutal exchange of anger; from another the radio blares out a religious service; and from another there comes the faint echo of tears.

My daughter, she whispers, licking her lips slowly.

Yes, but which one? I press on, leaning over her gently.

I had three, she says, a long way away.

I press my cheek lightly into hers. *But what's my name?*

You're the other one, aren't you? I love her when she is like this, when I can feel so strongly that she is still playing with me, teasing me that I am only one of many, making me come down off my high horse and wait in line, just like everyone else, for what is my due.

Mum, don't you know? I ask, mock-dramatically. *Don't you remember?*

We often play this game with her, teasing her back to life with silly questions and challenges.

Come on, Mum, we'll say, trying to rouse her. *Who's this? And who is that?*

Cathie is better at it than I am. Her life force is strong and vibrant like our grandmother's was. Paul, Kim and the boys never have to try at all; they do it just by coming, a tumult of fun and activity, into Mum's room. Janice can do it with gusts of laughter. Stephen usually just sits beside Mum and gently taps her arm with his forefinger, and she will know that it is him. We all have a way of making ourselves known, our signature tune, so to speak, our personal melody.

With great effort she lifts open her right eyelid. *Mmm . . .* she mumbles, moving her lips slowly in the chewing motion she makes as she begins the effort of speaking.

Have you forgotten then, Mum? Have you forgotten who I am? I say as I lean my head down on her shoulder, which is so brittle now that I feel I could break her with too heavy a touch.

Your name . . . means 'beautiful', she whispers, swallowing the last word in her effort to say it. I don't get up from her. I only lift my weight so she will not be hurt by my head leaning on her. She doesn't grimace or grumble in pain as she often does these days. She lets me lie there with her, a favour to me on Christmas Day.

There is a sense sometimes of being able to do something justice, and then there's another sense that tells you not to even try. I wonder then whether such times need to be noted or spoken of, or whether they are just there, as they always have been, in the brushing of my cheek against the soft cotton of her nightie, in my hand reaching out and holding on to her other bony shoulder, in her quiet sighs that seem to die away to nothing as she falls asleep opposite the small photograph of my father emerging, smiling, out of a bright blue pool of light, while Cathie and Steve laugh in the next room, and my violin lies, full with song, at the end of my mother's bed.

ACKNOWLEDGMENTS

I would like to extend my deepest thanks to the many people who contributed to the making of this book:

To my mother, Joan Neil, for graciously allowing me to share this sometimes difficult part of her life, and – from the very start of my life – for the music.

To my father, Ben Neil, for the rich legacy of his life; to my grandmother Chris Cottrell, for also passing on to me the fruits of her long life; to my sisters and brothers and extended family, to my sister Cathie, who kindly shared her words and memories with me; to Mum's friends and colleagues, and to the many other friends, students, carers, nurses and doctors with whom my family and I went through the highs and lows of this experience.

For the writing of the book itself I would like to thank Jan McKemmish, whose support for me as a writer brought forth the first lines of this book, to Amanda Lohrey, for her belief in the story, and to Bronwyn Lea, whose empathetic response helped me to keep going when I was ready to give up.

Thanks also to the Literature Board of the Australia Council and to Arts Queensland for its support during the early stages, to the University of Queensland, which gave me an opportunity to work on later drafts, and to the staff of the School of English, Media Studies and Art History at the University of Queensland. Thanks also to Sharon Davis, Radio Eye and ABC Radio National. I would like to thank Madonna Duffy, who first brought the book to the attention of UQP, Alexandra Payne, non-fiction publisher at UQP, whose enthusiasm for the book has been consistently welcoming and warm, as well as Rebecca Roberts and Jo Jarrah for their editorial eye, empathy and patience. Thanks also to Marion Campbell and Gail Jones for their support.

Thanks to the many others who contributed with their love, kindness, belief and support, especially Ross Ebert, Louella Linkson, Jamila Bonvegna, Joanne and James Douglas, Gabriel P, Estelle Castro, Mary Maher and Phil Vanderzeil.